The Perennial Philosophy

Series

# About this Book

"We sincerely congratulate the editor, Barry McDonald, for this very thoughtful selection of essays written by many well-known authors. The American reader, still surrounded here and there by virgin nature, will appreciate this book because it provides a more convincing argument for the protection of the environment and the survival of Mother Earth and its inhabitants. This book gives a valuable basis for any serious spiritual ecology. Besides, its presentation beautifully reflects its spirit."

—**Jean-Pierre Lafouge**, Marquette University

"Nature is the first and last revelation because it is the 'scripture' of the Eternal. As this remarkable collection of essays teaches, the trace of His hand is found in every rippling field of grass or fluttering leaf or silent flower; to read them is to help recover our roots of immortality."

—**Mark Perry**, author of *On Awakening and Remembering*

"This collection of essays by some of the most important scholars and religious authorities of our time points to the necessity of understanding the current environmental crisis through the lens of spiritual vision: its basic thesis is that the earth itself is sacred, and that to overcome the current agendas of exploitation and waste, we must see the creation as the work of the Creator. This book is essential reading for anyone who has ever felt the presence of God in nature."

—**Michael Oren Fitzgerald**, author of *Yellowtail, Crow Medicine Man and Sun Dance Chief* and editor of *Light on the Indian World* and *Indian Spirit*

"In the face of such evidence the scientific worldview that underpins the desacralization of nature is challenged to explain why it is that the deepest wisdom the human race is heir to unfailingly declares that we deviate from the vision of the natural world as our sacred home at our peril."

—**Brian Keeble**, co-founder of the Temenos Academy, founder of Golgonooza Press, and author of *Art: For Whom and For What?*

# World Wisdom
# The Library of Perennial Philosophy

The Library of Perennial Philosophy is dedicated to the exposition of the timeless Truth underlying the diverse religions. This Truth, often referred to as the *Sophia Perennis*—or Perennial Wisdom—finds its expression in the revealed Scriptures as well as the writings of the great sages and the artistic creations of the traditional worlds.

The Perennial Philosophy provides the intellectual principles capable of explaining both the formal contradictions and the transcendent unity of the great religions.

Ranging from the writings of the great sages of the past, to the perennialist authors of our time, each series of our Library has a different focus. As a whole, they express the inner unanimity, transforming radiance, and irreplaceable values of the great spiritual traditions.

*Seeing God Everywhere: Essays of Nature and the Sacred* appears as one of our selections in The Perennial Philosophy series.

# The Perennial Philosophy Series

In the beginning of the Twentieth Century, a school of thought arose which has focused on the enunciation and explanation of the Perennial Philosophy. Deeply rooted in the sense of the sacred, the writings of its leading exponents establish an indispensable foundation for understanding the timeless Truth and spiritual practices which live in the heart of all religions. Some of these titles are companion volumes to the Treasures of the World's Religions series, which allows a comparison of the writings of the great sages of the past with the perennialist authors of our time.

# Seeing God Everywhere

## Essays on Nature and the Sacred

*Edited by*
Barry McDonald

Foreword by Philip Zaleski

Introduction by Satish Kumar

**World Wisdom**

Seeing God Everywhere:
Essays on Nature and the Sacred
© 2003 World Wisdom, Inc.

Library of Congress Cataloging-in-Publication Data

Seeing God everywhere : essays on nature and the sacred / edited by Barry McDonald ;
foreword by Philip Zaleski ; introduction by Satish Kumar.
    p. cm. — (The perennial philosophy series) Includes bibliographical references and
index.
  ISBN 0-941532-42-9 (pbk. : alk. paper)
  1. Nature—Religious aspects. 2. Human ecology—Religious aspects. I. McDonald, Barry,
1952- II. Series.
  BL65.N35S42 2003
  291.2'4–dc21

2003014016

Printed on acid-free paper in Canada

For information address World Wisdom, Inc.
P.O. Box 2682, Bloomington, Indiana 47402-2682

www.worldwisdom.com

For Thomas Yellowtail (1903-1993)
(Crow Medicine Man and Sun Dance Chief)

So high an eagle rises in the light
It disappears, and yet it is not gone.
Its wings outspread to vanish in the sun
And there are men who sing to know its flight
*Nothing lives long except the earth and sky.*

Round campfires in the night the old men rest.
Their tipis softly lit: of victory
They sing with solemn voices high and free.
Each naked warrior is with glory dressed,
*Brave hearts there is no better day to die.*

And there are men who dance to ancient song
While others drum and dream an eagle's cry.
The mountains turn under an eagle's eye
And to that height all things on earth belong.

—Barry McDonald

# Table of Contents

# Poetry

# Preface

When we think of nature and the sacred, several images come to mind: the first Christian monks who fled to the Egyptian desert in the fourth and fifth centuries, Vedic sages meditating upon truth and seeking union with the Divine in the deep forests of India, a solitary Lakota crying for a vision upon a remote precipice in the Black Hills of South Dakota, or the T'ang poet Han Shan writing Zen verses on scraps of bark and leaving them along the path that climbs Cold Mountain.

All of these scenes, and others too numerous to mention, remind us that throughout the centuries, and across many religious traditions, we have sought the presence of the Real in wilderness landscapes. Deserts, forests, mountains and oceans are all places where the eye of the heart has opened and we have caught a glimpse of the beauty and the majesty of the Divine. Immersed in the silence of the great forest cathedrals and listening to the pure song of a mountain stream, we have come to know the inner man who has always lived upon the threshold of Heaven. And it is not only through the large and dramatic manifestations of nature that we have perceived the sacred: what wisdom did not the Buddha transmit by silently holding up a simple flower to the venerable Kashyapa?

Why are we drawn into the heart of nature? Why do we feel uplifted and spiritually renewed after spending time in some wild place far removed from the ordinary business of men? There are many answers to these questions, ranging from the healthful benefits associated with the exhilarating effects of fresh air and exercise to the pleasure of sitting by an evening campfire and gazing at the stars.

There is another reason, however, and it is far more profound. In the opening pages of this book, Frithjof Schuon speaks of "seeing God everywhere". The "remembrance of God in all things" and the "metaphysical transparency of phenomena" are other pertinent expressions which Schuon uses to underline the immanence of God in the world. These words remind us that it is not only through

*Preface*

sacred books like the Bible, the Upanishads, and the Quran that God reveals Himself to man. He also shows us the shining facets of His Reality through the beauties of the natural world; and just as we learn something about the nature of an artist through his art, we may discover the presence of the Creator in His creation. Whether the Absolute was referred to as God, Brahman, Allah, Wakan Tanka, Shunyamurti, Tao, or by some other Name, every branch of human society has, without doubt, seen traces of the One in the many wonders of nature.

This vision of the immanence of God, which is most often associated with the mystical dimension of religion, finds one of its greatest voices in the 12th century Sufism of Ibn 'Arabi, whose metaphysical writings on the Oneness of Being and the Self-Disclosure of God are among the most profound and comprehensive treatments of the subject in the history of spiritual literature.[1] As Toshihiko Izutsu explains in his article in this book, Ibn 'Arabi's cosmology teaches "that the very root of creation is the singleness of the Absolute." This subject is far too vast to be explored in our brief Preface; however, I would point the interested reader to the many examples of the same doctrine which may be discovered in the mystical literature of both Eastern and Western religious traditions, including the visions of Hildegard of Bingen, the Canticle of Saint Francis, the Kashmiri Shaivism of Abhinavagupta, the Taoism of Lao Tzu, the Kabbalah of Issac Luria, the angelophany of Zoroastrianism,[2] and the Hua-Yen Buddhism of Tu Shun. One of the most beautiful articulations of the doctrine of the Oneness of Being is found among the Lakota Indians of the American West. Their expression *mitakuye oyasin* (we are all related) extends beyond tribal members to all living things. When the Onondaga Elder, Oren Lyons, writes in his essay "Our Mother Earth" that, "the bears and the wolves and the eagles are Indians" he is directly underlining the metaphysical Reality of the fundamental unity and spiritual kinship of all creation. North American Native Traditions, as well as all

1. *Sufism and Taoism: a Comparative Study of Key Philosophical Concepts* by Toshihiko Izutsu (Berkeley: University of California, 1983). Also, *The Self-Disclosure of God: Principles of Ibn 'Arabi's Cosmology* by William C. Chittick (Albany: State University of New York, 1998).
2. See S.H. Nasr's *Religion and the Order of Nature* (Oxford: Oxford University Press, 1996), pp.48-50 for an illuminating explanation of Zoroastrianism. *Angelophany* refers to the idea that the earth is an angel.

other forms of Shamanism, are founded upon the holiness of creation, which is directly based upon the idea of the immanence of God.

If we understand that creation is the sacred art of the Creator, what should be our role in relationship to the surrounding world? And what must we do to fulfill that role? According to the Bible and the Quran, the nature of man is theomorphic; we are "made in the image of God." Consequently, we have a sacred responsibility towards the creation because we are providentially destined to serve as pontiff, or viceregent; we are created with a free will and we are responsible to God for our treatment of the earth. Virtually all of our ancestors realized that holiness is the defining characteristic of creation, and through their reliance upon Mother Earth to provide them with the necessities of daily life, they cultivated a deep and sustaining relationship with the natural world. They saw the Hand of God touching everything and they understood that their existence, as well as the existence of all other forms of life, was totally dependent upon the harmonious inter-relationship of all living things. The very root of the word nature, which comes from the Latin *nascitura*, means, "to give birth." Our ancestors, who lived out of doors in constant communion with the elements, understood concretely that nature is the progenitor of life. And as the sacred source of life, nature was revered as a beloved Mother. Today, many people are interested in whole foods and wholistic medicine and this is easily understood as a contemporary echo of the ancient belief in the inter-relatedness of all things.

Entering the portal of the 21st century, we are facing one of the most serious problems in the history of man. The current environmental crisis stems from our forgetfulness of who we are and what creation is. The causes of this forgetfulness are many; however, in large part it may be traced back to that point where we lost touch with the sacred quality of nature and began to view the world as a vast mechanism which could be best understood through the lens of physical science. This world-view, which has many of its roots in the Renaissance, has brought us to a point where we no longer understand the connection between the physical and the metaphysical. We have forgotten that the physical cannot be separated from the metaphysical without suffering potentially disastrous consequences. Assuming, as we do, an infinite supply of natural resources, we exercise power over the earth and forget that with this power comes our sacred responsibility to serve as shepherds of the creation. As Seyyed Hossein Nasr, a world-renowned authority on Sufism and the *Religio Perennis* has repeatedly pointed out in his many profound studies on religion and nature, as well as in his essay in this book, the current environmental crisis is, in fact, a spiritual crisis.[3] Dr. Nasr writes, "The ultimate question for us, the ultimate challenge, is: who are we? What are we doing here? And the response has always been that we are here first of all to remember who we are; we are here to remember what the world is in its spiritual reality; and above all we are here to remember God who is the source of both the world and ourselves."

As various forms of secularism gained ascendancy in the 20th century, so did their underlying presuppositions—that nature is a purely quantitative phenomenon which can be defined and measured by physics and mathematics. This perspective, which René Guénon called the "reign of quantity" more than fifty years ago,[4] created a spiritual myopia preventing us from seeing the presence of God in the world. As modern men, we are the first collectivity in the history of humanity to fail to see the Reality of the Creator in His creation, and to draw the consequences of that vision. This blindness has spread into nearly every aspect of human life, but nowhere is there more tangible evidence of the greed and gross materialism that stems from this quantitative world-view than in our exploitation of the earth. We have been lulled into a false sense of security by a scientism which tells us that all obstacles to future progress and prosperity may be overcome in a test tube. And despite the positive efforts made by certain ecological groups to reverse the disastrous consequences of numerous agendas based upon modern science and the quantification of nature, most of these well-intentioned efforts have not gone far enough. We are desperately in need of a deeper ecological vision founded upon spiritual insight into the profound order of nature. Some 300 years before the birth of Christ this ecological vision was summarized by the Chinese sage Chuang

3. See, for example, *Man and Nature: The Spiritual Crisis in Modern Man* (Chicago, IL: Kazi, 1997) and *Religion and the Order of Nature* (Oxford: Oxford University Press, 1996).

4. *The Reign of Quantity and the Signs of the Times* by René Guénon, trans. Lord Northbourne (London: Luzac & Co., 1953; New York: Sophia Perennis et Universalis, 1995).

Tzu who said, "Heaven and earth and I spring from the same root, and all things are one with me."[5]

The fundamental thesis of this book is that our continuing physical and spiritual well-being is ultimately linked with our ability to "see God everywhere" and "remember Him in all things." From the non-theistic perspective of Buddhism, Tenzin Gyatso, His Holiness the 14th Dalai Lama speaks in his article, "A Tibetan Buddhist Perspective on Nature," about the principle of the interdependence of all things and the exchange between human spirit and nature. He states that the "Buddhist literature mentions the sanctity of the environment as inspiring and blessing the practitioner, and in turn the practitioner's spiritual realization blessing the environment." This thesis is clearly and beautifully articulated in the cosmology of Hua-Yen, which teaches that the entire universe is like a net of dazzling jewels, infinitely complex and totally interdependent.[6] Every part of life is joined to every other part of life and each is reflected in the other. This means that we cannot plunder the earth without robbing ourselves. We cannot deplete natural resources without diminishing ourselves. To continue to live from generation to generation we need to recognize and embrace this interdependence, and we need to extend our definition of the spiritual into the ecological. Among the many ecological perspectives which have been brought to bear upon the current environmental crisis, this vision of the immanence of God in nature, and its implicit understanding of the interdependence of all things, is the most radical because it points to the Origin of all that is. The future of the earth may be determined by the degree to which we understand this vision, which clearly underlines the deepest relationship between nature and the sacred.

In "Christianity and the Survival of Creation" Wendell Berry reminds us that the Bible is not "enough appreciated as an outdoor book." He states that "it is a hypaethral book, such as Thoreau talked about—a book open to the sky. It is best read and understood outdoors, and the farther outdoors the better." This is good advice. We should also remember that our ancestors knew that nature is a

---

5. *The Golden Age of Zen* by John C.H. Wu (Bloomington, Indiana: World Wisdom, 2003).

6. *Entry into the Inconceivable: An Introduction to Hua-Yen Buddhism* by Thomas Cleary (Honolulu: University of Hawaii, 1983).

holy book and that Heaven speaks to us through the manifestations of the natural world. They knew that just as the many return to the One, the One returns to the many. It is this spiritual vision which defines the wisdom of the human state, and to heal nature and ourselves we must reclaim this wisdom. Every essay in this collection, each in its own way, calls attention to the pressing urgency of this necessity. And each short poem is meant to be a flower through which God wants to be known. I would encourage every reader to take this book outdoors and read it under the open sky. To appreciate and understand the message contained in these pages you could do no better than to start by closing your eyes and feeling the sunlight on your face. That sunlight, shining everywhere, is the signature of God.

Barry McDonald
July 2002

# Foreword

That the earth is in trouble few of us deny. The evidence mounts on every side, and the dread litany of our self-destruction has become a daily staple: acid rain, air pollution, water pollution, deforestation, global warming, the extinction of species. The timetable for degradation may be uncertain; the ability of the planet to renew itself may be greater than we realize; but there can be no doubt that the earth is in trouble.

How should we respond to this crisis? Much can be learned by listening to societies more at ease with nature than our own. I am thinking of groups as diverse as the hunters of the Great Plains, the peasant-farmers of Eastern Europe, the fishermen of the South Pacific. One learns some surprising lessons, often at odds with the *credo* of the contemporary environmentalist movement. None of these peoples advocate a hands-off policy toward nature; every culture since the Neolithic, and perhaps before, has transformed the environment and curtailed the wilderness. Nor do these societies support animal rights. They value and even revere animals as creatures of God, as divine messengers, as symbols of the divine attributes, but they never mistake animals as members of the *polis*. Hierarchical distinctions remain intact, as does the position of the human being as nexus of heaven and earth. However, as these observations may suggest, traditional societies do hold one thing— the one thing which explains all things—in common: a metaphysics that embraces, in one glance, both heaven and earth, and that finds both radiant with the presence of God.

Lately I have been reading in the *Carmina Gadelica* (1900-1954), Alexander Carmichael's magisterial compilation of Gaelic hymns, prayers, and blessings, the fruit of sixty years of travel along the sheep-tracks and bridle-paths and trackless moors of the Scottish Highlands and islands. The crofters that Carmichael befriended, most of who were unlettered, untraveled, and, by the standards of the world, utterly destitute, exemplify the sensitivity to sacred realities that I have been describing. The presence of God, the Holy Trinity, suffuses every created realm:

The Three Who are over me,
The Three Who are below me,
The Three Who are above me here,
The Three Who are above me yonder,
The Three Who are in the earth,
The Three Who are in the air,
The Three Who are in the heaven,
The Three Who are in the pounding sea.

Every aspect of nature contains something of God. Carmichael tells us, for example, that the old men and women, in whom the ancient customs still survived, addressed daily hymns to sun and moon, often tramping several miles to the shore, winter or summer, "to join their voices with the voicing of the waves and their praises with the praises of the ceaseless sea." There they celebrated the power of the sun and the intelligence of the moon, that warmed the soil by day and guided ships home by night, and they gave thanks to God, who created and dwells in every heavenly orb. "Is it not much meeter for me," asked one crofter, "to bend my body to the sun and to the moon and to the stars, that the great God of life made for my good, than to the son or daughter of earth like myself?" There are traces of paganism in the *Carmina Gadelica*, but the presence of the one God lies behind every utterance, and in its pages all creation sings His praise. This is Christian environmentalism, and thus of particular interest to those who believe that Christianity is responsible for the current crisis and offers no way out. Here the eternal self-giving of the three Persons of the Trinity is the divine template against which all earthly relationships (including those between human beings and the other orders of being) must be measured. Here the saints, especially the Blessed Virgin and St. Bride, embody this environmentalism born of love; thus Bride—the most popular of all Gaelic saints—heals "as Christ did," and, in turn, the crofter heals "as Bride did." This is, then, an environmentalism whose motive is love, whose means is sanctity, whose fruit is beauty—the physical beauty of the natural world reflected in the moral beauty of its saints—and whose heart is the Eucharist, where divine and human unite, and where the fallen earth is restored to heavenly glory.

The culture portrayed in the *Carmina Gadelica* provides one set of clues to the resolution of the environmental crisis. There are many others, to be found in every authentic religious tradition. In *Seeing God Everywhere*, Barry McDonald has done us the great favor of gathering voices from many streams, ranging from Tibetan Buddhism to the Kabbalah to Orthodox Christianity to exponents of the perennial philosophy. Together, they constitute a universal chorus proclaiming some irreducible truths: that God abides above and yet within His creation; that every part of nature, even to the smallest sparrow playing in the dust, is a theophany, a "trace of God's passing" (St. John of the Cross); that our only hope lies in repairing the world, not as an engineer repairs a machine, but as an artist restores an icon. These truths are proclaimed here with intelligence, beauty, and prophetic force. They will give rise, in thoughtful readers, to a number of disturbing speculations: about how the world has come to such a sorry state and what radical adjustments may be necessary to rectify it; about how traditionalists might best press their views in a hostile secular culture; about the relationship between environmental recklessness and various moral issues such as cloning, euthanasia, and abortion.

How good it would be if this book were to come into the hands of everyone involved with the natural world: environmentalists, naturalists, scientists, hunters, fishers, farmers, every mother with a baby playing in the garden, every father mowing the lawn, every human being who breathes air, drinks water, eats of the earth. That is to say, this book speaks to us all. If its lessons were heard and heeded, wonders might result. All of us long for a way out of this self-imposed crisis, and we are hungry for any message that offers hope (witness the stunning success of Tolkien's *The Lord of the Rings*, a tale at least in part about environmental degradation and its resolution through courage, love, and divine grace). This splendid collection points the way and fills us with hope. As such, it deserves our attention and our thanks.

Philip Zaleski
Smith College
Senior Editor of Parabola

# Introduction: Sacred Nature

In an ancient Indian text of *Upanishad* it is said that the entire existence is imbued by the sacred. From a blade of grass to Mount Everest, all and everything is permeated by the divine. *Each and every particular to the totality of the Universe is the home of the Holy Spirit.* The god is not outside the world but the world is an embodiment of the divine. There is no separation, no division, no duality and no fragmentation. Everything is connected to everything else and the existence of one is dependant on the existence of the other. Thus, the earth and heaven and the entire cosmos are a seamless whole.

This deep realization of the unity of life and diversity of its manifestation is common to most traditional cultures. The American Indians saw the earth as mother, the sky as father and animals as brothers and sisters. The Aboriginals of Australia looked at the world and saw it as one wonderful dream. The Bushmen of the Kalahari and other tribes of Africa related to the land and to all its creatures as one family.

Tao in China also appreciated the working of the world as an intricate web of life to be handled with humility and care. Buddhists came to the same conclusion, they called it dependant co-arising: clouds arise from the sea, fall on the ground, nurture and nourish life and return to the sea again. This is the sacred cosmic cycle.

The Jains observed the profound truth of life nurturing life; through mutuality we maintain each other, through spirituality we sustain each other, through reciprocity we renew each other. There is a dance between conflict and compassion, between anger and appreciation and between creation and destruction. In the end there is balance and harmony within the big picture of eternal time and infinite space.

This is the perennial wisdom of saints and poets, wise and elder, which has served and nourished all aspects of existence. But at some point in human history hubris entered, particularly with the rise of scientific rationalism, the Age of Enlightenment and the Industrial Revolution. An idea emerged that nature "out there" is a separate object and humans "in here" are endowed to see nature as a resource for the benefit of humankind. It is our right to know the laws of nature and use it, control it and manipulate it to the benefit of humanity. We can take the gifts of nature and own them as ours and then do what we like with them. We are the masters of creation—its forests, rivers, mountains, fishes, fossils, animals, birds, gas, oil, coal and all. We have dominion over the land and the sky. We can split the atom and walk upon the moon; we can diminish the wild and enslave the animals. There are no limits to our power.

To exercise this power we developed mathematics and measurement. Nature must be measured, quantified and analyzed in order to control it and distill its secrets. How can this be done? The earth was not an empty space. Humans inhabited it. So those who got the notion of controlling nature also had to control people living in nature; and so boats and weapons were developed to occupy the Americas, Australia and Africa. The techniques of trade were developed to colonize Asia. This was the rise of the European project to amass political power and rule the world with the ideology of materialism.

This has lasted for the past 500 years and even now it continues to dominate the earth in the name of economic growth, progress, development, technological innovation, scientific inventions, globalization, free market and ever rising living standards.

However, there is a backlash from nature. The threat of climate change and global warming is causing deep unease across the world. The decrease of human health and increase of Aids, cancer, obesity and other diseases have already started to take their toll. Stress, anxiety, social breakdown and crime are defeating the political administrations across the world. Terrorism, regional conflicts, wars, and general insecurity are becoming a crippling preoccupation of policy makers, business leaders and armed forces.

Is this the dream of the founders of the American Dream, Enlightenment and the Industrial Revolution? Where is the joy of life which one can enjoy when one is not busy with making money and feeling anxious?

The experiment to create a religion of materialism has clearly failed. The fundamental human need to be happy is not met. In spite of all the gadgets of comforts, conveniences and gratifications, humanity is not at ease with itself. An increasing number of people are asking the question, "what is it all about and what is it all for?"

Now we are at a turning point. We are faced with a choice: either we can continue to follow the same path and live in the illusion of perpetual economic growth, remaining addicted to our gadgets, pursuing genetics, robotics and nanotechnology and ultimately reach the abyss; or we can turn towards sacred ecology; the path of values, ethics and aesthetics.

If we make the second choice then we need to follow some principles, which can help us along the way. The Jains have three guidelines:

1. **Reverence.** The materialistic worldview looks at nature and values it in terms of its usefulness to humans. In reverential ecology we see the intrinsic value of nature. A tree is good not just because it provides oxygen to humans and wood for furniture or fire (and therefore we take care of it), but a tree is good in itself, irrespective of its market value or human usefulness. A profound reverence for all life is essential for sustainability, for human survival, for mental serenity and for spiritual fulfillment. When we have deep reverence in our hearts we do least harm to others and we develop a non-violent way of relating to the world.

2. **Restraint.** The notion of perpetual economic growth knows no limits. We will clear the forests, and turn them into prairies, we will sweep the deepest parts of the oceans to get our fish, we will eliminate all wild life to build our cities and accommodate our cars. If the resources of this planet earth are not enough we will conquer the Moon and occupy Mars. This is a recipe for ruin. We need to learn the principle of restraint, and celebrate the joy of simplicity. As Mahatma Gandhi said, "there is enough in the world for everybody's need but not enough for anybody's greed."

3. **Replenishment.** The current mode of our living necessitates the idea of take, make and throw away. The linear thinking has permeated all aspects of our lives. The landfills are full of rubbish and waste has become the curse of modern civilization. We need to learn from nature. In nature there is no waste. Decaying material replenishes new growth. So we need to move away from our obsession with quantity of materials and possessions in our homes and towards quality of life. The beauty of reusing, repairing and recycling should be a joy in itself.

*Introduction*

In the context of practicing reverence, restraint and replenishment, *Seeing God Everywhere* is a wonderful collection of essays and poems which will inspire anyone who cares to read them. This book is a bouquet of fragrant flowers which will nourish the hearts and minds of spiritual seekers and earth pilgrims alike. The book honors many traditions, distills their insights and yet transcends their boundaries. Essays of this book leave the reader in no doubt that there are no short cuts, there are no technological fixes, there are no easy answers to rebuild human–nature relationships. It is a big challenge and this book is a noble attempt to meet that challenge.

Satish Kumar
Editor of *Resurgence* and
Programme Director of Schumacher College,
Devon, U.K.

# Chapter 1

# Seeing God Everywhere

## *Frithjof Schuon*

One often hears it said that it is necessary to "see God everywhere" or "in everything." For men who believe in God this does not seem a difficult conception; nevertheless there are many degrees involved, extending from simple reverie to intellectual intuition. How can one attempt to "see God," who is invisible and infinite, in what is visible and finite without the risk of deluding oneself or falling into error, or without giving the idea a meaning so vague that the words lose all significance? That is the question we propose to clarify here, though this means returning to certain points we have already treated elsewhere.

First of all, we must consider in the things around us—and also in our own soul insofar as it is an object of our intelligence—the something that might be called the "miracle of existence." Existence is miraculous: it is through existence that things are, so to speak, separated from nothingness; the gap between them and nothingness is infinite, and seen from this angle the least speck of dust possesses something of the absolute, and thus of the "Divine." To say that one must see God everywhere means above all that one must see Him in the existence of beings and of things, our own included.

But phenomena do not possess existence alone, for otherwise they would not be distinct; they also possess qualities which are as it were superimposed on existence and deploy its virtualities. The quality which distinguishes a good thing from a bad resembles, though on a lesser scale, the existence which distinguishes each thing from nothingness;[1] in consequence positive qualities repre-

---

1. We speak here of nothingness as if it had some reality, which is metaphysically necessary in certain cases although logically absurd. If there is no nothingness, there is nevertheless a "principle of nothingness," a principle which—since nothingness does not exist—always stops halfway. This principle is like the inverse shadow of the infinitude of Beyond-Being; it is *Mâyâ* which is illusorily detached from *Âtmâ*, though not able to emerge from *Âtmâ*, still less to abolish *Âtmâ*.

*1*

sent God, as does pure and simple existence. Beings are attracted by qualities because they are attracted by God; every quality or virtue, whether the slightest of physical properties or the most profound of human virtues, transmits to us something of the Divine Perfection which is its immutable source, so that, metaphysically speaking, we can have no motive for love other than this Perfection.

But there is yet another "dimension" to be considered by the man who seeks the remembrance of God in things. The enjoyment that qualities afford us shows that these not only exist around us, but also concern us personally through Providence; for a landscape which exists out of our sight is one thing, and a landscape we can see is another. There is thus a "subjective-temporal" dimension which is added to the "objective-spatial" dimension, if one may express oneself in this way: things recall God to us, not only insofar as they are good or display an aspect of goodness, but also insofar as we can perceive this goodness or enjoy it directly. In the air we breathe, which might be denied us, we meet God in the sense that the Divine Giver is in the gift. This manner of "seeing God" in His gifts corresponds to "thanksgiving," while the perception of qualities corresponds to "praise"; as for the "vision" of God in existence alone, this gives birth in the soul to a general or fundamental consciousness of the Divine Reality.

Thus, God reveals Himself not only by the existence and qualities of things, but by the gift He makes of them to us; He reveals himself also by contraries, namely, by the limitation of things and by their defects,[2] and again by the absence or disappearance of something which, being good, is useful and agreeable to us. It will be noticed that the concrete opposite of existence is not nothingness—the latter is only an abstraction—but limitation, the limitation which prevents existence from extending to pure Being and thus becoming God. Things are limited in multiple ways, but above all by their existential determinations, which, on the terrestrial level, are matter, form, number, space, time. A clear distinction must be made between the aspect of "limit" and the aspect of "defect"; the ugliness of a creature is not of the same order as the spatial limitation of a perfect body, for the latter expresses a form, a normative principle, or a symbol, while the former corresponds

---

2. It is in this sense that Meister Eckhart could say: "The more he blasphemes, the more he praises God."

only to a lack and merely confuses the clarity of the symbolism. However that may be, what God reveals by the limitation of things, by their defects, and also, in relation to the human subject, by the privation of things or of qualities, is the "non-divine", hence "illusory" or "unreal" character of all that is not He.

\*

\* \*

All things are only the accidentalities of a unique and universal substance, Existence, which remains always virgin in relation to its products; it manifests, but is not itself manifested; that is, it is the Divine act, the creative act, which, starting from Being, produces the totality of creatures. It is Existence that is real, not things; substance, not accidents; the unvarying, not the variations. Since this is so, how could things not be limited, and how could they not proclaim, by their multiple limitations, the unicity of the Divine Word, and thereby of God? For universal Substance is none other than the creative Word, the word "Be!" from which all things spring.

To say "exist" is to say "to have qualities," but it is also to say "to have limitations," even defects. We have already noted that things are limited, not only in themselves, but also in relation to us; they are limited and ephemeral, and at the same time they elude our grasp, whether by their remoteness in space or by the destiny that carries them away. This again allows us to "see God in everything," for if God manifests His Reality, His Plenitude, and His Presence in His act of giving, He manifests our relativity, our emptiness, our absence—in relation to Him—in removing, that is, in taking back what He has given.

Just as qualities express existence on the actual level of the latter, so too limitations express, in an inverse sense, the metaphysical unreality of things. Herein lies a new manner of "seeing God everywhere": for each thing, in existing, is by that very fact "unreal" in relation to absolute Reality; we should therefore discern in all things not only their existential aspects, but also their "nothingness" before God, or in other words the metaphysical unreality of the world. And it is existence[3] itself which furnishes us with the "substance" of this "nothingness"; things are unreal or illu-

---

3. Existence is positive and "Divine" in relation to existing things and insofar as it is cause, but it is limitative and "demiurgic" in relation to God, who, in the act of

*3*

sory to the exact extent that they are embedded in existence and that their contact with the Divine Spirit thereby becomes more and more indirect.

Quality, we have said, expresses existence on the level of existence itself; and we could say analogously that a defect expresses limitation in a manner which is solely negative and accidental. For limitation stands in a certain manner between existence and nothingness: it is positive insofar as it delineates a form-symbol, and negative insofar as it disfigures this form in seeking to bring it back, as it were, towards the indistinction of the essence, but "from below"; this is the classical confusion between the supra-formal and the formless, a confusion which, let it be said in passing, is the key to "abstract" or "surrealist" art. However, although form has a positive function thanks to its power of expression, it limits at the same time what it expresses, which is an essence: the most beautiful body is like a congealed fragment of an ocean of inexpressible bliss.

\*

\* \*

To all these categories of existence, subjective as well as objective, we can add those of symbolism. Although every phenomenon is of necessity a symbol, since existence is essentially expression or reflection, we must nevertheless distinguish degrees of content and of intelligibility: for example, there is an eminent—and not a merely quantitative—difference between a direct symbol such as the sun and an indirect, quasi-accidental symbol; further, there is the negative symbol, the intelligibility of which may be perfect, but its content obscure; nor should we forget the double meaning of many symbols, though not of those that are most direct. The science of symbols—not simply a knowledge of traditional symbols—proceeds from the qualitative significances of substances, forms, spatial directions, numbers, natural phenomena, positions, relationships, movements, colors, and other properties or states of things; we are not dealing here with subjective appreciations, for the cosmic qualities are ordered in relation to Being and according to a hierarchy which is more real than the individual; they are therefore inde-

creating, limits Himself in a certain illusory sense, if such an expression is allowable; an illusory sense, we say, since God is immutable, impassible, inalterable.

pendent of our tastes, or rather they determine them to the extent that we are ourselves conformable to Being; we assent to the qualities to the extent that we ourselves are "qualitative."[4] Symbolism, whether it resides in nature or is affirmed in sacred art, also corresponds to a manner of "seeing God everywhere," on condition that this vision is spontaneous thanks to an intimate knowledge of the principles from which the science of symbols proceeds; this science coincides at a certain point with the "discerning of spirits," which it transposes onto the plane of forms or phenomena, whence its close connection with religious art.

How, then, do things symbolize God or "Divine aspects"? One cannot say that God is this tree, nor that this tree is God, but one can say that the tree is, in a certain aspect, not "other than God," or that, not being non-existent, it cannot not be God in any fashion. For the tree has firstly existence, then the life which distinguishes it from minerals, then its particular qualities which distinguish it from other plants, and finally its symbolism; all of these are for the tree so many manners, not only of "not being nothingness," but also of affirming God in one or another respect: life, creation, majesty, axial immobility, or generosity.

In a certain sense, God alone is "that which is not nothing"; He alone is "non-inexistence"—two negatives at once, but having their precise function. Truths of this kind can give rise, indirectly and by deviation, to pantheism and idolatry, but this does not prevent them from being true and therefore, to say the least, legitimate on their own level.

Symbolism would have no meaning if it were not a contingent, but always conscious, mode of perception of Unity; for "to see God everywhere" is to perceive above all the Unity—*Âtmâ*, the Self—in phenomena. According to the *Bhagavad-Gita*, "The cognition which recognizes in all beings an essence that is unique, imperishable, indivisible, although diffused in separate objects, proceeds from *Sattva*" (the tendency that is "luminous," "ascendant,"

---

4. A man must be quite perverse to see no qualitative and objective difference between what is noble and what is mean, unless he takes his stand at the transcendent point of view of the non-differentiation of *Âtmâ*, which is an absolutely different thing from a subversive and iconoclastic egalitarianism. However that may be, it is this science of qualitative phenomena which allows the aberrations of contemporary art to be "placed" inexorably and the veil of its false mystery to be torn aside.

"conformable to Being," *Sat*); and the same text continues: "But the cognition which, led astray by the multiplicity of objects, sees in all beings diverse and distinct entities proceeds from *rajas* (the 'fiery,' 'expansive' tendency). As for that shuttered cognition which, without returning to causes, is attached to a particular object as if it were all in all, this proceeds from *tamas* (the 'dark' and 'downward' tendency)" (18:20-22). It is necessary here to take into account the angle from which things are envisaged: the cosmic tendencies (*gunas*) are not only in the mind of man; they clearly enter also into his faculties of relative knowledge and the realms corresponding to them, so that reason can no more escape diversity than can the eye; further, to say that such and such a cognition "recognizes a unique essence in all beings" amounts to affirming that these beings exist on their own plane. It is a question, then, of admitting not that there are no objective differences around us, but that the latter are in no way opposed to the perception of the unity of the essence; the "passional" perspective (*rajas*) is at fault, not because it perceives differences, but because it lends them an absolute character, as if each being were a separate existence; so also does the eye in a certain way, precisely because it corresponds existentially to a "passional" view insofar as it belongs to the ego, which is "made of passion." The Intellect, which perceives the unity of essence in things, discerns at the same time the differences of modes and degrees as a function of this unity, apart from which the distinction between the *gunas* would be excluded.

We have alluded above to the conditions of sensory or psychophysical existence: space, time, form, number, substance—modes which moreover are not all reducible to our plane of existence (since the latter could not be a closed system), any more than they enclose man wholly, since man extends towards the Infinite. These conditions denote so many principles which allow one to "see God in things"; space gives extension and conserves, while limiting by form; time limits and devours, while giving extension by duration; form both expresses and limits at the same time; number is a principle of expansion, but without the force of quality or, it could be said, the virtue of form; and finally substance, which on the physical plane becomes "matter,"[5] denotes existence on such and such a level, hence the "level of existence."[6] Form, in itself qualitative, has something quantitative about it when it is material; number, in itself quantitative, has something qualitative when it is abstract. The materiality of form adds size and so quantity to the latter; the symbolic character of number frees it from its quantitative function and confers on it a principial value, hence a quality.[7] Time, which is "vertical" in relation to space, which is "horizontal"— although a geometrical symbolism is barely proper to a consideration which clearly goes outside the spatial condition—exceeds the limits of terrestrial existence and is projected in a certain fashion and within certain bounds into the "beyond," a fact of which the connection in terrestrial life between psychic life and time already offers a foretaste; this connection is more intimate than that which links the soul with the space surrounding us, as is shown by the fact that it is easier to abstract oneself, in concentration, from spatial extension than from duration; the soul of a blind man is as it were cut off from space, but not from time. As for matter, it is, still more directly than the subtle or animic substance, universal substance "congealed"[8] or "crystallized" by the cold proximity of "nothingness"; this "nothingness" the process of manifestation could never reach, for the simple reason that absolute "nothingness" does not

5. This fifth condition has sometimes been called "life," doubtless to express the idea that inertia could not be absolute or that the ether possesses a certain vital potentiality, without which life—"breath" (or *prâna*)—would find no receptacle.

6. The Sanskrit word for "matter," *bhûta*, includes a meaning of "substance" or "subsistence"; matter derives from substance; it is a reflection of it on the plane of "gross" coagulation and is connected, through substance, with Being.

7. This is number in the Pythagorean sense, of which the universal rather than the quantitative import is already to be divined in geometrical figures; the triangle and the square are "personalities" and not quantities; they are essentials and not accidentals. While one obtains ordinary number by addition, qualitative number results on the contrary from an internal or intrinsic differentiation of principial unity; it is not added to anything and does not depart from unity. Geometrical figures are so many images of unity; they exclude one another, or rather they denote different principial qualities; the triangle is harmony, the square stability; these are "concentric" not "serial" numbers.

8. This "congealing" does not affect substance itself, any more than, in the order of the five elements, "solidification"—or the diversification of the elements in general—affects the ether which subsists in them. All the same this comparison is not adequate, since ether is an element and is not then situated on another plane, despite its "central" position and its "virginity," while universal substance is transcendent in relation to its productions.

exist, or rather it exists only by the way of "indication," "direction," or "tendency" in the work of creation itself; an image of this is seen in the fact that cold is merely a privation and thus has no positive reality, though it transforms water into snow and ice, as if it had the power to produce bodies.

Space "sets out" from the point or the center; it is "expansion," and it "tends" toward infinitude without ever being able to attain it; time sets out from the instant or the present;[9] it is duration, and it tends toward eternity; form sets out from simplicity; it is differentiation or complexity, and it tends toward perfection; number sets out from unity; it is multiplicity or quantity, and it tends toward totality;[10] finally, matter sets out from ether; it is crystallization or density, and it tends toward immutability, which is at the same time indestructibility. In each of these cases, the "middle term"—what the respective condition "is"—seeks in short the perfection or virtue of the "point of departure," but it seeks it on its own level or rather in its own movement, where it is impossible that it should be attained: if expansion had the virtue of the point, it would be infinity; if duration had the virtue of the instant, it would be eternity; if form had the virtue of simplicity, it would be perfection; if number had the virtue of unity, it would be totality; if matter had the virtue—immutable because omnipresent—of ether, it would be immutability.

If it is objected that, on the formal plane, perfection is attained by the sphere, we reply that formal perfection could not be restricted to the simplest form, for what distinguishes a beautiful form of complex character—such as the human body—from the

---

9. In relation to the "point" and the "instant," the "center" and the "present" denote a perspective at once qualitative and subjective: qualitative subjectivity, because the subject is the Self. The objective terms—"point" and "instant"—certainly imply this same "quality," but the spiritual relationship—not the metaphysical relationship—is less direct and less apparent, precisely because the respective notions are detached from life.

10. In these two conditions, form and number, the respective points of departure—simplicity and unity—have a concrete existence, doubtless because these conditions are "contents" in relation to space and time, which are "containers"; on the other hand, the points of departure of these latter conditions—the point and the instant—have respectively neither extent nor duration. Nonetheless, spherical simplicity is not one form among others, since it is incomparable, any more than unity is a quantity properly speaking, since it is not added to anything; if there were only simplicity and unity, there would be neither form nor number.

sphere is in no way a lack of perfection, the less so since the formal principle tends precisely towards complexity; it is only therein that it can realize beauty. But this in no way signifies that perfection could be obtained on this plane; in fact, complex perfection demands a form which combines the most rigorous necessity or intelligibility with the greatest diversity, and this is impossible because formal possibilities are innumerable to the extent that they move further and further, by means of differentiation, from the initial spherical form. In plunging into complexity, one can certainly attain the "unilateral" or "relatively absolute" perfection of a given beauty, but not the integral and absolute perfection of all beauty; the condition of pure necessity is realized only in the spherical and "undifferentiated" proto-form.

What enters into space enters also into time; what enters into form enters also into number; what enters into matter thereby enters into form, number, space, time. Space, which "contains" like a matrix[11] and which "preserves," recalls Goodness or Mercy to us; it is connected with love; time, on the contrary, ceaselessly throws us into a "past" which is no more and carries us towards a "future" which is not yet, or rather will never be, and which we do not know, save for death, the sole certainty of life; this implies that time is associated with Rigor or Justice and that it is connected with fear. As for matter, it recalls Reality to us, for it is that mode of "non-inexistence" which is everywhere apparent to us, in our body just as in the sight of the Milky Way; form reminds us of the Divine Law or the universal norm, for it is either veridical or erroneous, exact or false, essential or accidental; finally, number unfolds before us the limitlessness of All-Possibility, which like the sand of the desert or the stars of the sky is not to be numbered.

However much space may limit its contents, it cannot prevent them from existing; and however much time may prolong its contents, they will one day cease to exist just the same. Duration does not abolish ephemerality any more than spatial limitation abolishes extension. In space, nothing is ever wholly lost; in time, all is irremediably lost.

Existence is manifested *a priori* by substance. The latter has two containers, space and time, of which the first is positive and the

---

11. It is for us like a "womb of immortality," death being birth into eternal Life.

second negative; it has also two modes, form and number, of which the first is limitative and the second expansive. Number reflects space, since it extends; form reflects time, since it restricts.

If man could live a thousand years, he would doubtless end by feeling himself crushed by the limits of things, hence also by space, time, form, number, matter; by compensation, he would see in contents only essences. A child or indeed an ordinary man sees, on the contrary, only contents, without essences and without limits.

*<br>* *

These conditions of our existence on earth have, each one of them, two "openings" toward God: space implies, on the one hand, the geometric point or the "center" and, on the other, limitless extension, the "infinite"; likewise time implies the instant or the "present," as well as indefinite duration, "eternity"; in space we are as it were between the center and the infinite, and in time, between the present and eternity, and these are then so many dwellings of God which take us out of the two "dimensions of existence"; we cannot prevent ourselves from thinking of them when we are conscious of these conditions in which we live and which so to speak live in us. The center and the infinite, the present and eternity, are respectively the poles of the conditions of space and time, but equally we escape these conditions by these very poles: the center is no longer in space, strictly speaking, any more than the geometric point has extension, and the absolute present or the pure instant is no longer in duration: as for the infinite, it is in a way "non-space" as eternity is "non-time."

But let us consider the formal condition; in form there lie geometrical perfection and bodily perfection, and both reveal God; the Creator manifests Himself in the "absoluteness" of the circle, the square, the cross, as in the beauty—the infinity—of man or a flower; geometrical beauty is "cold," bodily beauty "warm." But strictly speaking, the "center" of the formal condition is the void; elementary geometrical forms, starting with the sphere, represent the first "issuing forth" of form out of the void, thus at the same time the first "expressions" and "negations" of the latter. The sphere is the form which remains nearest the void, whence its perfection of simplicity; the human body, in its normative beauty—and the varied modes which it comprises—is what approaches most nearly to plenitude, corresponding to the opposite perfection, that of complexity. Plenitude is that which brings together a maximum of homogeneous aspects or which introduces totality into form: the sphere and man correspond, in formal mode, to unity and totality; what number expresses in abstract, separative, and quantitative mode, form expresses in concrete, unitive, and qualitative mode. Zero is to unity what the void is to the sphere; unity denotes God, while totality is equivalent to His manifestation, the cosmos.

*<br>* *

"To see God everywhere" is to see Oneself (*Âtmâ*) in everything; it is to be conscious of the analogical correspondences—insofar as they are "modes of identity"—between the principles or possibilities which, included first in the Divine Nature, spread out or reverberate "in the direction of nothingness" and constitute the microcosm as well as the macrocosm, of which they create at one and the same time the receptacles and the contents. Space and time are receptacles; form and number appear as contents, although they are containers in relation to the substances which they coagulate or which they segment. Matter is, in a more visible way, both container and content at the same time; it "contains" things, and it "fills" space; its contents are gnawed and devoured by time, but it itself remains quasi non-temporal, so that it coincides in effect with the whole of duration.

The problem of time is intimately linked with that of the soul and can give rise to the following question: what meaning must be given to the dogmatic doctrine of the soul held by Monotheists, according to which the soul is said to have no end, while having had a beginning? The metaphysical absurdity of an eternity created in time, or of a purely "unilateral" perpetuity, is evident; but since theological orthodoxy excludes pure and simple absurdity, one must seek beyond the words and in symbolism for the explanation of a doctrine so contradictory. Let us say at once that Monotheism includes in its perspective only what directly interests man, so that it appears as a "spiritual nationalism" of the human race; but since the state preceding our birth on earth was as little human as are the animal or angelic states, it is treated as non-existent, exactly as are the souls of animals and plants; hence, we are called "soul" only from the moment of our human birth, or rather from entry into the womb. But there is something else of much more importance; the creation of the soul in time—that is, its entry into the human state—expresses our relativity; by contrast, the celestial perpetuity of the soul, or its eternity with God, concerns its absolute side, the "uncreated" quality of its essence; we are relative and absolute at the same time, and this fundamental paradox of our being explains what the theological doctrine of the soul contains that is illogical or "mysterious" in its very formulation. It must not be forgotten, on the other hand, that *creatio ex nihilo* affirms above all a Divine causality in the face of an ever threatening "naturalism"; and to say that the soul is "eternal" can mean only, on the level of absolute truth, that it is "essentially" the Self.

*

\* \*

The faculty of "seeing God in everything" can be independent of all intellectual analysis; it can be a grace, the modes of which are imponderables and which springs from a profound love of God. When we say "intellectual analysis" we do not mean speculations in the void: the "categories" of which we have spoken are by no means "abstract," but their perception evidently depends on a discernment which appears to be abstract from the point of view of sensations and which, though far from delighting in sterile dissections, is nevertheless obliged to "separate" in order to "unite." Separation and union alike are in the nature of things—each, it might be said, on its own level; the eye, the better to see a mountain, needs a certain distance; this distance reveals differences; it permits visual analysis, but at the same time it "unites" or synthesizes in furnishing the adequate and total image of the mountain.

To see God everywhere and in everything is to see infinity in things, whereas human animality sees only their surface and their relativity; and it is to see at the same time the relativity of the categories in which man moves, believing them to be absolute. To see the infinite in the finite is to see that this flower before us is eternal because an eternal spring is affirmed through its fragile smile; to see relativity is to grasp that this instant that we are living in is not "now," that it is "past" even before it has arrived, and that, if time could be stopped—with all beings remaining fixed as in a river of ice—the human masquerade would appear in all its sinister unreality; all would seem absurd, save only the "remembrance of God," which is situated in the immutable.

To see God everywhere is essentially this: to see that we are not, that He alone is. If from a certain angle humility can be called the greatest of the virtues, this is because it implies in the last analysis the cessation of egoity, and for no other reason. With a small change of viewpoint one could say as much of each fundamental virtue: perfect charity is to lose oneself for God, for one cannot lose oneself in God without giving oneself in addition to men. If love of one's neighbor is fundamental on the strictly human plane, it is not only because the "neighbor" is in the final analysis "Self" as are "we," but also because this human charity—or this projection into the "other"—is the sole means possible for the majority of men of being detached from the "I"; it is less difficult to project the ego into the "other" than to lose it for God, although the two things are indissolubly linked.

Our form is the ego: it is that mysterious incapacity to be other than oneself, and at the same time the incapacity to be entirely oneself and not "other-than-Self." But our Reality does not leave us the choice and obliges us to "become what we are," or to remain what we are not. The ego is, empirically, a dream in which we ourselves dream ourselves; the contents of this dream, drawn from our surroundings, are at bottom only pretexts, for the ego desires only its own life: whatever we may dream, our dream is always only a symbol for the ego, which wishes to affirm itself, a mirror that we hold before the "I" and which reverberates its life in multiple fashions. This dream has become our second nature; it is woven of images and of tendencies, static and dynamic elements in innumerable combinations: the images come from outside and are integrated into our substance, whereas the tendencies are our responses to the world around us; as we exteriorize ourselves we create a world in the image of our dream, and the dream thus objectivized flows back upon us, and so on and on, until we are enclosed in a tissue, sometimes inextricable, of dreams exteriorized or materialized and of materializations interiorized. The ego is like a watermill whose wheel, under the drive of a current—the world and life—turns and repeats itself untiringly in a series of images always different and always similar.

The world: it is as if the "conscious Substance" which is the Self had fallen into a state which would split it up in many different ways and would inflict on it endless accidents and infirmities; and in fact the ego is ignorance floundering in objective modes of ignorance, such as time and space. What is time, if not ignorance of what will be "after," and what is space, if not ignorance of what escapes our sense? If we were "pure consciousness" like the Self, we would be "always" and "everywhere"; that is, we would not be "I," for that, in its empirical actuality, is entirely a creation of space and time. The ego is ignorance of what is the "other"; our whole existence is woven of ignorances; we are like the Self frozen, then hurled "to earth" and broken into a thousand fragments; we observe the limits which surround us, and we conclude that we are fragments of conscious-ness and of being. Matter grips us like a kind of paralysis; it imposes on us the heaviness of a mineral and exposes us to the miseries of impurity and of mortality; form shapes us according to such and such a model; it imposes on us such and such a mask and cuts us off from a whole to which we are none the less tied, though at death it lets us fall as a tree lets fall its fruit; finally, number is what repeats us—inside ourselves as also around us—and what, in repeating us, diversifies us, for two things can never be absolutely identical; number repeats form as if by magic, and form diversifies number and must thus create itself ever anew, because All-Possibility is infi-nite and must manifest its infinitude. But the ego is not only mul-tiple externally, in the diversity of souls; it is also divided within itself in the diversity of tendencies and thoughts, which is not the least of our miseries; for "strait is the gate," and "a rich man shall hardly enter into the kingdom of heaven."

And since we are "not other" than the Self, we are condemned to eternity. Eternity lies in wait for us, and that is why we must find again the Center, that place where eternity is bliss. Hell is the reply to the periphery which makes itself the Center, or to the multitude that usurps the glory of Unity; it is the reply of Reality to the ego wanting to be absolute and condemned to be so without being able to be so. The Center is the Self "freed," or rather that which has never ceased to be free—eternally free.

*Nothing is without voice:*
*God everywhere can hear*
*Arising from creation*
*His praise and echo clear.*

*You travel far and wide*
*To scout and see and search;*
*If God you fail to see,*
*You have nothing observed.*

*— Angelus Silesius*

## Chapter 2

# A Tibetan Buddhist Perspective on Spirit in Nature

*Tenzin Gyatso, His Holiness the 14th Dalai Lama*

Brothers and sisters, I am very happy to be here with you, to come to this beautiful place once more. I have enjoyed the last few days very much. The speeches from the leaders of the various traditions have been very impressive.

Although I have prepared a speech myself, a large number of people have come here today, and I think you may have different interests. This creates confusion in my mind right now; just what subject should I address to be most helpful to all of you?

The first thing that will relieve my small anxiety is to confess that I am not an expert or a specialist on ecology or the environment. So I will address a broader subject. And if you have come here with some expectation on that score, I can say that, essentially, I have nothing to offer to you. I can simply try to share some of my own views and experiences, and then maybe some of you will find some benefit; or at least some new ideas to think about.

Now, first I will try to explain briefly the Buddhist attitude and approach to the environmental crisis. In dealing with this subject I would like to divide my talk in three stages. First, I will talk about the Buddhist perception of nature and reality. Second, I will discuss what kind of ethical principle an individual should adopt, based on that view of reality and nature. Third, I will talk about what kind of right conduct, what kind of measures individuals and society should take to restore and correct the degradation of nature and the earth, based on such an ethical principle.

When talking about developing a correct understanding or correct view of reality and nature, Buddhism emphasizes the applica-

---

* Editor's Note: This talk was delivered at the Symposium on "Spirit and Nature" held at Middlebury College in Middlebury, Vermont in 1990.

tion of reasoning and analysis. It talks about four avenues of reasoning or analysis through which one can develop a correct understanding of reality and nature. These four can be called natural, relational, functional, and logical avenues of reasoning. Reasoning and analysis have to take into account the natural laws of the universe, the interrelationships that exist in the universe, the functional properties of things in reality, and the processes of reason itself, with which it understands the universe.

First one takes into account the fundamental laws of nature, such as the fact that things exist, the fact that matter differs from consciousness, the fact that mind exists in a certain way, and so on. Second, reason takes into account the interdependence between these various entities that exist in the world, the interdependence between causes and conditions, the interdependence between parts that constitute a whole, and so on. Third, reason takes into account the functional properties that we see in reality, the properties which emerge as a consequence of the interaction between multiple factors. Fourth, based on these three levels of understanding nature, Buddhism emphasizes understanding the process of human reasoning and analysis itself. For example, reason can understand how reliable knowledge is generated through inference, either about the probable nature of a cause from the observed nature of its effect, or about a probable future state of affairs from an observed state of its cause. In short, while Buddhism is usually thought of as a religion, it is actually a way of thought that emphasizes the necessity for human reason to be applied to human problems.

When talking about the fundamental nature of reality, one could sum up the entire understanding of that nature in a simple verse: "Form is emptiness, and emptiness is form" (The Heart Sutra). This simple line sums up the Buddhist understanding of the fundamental nature of reality. In appearance, we see the world of existence and experience. In essence, all those things are empty of intrinsic reality, of independent existence. Superficially, if we were to look at the words "emptiness" and "form" or "appearance," they might seem to be contradictory. If anything has appearance, how can it be empty? If anything is empty, how can it have a form or appearance? To overcome this contradiction, one must understand the meaning of emptiness to be interdependence. The meaning of interdependence is emptiness of independent existence. Precisely because things and events exist relatively and appear as having form, they are empty of independent existence.

Events and things come into being as a result of the aggregation of many factors, causes and conditions. But because they lack independent or absolute existence, it is possible for experiences such as our sufferings—which we do not desire—to come to a cessation. And because they lack independent or absolute existence, it is possible for pleasant experiences such as our happiness—which we do desire—to be created within ourselves.

Fundamental to attaining the Buddhist perception of reality, which ultimately is emptiness, is the understanding of relativity, the principle of interdependence. And the meaning of interdependence has three levels. At its subtlest level, it is the interdependence of things with thought and conceptual designations. At its middle level, it is the interdependence of parts and wholes. And at the surface level, it is the interdependence of causes and effects.

I think there is a direct connection between the correct understanding of ecology and the natural environment and the Buddhist principle of interdependence in terms of causes and effects and in terms of parts and wholes, factors and aggregates. But the correct understanding of the subtlest level of interdependence—that of the interdependence of things and conceptual constructions—has more to do with maintaining the balance of the outer and the inner world, and with the purification of the inner world.

I believe that every individual living being, whether animal or human, has an innate sense of self. Stemming from that innate sense of self, there is an innate desire to enjoy happiness and overcome suffering. And this is something which is innate to all beings. I believe it is a natural phenomenon. But if we tried to examine why such innate faculties are there within living beings, I do not think we could ever find a convincing answer. I would rather stop there and say that it is a natural fact. Various different philosophies have tried to examine that nature of living beings. And still, after centuries, this is not yet finally solved. So I think it is better to accept this as something natural, as a reality.

Therefore, we can say that the purpose of life is happiness, joy, and satisfaction, because life itself, I think, exists on the ground of hope, on the basis of hope. And hope is, of course, for the better, for the happier. That is quite natural, isn't it? In that case, relations with one's fellow human beings—and also, animals, including insects (even those which sometimes seem quite troublesome)—should be based on the awareness that all of them seek happiness, and none of them want suffering. All have a right to happiness, a right to freedom from suffering. And generally speaking, all beings seem beautiful to us, beautiful birds, beautiful beasts. Their presence gives us some kind of tranquility, some kind of joy; they are like an ornament to our lives really. And then the forest, the plants, and the trees, all these natural things come together to make our surroundings pleasant. All are heavily interdependent in creating our joy and happiness, in removing our sufferings.

Our human ancestors survived by depending on trees, on wood. Their fires depended on the wood. The trees gave them shelter and protection. When a dangerous animal threatened them, they could climb up to safety. Some trees bear beautiful flowers, which are ornaments, which they picked and wore in their hair, something like our modern jewelry. Then, of course, there's the fruit of the trees, and nuts, which are nourishing. And finally, of course, there are sticks made from the branches; when someone attacks, it's a weapon; when you get older, it is a cane, like a reliable friend. Such examples, I think, show the historical basis of human nature. Later, as human culture developed, we made something more beautiful out of it, something poetical. During our ancestors' time, human survival and welfare were very dependent on trees. But as society and culture became more developed and sophisticated, this dependence became less and less, and trees became the subject of poetry.

So, therefore, this shows that our very existence is something heavily dependent on the environment. Now since we are seeking happiness and joy, we must be able to distinguish the different causes and conditions that lead to happiness and joy, causes both immediate and long-term. One finds that, although the ultimate aim of the major world religions is the achievement of the happy life after death, eternal life, they do not encourage their adherents to neglect the well-being of the present life. The expressed aim of Buddhism is the purification and development of the mind through mental training in order to attain supreme liberation. But the meditation manuals place great emphasis on finding an ideal environment for the practice of training the mind because a cleaner environment does have a tremendous impact on one's spiritual progress. The Buddhist literature mentions the sanctity of the environment as inspiring and blessing the practitioner, and in turn the practitioner's spiritual realization blessing the environment. There is an exchange between human spirit and nature. In tune with such awareness, we find in Buddhist practice specific rituals aimed at regenerating the vitality of the earth, at purifying the environment, wherein certain precious minerals are buried underground, and then consecration rituals are performed.

I think that in ancient time, the human ability to measure the imbalance of nature was very limited, almost none. At that time, there was no need for worry or concern. But today, the human ability to disturb the balance of nature is growing. World population has increased immeasurably. Due to many factors, nature, even the Mother Planet herself, it seems, is showing us a red light. She is saying, "Be careful, you should realize there are limits!"

Taking care of the planet is nothing special, nothing sacred or holy. It's just like taking care of our own house. We have no other planet, no other house, except this one. Even if there are a lot of disturbances and problems, it is our only alternative. We cannot go to any other planet. If the moon is seen from a distance, it appears quite beautiful. But if we go there to stay, I think, it would be horrible. So, our blue planet is much better, much happier. Therefore, we have to take care of our own place. This is not something special or holy. This is just a practical fact!

*

\*  \*

Now I will go on to the second part of my talk, the development of an ethical principle based on the Buddhist understanding of reality and nature as emptiness and interdependence.

Essentially, nature's elements have secret ways of adapting. When something is damaged, another element helps out and improves the situation through some kind of evolution. This is nature's way of adjustment. But then, human intervention creates certain changes which do not give nature and its elements time to cope. So the main troublemaker, the major cause of imbalance, is we human beings ourselves. Therefore, the responsibility should be borne by us. We must find some way to restrain our destructive habits. We cause these problems mainly with our modern economy. With different kinds of factories and chemicals, we have a strong negative impact on the balance of nature. The next question is, if that is the case, whether we have to stop all factories, all chemicals.

Of course, we cannot do that. While there are negative side effects, there are also tremendous benefits. True science and technology bring humanity a lot of benefit.

So what to do? We must use our human intelligence. And in some cases, we must have more patience. We must cultivate more contentment. And we must handle new progress and development in a proper way, keeping the side effects to a minimum. At the same time, we must take care of the earth and its basic elements in a more balanced way, no matter how expensive the cost. I think that's the only way.

Here I have come to the third part of my talk. Based on a practical ethic of caring for our home, grounded in our understanding of interdependence, what kind of measures can we take to correct these imbalances in nature? Generally speaking, crises emerge as a consequence of certain causes or conditions. Principal among them is ignorance of the real situation. In order to overcome that, the most effective means is to develop knowledge and understanding. Presently, older people like myself are speaking out about these dangers—but I think that is very limited in effect. The greater responsibility, I feel, lies with the scientists, especially those who are trained in this field. Through their research, with their experimental data, they should make clear the real long-term consequences of certain negative practices and positive measures. Scientists and environmental experts should prepare a very specific and detailed global study of the long-term dangers and benefits our society will face in the future. Materials based on such studies should then be thoroughly learned by young students in school right from the start. Young children should take the environment into account when they study about geography, economics, or history. I feel it's very important to introduce ecology into the school curriculum, pointing out the environmental problems that the world currently faces. Even at a very early age, children should be exposed to the understanding and knowledge of the planetary environmental crisis. The various media—newspapers, television—all should be responsible for communicating the reality of this threatening situation.

In some cases, we might be able to overcome ignorance, understand reality, and reach the situation where everyone knows what is going on. But still we do not act to prevent disaster. Such a lack of will to act—in spite of having the knowledge and understanding—

stems, I think, either from negligence (becoming totally oblivious to the crisis) or from discouragement (the feeling that "I have no ability, I simply cannot do anything").

I firmly believe that the most important factor is our attitude and human motivation. Genuine human love, human kindness, and human affection. This is the key thing. That will help us to develop human determination also. Genuine love or compassion is not a feeling of lofty pity, sympathy tinged with contempt toward the other, a looking down on them; it is not like that. True love or compassion is actually a special sense of responsibility. A strong sense of care and concern for the happiness of the other, that is genuine love. Such true love automatically becomes a sense of responsibility.

So, how should we develop compassion? How should we expand our love? First, it is very important to know that within the meaning of "love" there are various emotions. What is commonly called "love" is often merely blind love, or blind attachment. In many cases, it involves unconscious projections on the other, possessiveness, and desire; it is usually not at all good. There is a second level of love or compassion, which is a kind of condescending pity. But that is not really positive compassion. We feel genuine compassion and love not just for beings close to us, but for all persons and animals. Such true compassion develops from the recognition that everyone does not want suffering and does want happiness, just like us. When we really feel that, we feel that they have every right to be happy and every right to overcome suffering. Realizing that, we naturally develop a genuine concern for their suffering and their right to be free from it.

We can feel this kind of genuine love for others no matter what their attitude toward us. That love is steady; so long as any person or being suffers, we feel responsible, even if he or she is our enemy. Love mixed with attachment makes us concerned only for beings close to us. That kind of love is biased and always narrow and limited. But genuine love is much wider and stronger. And it can be developed. If we analyze the situation in various ways, we can develop a firm conviction about the need for such a mental attitude, even out of self-interest. In our daily life, it is the energy of genuine love and compassion that is the source of hope, the source of happiness, the source of joy, and the source of inner strength. When we have that kind of love with its strong sense of responsibility, we will never lose our hope or our determination. The more we are challenged by negative forces, the more determination we will develop. So it is really the source of every success. That is what I always feel.

In our daily lives, we love smiles. I especially love a genuine smile, not a sarcastic smile, or a diplomatic smile, which sometimes even increases suspicion. But I consider the genuine smile something really precious. It is the great bridge of communication. Whether you know the same language or not, whether you are from the same culture, or nation, or race all that is secondary. The basic thing is to realize that the other is a human being, a gentle human being who wants happiness and does not want suffering, just like ourselves. At that basic level, we just smile—we can exchange smiles. Then immediately the barrier is broken and we feel close.

After all, a human being is a social animal. I often tell my friends that there is no need to study philosophy or other complicated subjects. Just look at those innocent insects, like ants or bees. I am very fond of honey so I am always exploiting the bees' hard work. Therefore, I have a special interest in the lives of bees. I learned many things about them and developed a special relationship with them. They amaze me. They have no religion, no constitution, and no police force, but their natural law of existence requires harmony, and they have a natural sense of responsibility. They follow nature's system.

So what is wrong with us, we human beings? We have such a great intelligence, our human intelligence, our human wisdom. But I think we often use our human intelligence in the wrong way, we turn it in the wrong direction. As a result, in a way we are doing certain actions which are essentially contrary to our basic human nature. And here I always feel that basic human nature is compassion or affection. This is quite simple. If we look closely at the beginning of human life, at the conception of a child, we see that sexual relations and the forming of a family are connected with real love. From the biological perspective, according to natural law, the main purpose is reproduction. And I think that the beneficial kind of love—even of sexual love—is love with a sense of care and responsibility. Mad love is not lasting, I think, if it lacks a sense of responsibility.

Look at those beautiful wild birds. When two birds come together, it is to build a nest and raise their young. When they have chicks, the male and the female both assume the same responsibility to feed the little ones. Sometimes mad love is just wild, just like dogs, completely careless about the consequences. I think it is not very good for people. If that was all there was to it, there would be no use for marriage. And yet look how people consider the marriage ceremony something very important. If we really consider it important, then we should have the love that is a sense of responsibility. If we did develop that, I think there would be fewer divorces, wouldn't there? Marriages would last longer—I think until death.

At any rate, we can see that human life begins with affection, with love, a sense of responsibility and care. We are in the mother's womb for many months. During this time the mother's mental calmness is said to be a very important factor for the healthy development of the unborn child. And after birth, according to some neurobiologists, the first few weeks are the most important period for the healthy development of the child's brain. And they say that, during that time, the mother's actual physical touch is a crucial factor. This does not come from religious scripture or ideology. It is from scientific observation. Therefore, I believe that this human body itself very much appreciates affection. The first action of the child is the sucking of the mother's milk. And the mother, in spite of pain or exhaustion, is very willing to give milk to her child. So milk is a profound symbol of affection. Without mother's milk we cannot survive. That is human nature.

During the process of education, it is quite easy to notice how much better we learn from a teacher who not only teaches us but also shows a real concern for our welfare, who cares about our future. The lessons of such a teacher go much deeper in our mind than lessons received from a teacher who just explains about the subject without any human affection. This again shows the power of affection in nature.

The art of medicine is another good example. During this trip, I visited a hospital in New York about a problem in my left nostril. The doctor who examined me and removed the blockage was so gentle and careful, in addition to having a beautiful machine. His face was full of life—and he had a genuine smile. In spite of some pain from that small operation, I felt very fresh, quite happy and confident. In some cases when we visit doctors, they may be very professional, but if they show no human affection, we feel anxious, suspicious, and unsure how it will turn out. Haven't we all noticed that?

In our old age we again reach a stage where we come to depend heavily on others' affection. We appreciate even the slightest affection and concern. And even when we face death, on our last day, even though all efforts are now exhausted, though there is no hope, still, if some genuine friend is there at our bedside, we feel much happier. Although there is no more time to do anything, we still feel much happier—because of human nature. So, from the beginning of human life to the end of human life, during all those years, it is clear that human affection is the key for human happiness, human survival, and human success. What do you think? This is how I feel.

Therefore, affection, love, and compassion—they are not a matter of religion. Various religions do teach us the importance of love and compassion because the basic aim of religions is the support and benefit of human beings. Since human nature is love, since genuine love and compassion are so important for life, every religion, in spite of different philosophies, traditions, and ideologies, teaches us about love and compassion. But human affection as essential for human nature is something deeper than matters of religious belief or institutional affairs. It is even more basic for human survival and success than any particular religion. Therefore, I always used to tell people that whether they are believers or nonbelievers, that's up to them. From a certain point of view, religion is a little bit of a luxury. If you have religion, that's very good. But even without religion, you can survive, you can manage to live and even sometimes succeed. But not without human affection; without love, we cannot survive. Therefore, affection, love, and compassion, they are the deepest aspect of human nature.

Some of you here may doubt this. You may feel that anger and hatred are also part of human nature. Yes, of course anger is a human habit. But if we carefully investigate, I think we will find the dominant force of the human mind is affection. As I mentioned earlier, when we are first born, if the mother feels the agitation of resentment or anger toward the child, then her milk may not flow freely. I noticed when I visited Ladakh that sometimes when people milk their cow, the cow's calf is brought in the front of the cow first. This way they cheat the cow; in her mind, she is giving milk to her own baby. So that shows that there is a natural condition where without a tender loving feeling of closeness, the milk may not come. So milk is the result of affection and is blocked by anger.

Again I have another reason, if we look carefully at daily life. When something happens which horrifies our minds, a murder case or terrorist attack, it is immediately reported in all the news because an event like this makes such a forceful impression in the mind. And yet every day thousands and millions of undernourished children are given food; they are nourished and they survive another day. But no one reports that because it is something normal; it should be a routine happening. We take it for granted. These facts also demonstrate our human nature and that affection is something normal. Killing, and other actions born of anger and hatred are unusual for us. And so such unfortunate events strike our minds more forcefully. The basic human nature is gentle. And so I feel that there is a real possibility to promote and develop human affection on the global level. It is not unrealistic, because it is the most important part of human nature.

Each of us is an individual, naturally a part of humanity. So human effort must begin with our individual initiatives. Each of us should have a strong sense of the responsibility to create our own small part of a positive atmosphere. At the same time, we have more powerful social methods today with which to channel individual human insight and inspiration and thus to have a wider impact. There are different organizations on the national and international levels, governments, and United Nations organizations. These are powerful channels through which to implement new insights, to mobilize new inspirations.

This kind of conference is very helpful to such an end, though it would be unrealistic to expect that a few conferences could achieve any sort of complete solution. That's expecting too much. But, the constant effort of deep thought and broad discussion is very useful and worthwhile.

I climb the road to Cold Mountain,
The road to Cold Mountain that never ends.
The valleys are long and strewn with stones;
The stream broad and banked with thick grass.
Moss is slippery, though no rain has fallen;
Pines sigh, but it isn't the wind.
Who can break from the snares of the world
And sit with me among the white clouds?

— Han Shan

*Chapter 3*

# "The Firmament Sheweth His Handiwork"

## Re-awakening a Religious Sense of the Natural Order

*Harry Oldmeadow*

Thou art the fire,
Thou art the sun,
Thou art the air,
Thou art the moon,
Thou art the starry firmament,
Thou art Brahman Supreme:
Thou art the waters,
The creator of all!

Thou art woman, thou art man,
Thou art the youth, thou art the maiden,
Thou art the old man tottering with his staff;
Thou facest everywhere.
Thou art the dark butterfly,
Thou art the green parrot with red eyes,
Thou art the thunder cloud, the seasons, the seas.
Without beginning art thou, beyond time, beyond space.
Thou art he from whom sprang the three worlds.

*The Upanishads*[1]

The heavens declare the glory of God;
and the firmament sheweth his handiwork.

*Psalms*[2]

---

\* Editor's Note: This essay is a revised and expanded version of an article which first appeared in the journal *Sacred Web* 2 (December 1998), under the title "The Translucence of Nature."

1. *Svetasvatara Upanishad*, IV:2-4.
2. *Psalms*, XIX:1.

> Crazy Horse dreamed and went out into the world where there is
> nothing but the spirits of all things. That is the real world that is
> behind this one, and everything we see here is something like a
> shadow from that world.
>
> *Black Elk*[3]

For the sage each flower is metaphysically a proof of the Infinite.

*Frithjof Schuon*[4]

The modern mentality characteristically looks for solutions to
our most urgent problems in the wrong places; more often than
not the proposed remedies aggravate the malady. Various responses
to the so-called environmental crisis are of this type. Hardly anyone
is now foolish enough to deny that there is something fundamentally wrong with our way of "being in the world." The evidence is
too overwhelming for even the most sanguine apostles of
"Progress" to ignore. Much of the debate about the "environment"
(itself a rather problematical term) continues to be conducted in
terms derived from the secular-scientific-rationalist-humanist
world-view bequeathed to us by that series of upheavals which sub-
verted the medieval outlook—the Renaissance and Reformation,
the Scientific Revolution, the Enlightenment. As Seyyed Hossein
Nasr has observed:

> most Western intellectuals think about environmental issues as if
> everyone were an agnostic following a secular philosophy culti-
> vated at Oxford, Cambridge or Harvard and so they seek to
> develop a rationalist environmental ethics based upon agnosti-
> cism, as if this would have any major effect whatsoever upon the
> environmental crisis . . . the very strong prejudice against religious
> ethics . . . is itself one the greatest impediments to the solution of
> the environmental crisis.[5]

My purpose here is to turn our attention to some general principles
which informed traditional religious understandings of the natural
order and of the human place in it. No "solution" to the environmental crisis is proposed. However, it is perfectly evident to those
with "eyes to see and ears to hear" that the desecration (one uses
the word advisedly) of nature cannot be remedied without recourse
to the principles which governed traditional understandings of the

3. Black Elk in John Neihardt, *Black Elk Speaks* (London, 1974), p.67.
4. Frithjof Schuon, *Spiritual Perspectives and Human Facts* (London, 1969), p.10.
5. S.H. Nasr, *The Spiritual and Religious Dimensions of the Environmental Crisis*
(London, 1999), pp.7, 9.

natural order. These might offer some hope where modern scientism (the ideology of modern science) has so spectacularly failed.

# I. Traditional Cosmogonies

The first question which might present itself in any inquiry into religious perspectives on nature is this: how does this or that religion in particular, or how do religions in general, envisage the origin, the source of the universe? Generally speaking the different traditions, from both East and West, and from both primal and literate cultures, account for the beginnings of the universe through a mythological account, a cosmogony. In the Judeo-Christian tradition we find it in the Genesis story. While the narrative details vary, this is not essentially different from, let us say, the mythical accounts of the *Vedas*, or of the Aboriginal Dreaming.

These days "myth" is often a pejorative term meaning either a naive and childish fabrication or simply a story which is untrue. This kind of view is probably rooted in the 19th century where many scholars and theorists (anthropologists, folklorists, sociologists and the like) took this condescending and disabling view of mythology. Thus, Andrew Lang, for instance, took it that "primitive" mythologies were "a product of the childhood of the human race, arising out of the minds of a creature that has not yet learned to think in terms of strict cause and effect."[6] Myths were thus to be understood as a kind of fumbling proto-science.

We must return to earlier outlooks if we are to understand religious myths (from wherever they come) aright—as allegorical or symbolic narratives which articulate, in dramatic form, a world-view whose elements will necessarily include a metaphysic (an account of the Real; the metacosmic), a cosmology (an account of the visible world, in the heavens and here on earth; the macrocosmic) and an anthropology (an account of the human situation; the microcosmic). In combating the impertinent reductionisms of the anthropologists Ananda Coomaraswamy eloquently reminds us that,

> Myth is the penultimate truth, of which all experience is the temporal reflection. The mythical narrative is of timeless and placeless

6. Eric Sharpe, *Comparative Religion* (London, 1975), p.61.

validity, true nowhere and everywhere... Myth embodies the nearest approach to absolute truth that can be stated in words...[7]

Cosmogonies can be located on a spectrum one end of which might be labeled *creationist/ theistic* and the other *emanationist/ monistic*: the former type envisages the universe as a creation of a divine power or deity while the latter conceives of the universe as a spatio-temporal manifestation of an ultimate, spiritual reality. The Abrahamic monotheisms are of the former type, while Platonism and some forms of Hinduism represent the latter. In the *Mundaka Upanishad*, for instance, we are told that,

> As a spider sends forth and draws in its threads, as herbs grow on the earth, as hair grows on the head and the body of a living person, so from the Imperishable arises here the universe.[8]

Traditional cosmogonies necessarily deal with the relationship of spiritual and material realities, a relationship which lies at the heart of all religious understandings of nature. Philosophically speaking, religions posit the existence of two "worlds," one spiritual, immutable and absolute, the other material, mutable and relative, usually with an intermediary realm (which might variously be referred to as ethereal, subtle, astral and the like). Cosmogonies affirm the primacy of the spiritual: the material world derives from a divine creativity, or, at least, from a divine plenitude. In the religious context it is axiomatic that the material world did not and could not create itself; it is suspended, so to speak, within a reality which is immaterial and which is beyond time and space; the material world has no independent or autonomous existence. Consider a few quotes (one could easily assemble hundreds of such passages from all over the globe):

---

7. Ananda Coomaraswamy, *Hinduism and Buddhism* (New Delhi, 1996), pp.6, 33n21.

8. *Mundaka Upanishad*, I,i:7. Of the major religious traditions the one which has least to say about the origins of the universe is Buddhism which is generally suspicious of metaphysical speculation and eschews what the Buddha called the Indeterminate Questions, which is to say questions which are either unanswerable, at least in terms accessible to the ordinary human mentality, or which are distractions from the business at hand. Sometimes it is said by Buddhists that the universe "always was"; this perhaps is to be understood as being *upaya*—a kind of sufficient expedient, so to speak. However, as the *Prajna-Paramita* states, "the belief in the unity or eternity of matter is incomprehensible..."; quoted in Whitall Perry, *The Widening Breach: Evolutionism in the Mirror of Cosmology* (Cambridge, 1995), p.44.

There is something obscure which is complete
before heaven and earth arose;
tranquil, quiet, standing alone without change,
moving around without peril.
It could be the Mother of everything. I don't know its name,
and call it Tao.

(Tao Te Ching)[9]

The Imperishable is the Real. As sparks fly upward from a blazing
fire, so from the depths of the Imperishable arise all things. To the
depths of the Imperishable they again descend. Self-luminous is
that Being, and formless. He dwells within all and without all . . .
From him are born breath, mind, the organs of sense, ether, air,
fire, water and the earth, and he binds all these together.

(The Upanishads)[10]

This world, with all its stars, elements, and creatures, is come out
of the invisible world; it has not the smallest thing or the smallest
quality of anything but what is come forth from thence.

(William Law)[11]

Cosmogonies tell of the coming into being of the cosmos, a living,
organic unity displaying beauty, harmony, meaning, and intelligibility as against the chaotic and meaningless universe of modern science. ("Kosmos," in its original Greek and in archaic times meant
Great Man as well as "world": in the light of various cosmogonies,
particularly the Greek and the Indian, this is not without significance. In the *Vedas* we have but one of many accounts of the universe being created out of *Purusha*, a cosmic man, Primordial Man,
a Divine Archetypal figure.) One of the most beautiful expressions
of the idea of an underlying harmony in the universe is to be found
in the Taoist tradition and in the symbol of the *Tao* itself wherein we
see the forces of *yin* and *yang* intertwined, these being the two fundamental forces or principles or energies out of which the fabric of
the material universe is woven. In Hinduism the harmony, order
and intelligibility of the universe is signaled by the Vedic term *rta*
which we find in the earliest Scriptures. The beneficent influences
on humankind of the natural order, and the attunement of the sage
to natural rhythms, are particularly strong leitmotifs in Taoism but
are to be found in many Eastern Scriptures. By the same token,

9. *Tao Te Ching*, XXV.
10. *Mundaka Upanishad*, II,i:1-4.
11. *Selected Mystical Writings*, quoted in Whitall Perry, *A Treasury of Traditional Wisdom* (London, 1971), p.26.

humans are enjoined to play their part in the maintenance of the cosmic order, largely through their ritual life. This idea, everywhere to be found in the archaic worlds, makes no sense from a materialistic point of view which now determines the prevailing outlook— one completely impervious to the fact that, in Nasr's memorable phrase, "nature is hungry for our prayers."[12]

Religious doctrines (which might be expressed in any number of forms, not necessarily verbal) about the relationship of the spiritual and material worlds necessarily deal with the *transcendence* and *immanence* of the Absolute (whether this be envisaged in theistic, monistic, panentheistic or apophatic terms—God, *Allah, Brahman, Tao, Wakan-Tanka, nirvana,* or whatever): the "interplay" of these two "dimensions" varies from religion to religion but both are always present. Whatever accent a particular spiritual economy might place on these aspects of the Real the underlying principle is always the same. It might best be summed up by an old Rabbinic dictum: "The universe is not the dwelling place of God; God is the dwelling place of the universe."[13] In the light of such formulations we can also dispense with the sharp dualistic separation of the "two worlds": the world of phenomena is held together by a numinous spiritual presence—indeed, without it the world of "matter" would vanish instantly and completely. Eternity is ever-present within (so to speak) the phenomenal world. The mystic Jan van Ruysbroeck referred to this inner reality as,

> beyond Time; that is, without before or after, in an Eternal Now . . . the home and beginning of all life and all becoming. And so all creatures are therein, beyond themselves, one being and one Life . . . as in their eternal origin.[14]

A misunderstanding which bedevils many discussions of the beliefs of non-literate peoples is signaled by the term "pantheism," i.e., the worship of the natural order as co-terminous with "God." This, we are sometimes told (usually by anthropologists) was the practice of such and such a "primitive" people. In reality, pantheism, if ever it

---

12. S.H. Nasr, *The Spiritual and Religious Dimensions of the Environmental Crisis,* p.13.

13. Quoted in Sarvepalli Radhakrishnan, *Selected Writings on Philosophy, Religion and Culture* (New York, 1970), p.146.

14. Quoted in Philip Sherrard, *Christianity: Lineaments of a Sacred Tradition* (Brookline [Mass.], 1998), p.208.

existed as anything other than an anthropological fiction, could never have been more than a degenerate form of what is properly called "panentheísm," which is to say a belief in the overwhelming presence of the spiritual within the natural world—a quite different matter from the "pantheistic" fallacy that the natural world is somehow identical to (and thus exhausts) "God." Black Elk, the revered holy man of the Oglala Sioux, clearly articulated the panentheistic principle:

> We should understand that all things are the work of the Great Spirit. We should know that He is within all things; the trees, the grasses, the rivers, the mountains, all the four-legged animals and the winged peoples; and *even more important we should understand that He is also above all these things and peoples.*[15]

There are those who seek to develop an "eco-spirituality" which actually amounts to no more than a kind of secular pantheism, if one may be allowed such a term—a view of the natural order which retains some sort of "religiosity," surrendering to the view that it is possible to have an immanent "sacred" while dispensing with the transcendent, as if night and day can indeed be sundered from the sun, or as if there could be a circle with no center.[16] Equally absurd is the notion of a "secular scientific spirituality" which has recently been proposed.[17] Like all such concoctions this kind of naturism is a sentimental form of idolatry. As Philip Sherrard has so plainly put it,

> an agnostic and materialistic science of nature is a contradiction in terms ... its findings will necessarily correspond to the living reality of nature as little as a corpse corresponds to the living reality of a human being ...[18]

## II. The Sacred and the Profane

A category without which we cannot proceed very far in the study of religion is the sacred. There are many ways of defining it. Here is

---

15. Joseph Epes Brown, *The Sacred Pipe* (Baltimore, 1971), p.xx (my italics).

16. For a specimen see N. Hettinger, "Ecospirituality: First Thoughts" in *Dialogue & Alliance*, 9:2 (Fall-Winter, 1995), pp.81-98.

17. See, for example, Holmes Ralston III, "Secular Scientific Spirituality" in P.H. Van Ness (ed.), *Spirituality and the Secular Quest* (New York, 1996), pp.387-413.

18. Philip Sherrard, *Christianity: Lineaments of a Sacred Tradition*, p.19.

one from a discussion of Sacred Books by the sovereign metaphysician of our own time, Frithjof Schuon:

> That is sacred which in the first place is attached to the transcendent order, secondly possesses the character of absolute certainty, and thirdly, eludes the comprehension of the ordinary human mind . . . The sacred is the presence of the center in the periphery . . . The sacred introduces a quality of the absolute into relativities and confers on perishable things a texture of eternity.[19]

Of course, the category can apply to all manner of things: events, texts, buildings, images, rituals. In the context of our present concerns we might isolate two applications of this category or principle: to space and time, and to life itself. The traditional mind, especially in primal, non-literate societies, perceives and experiences space and time as "sacred" and "profane," which is to say that they are not uniform and homogeneous as they are for the modern scientific mind, but are *qualitatively* differentiated. A good deal of ceremonial life is concerned with entry into or, better, *participation in* sacred time and space.[20] Through ritual one enters into sacred time, into *real* time, the "once upon a time," *illo tempore*, a time radically different from a "horizontal" duration. Likewise with sacred places, remembering that a natural site can be *made* sacred through various rituals and practices, or it can be *recognized* as sacred—a place where the membrane, so to speak, between the worlds of matter and of spirit are especially permeable. Rivers, mountains, particular types of trees and places related to the mythological events are sites of this sort. The sacrality of Mt Kailas or Uluru, for instance, is not *conferred* but *apprehended*.

The sanctity of life itself is expressed in different ways in the various religious vocabularies. In the Judeo-Christian tradition this principle or theme begins in the affirmation in *Genesis* that man is made in the image of God, that the human being carries an indelible imprint of the Divine. Thence we have what might be called the principle of the spiritual equality of all human beings no matter what their station in life or their natural attributes and shortcomings—"all equal before God," as the Christian formula has it.

---

19. Frithjof Schuon, *Understanding Islam* (London, 1976), p.48.
20. One of the most useful expositions of archaic understandings of sacred and profane time and space is to be found in Mircea Eliade, *The Sacred and the Profane* (New York, 1959).

The Judeo-Christian tradition has primarily affirmed the sanctity of human life, sometimes to the neglect or abuse of other life forms. One of the lessons of the great Eastern and primal religions is the principle of the moral solidarity, if one may so express it, of all living forms: in Hinduism, Buddhism and Jainism this is embodied in the traditional Indian value of *ahimsa* (non-injuriousness). Here is what Gandhi had to say about the cow:

> The central fact of Hinduism . . . is "Cow Protection." Cow Protection to me is one of the most wonderful phenomena in all human evolution; for it takes the human being beyond his species. The cow to me means the entire sub-human world. Man through the cow is enjoined to realize his identity with all that lives . . . Hindus will be judged not by their correct chanting of sacred texts, not by their pilgrimages, not by their most punctilious observance of Caste rules, but by their ability to protect the cow . . . "Cow protection" is the gift of Hinduism to the world; and Hinduism will live so long as there are Hindus to protect the cow.[21]

"Man's identity with all that lives"—this is the key phrase to what appears at first sight to be a rather startling claim from the Mahatma. William Blake affirmed the same notion: "all that lives is holy."

## III. The Human Situation

The principle of the sanctity of life, and the "moral solidarity" of living forms should not blind us to the fact that all traditional wisdoms affirm, in their different ways, that the human being is especially privileged. The human is an axial or amphibious being who lives in both the material and spiritual worlds in a way which is not quite true of other living beings, and is thus a bridge between them. Seyyed Hossein Nasr reminds us that,

> Man's central position in the world is not due to his cleverness or inventive genius but because of the possibility of attaining sanctity and becoming a channel of grace for the world around him . . . the very grandeur of the human condition is precisely that he has the possibility of reaching a state "higher than the angels" and at the same time of denying God.[22]

21. Gandhi, quoted in Eric Sharpe, "To Hinduism through Gandhi" in Arthur Basham *et al.*, *Wisdom of the East* (Sydney, 1979), pp.61-2.
22. Seyyed Hossein Nasr, *Ideals and Realities of Islam* (London, 1966), pp.24-25.

This religious understanding is, of course, quite incompatible with the notion that man is simply another biological organism. By the same measure, it is utterly at odds with that most seductive and elegant (and certainly one of the most pernicious) of scientistic hypotheses, Darwinian evolutionism. As Blake so well understood, "Man is either the ark of God or a phantom of the earth and of the water." As "the ark of God" man is the guardian and custodian of the natural order, the pontifex, the caliph, "the viceregent of God on earth" in Qur'anic terms.[23]

The peculiar position of the human being can also be illuminated by recourse to the traditional cosmological principle of the microcosm/macrocosm, expressed most succinctly perhaps in the Hermetic maxim, "as above, so below." In brief, man is not only in the universe but the universe is in man: "there is nothing in heaven or earth that is not also in man" (Paracelsus).[24] The Buddha put it this way: "In truth I say to you that within this fathom-high body . . . lies the world and the rising of the world and the ceasing of the world."[25] Others have rendered the same truth poetically. Recall the beautiful lines of Thomas Traherne:

> You never enjoy the world aright, till the Sea
> itself floweth in your veins, till you are
> clothed with the heavens, and crowned with
> the stars: and perceive yourself to be the sole
> heir of the whole world, and more than so,
> because men are in it who are every one sole
> heirs as well as you.[26]

Similarly, from Blake:

> To see a world in a grain of sand,
> And Heaven in a wild flower,
> Hold infinity in the palm of your hand,
> And Eternity in an hour.[27]

23. See Jean-Louis Michon, "The Vocation of Man According to the Koran" in *Fragments of Infinity: Essays in Religion and Philosophy*, ed., Arvind Sharma (Bridport, 1991), pp.135-152. See also Kenneth Cragg, *The Mind of the Qur'an: Chapters in Reflection* (London, 1973).

24. Quoted in T.C. McLuhan, *Cathedrals of the Spirit: The Message of Sacred Places* (Toronto, 1996), p.270.

25. Quoted in Huston Smith, *Forgotten Truth: The Primordial Tradition* (New York, 1976), p.60.

26. Thomas Traherne, *Centuries of Meditation*, 1.29.

27. William Blake, "Auguries of Innocence."

One of the keys to this principle resides in the traditional understanding of consciousness as being infinite, as surpassing the temporal and spatial limits of the material world—which, in fact, is nothing other than a tissue of fugitive relativities, a world of appearances, a fabric of illusions, *Maya* in the Hindu lexicon.[28] At the same time we need to remember that while *Maya* is indeed "cosmic illusion,"

> . . . she is also "divine play." She is the great theophany, the "unveiling" of God "In Himself and by Himself" as the Sufis would say. *Maya* may be likened to a magic fabric woven from a warp that veils and a weft that unveils; she is the quasi-incomprehensible intermediary between the finite and the Infinite—at least from our point of view as creatures—and as such she has all the multi-colored ambiguity appropriate to her part-cosmic, part-divine nature.[29]

Thus,

> . . . the term *Maya* combines the meanings of "productive power" and "universal illusion"; it is the inexhaustible play of manifestations, deployments, combinations and reverberations, a play with which *Atma* clothes itself even as the ocean clothes itself with a mantle of foam ever renewed and never the same.[30]

These passages should immunize us to the preposterous but widely held view that the Eastern traditions are "negative," "pessimistic," "life-denying" and the like.[31]

This world of *Maya* is "illusory," but not in the sense that it is a mirage or a fantasy, but in that its "reality" is only relative: it has no independence, no autonomy, no existence outside the Divine Principle Itself. The sages of both East and West have never been

---

28. Furthermore, as Lama Anagarika Govinda reminds us, "If the structure of our consciousness did not correspond to that of the universe and its laws, we should not be aware either of the universe or the laws that govern it." *Creative Meditation and Multi-Dimensional Consciousness* (Wheaton, 1976), p.162.

29. Frithjof Schuon, *Light on the Ancient Worlds* (London, 1966), p.89. See also Ali Lakhani, "What Thirst is For" in *Sacred Web*, 4 (December 1999), pp.13-14.

30. Frithjof Schuon, *Logic and Transcendence* (New York, 1975), p89n.

31. Without pursuing the matter here we can note that the charge of "world-denial" directed against Buddhism rests on a very partial understanding of *samsara* to the neglect of its complement, *dharma*, by which is meant not simply the teachings of the Awakened One (its most familiar sense, at least to Westerners) but a pre-existent and eternal order to which these teachings testified and of which they are one expression. On this crucial point see Philip Novak, "Universal Theology and the Idea of Universal Order" in *Dialogue and Alliance*, 6:1 (Spring, 1992), pp.82-92.

seduced by the idea that the material universe is a self-existing entity, which is to say that they have ever understood that there is no such thing as "pure matter." Their understanding of the cosmos derives from all the sources of knowledge—mystical intuition and the revealed Scriptures, as well as the instruments of the mind and the senses. On the other hand, a profane, quantitative science (from whence the modern West derives its understanding of the universe), is

> . . . a totalitarian rationalism that eliminates both Revelation and Intellect, and at the same time a totalitarian materialism that ignores the metaphysical relativity—and therewith the impermanence—of matter and the world. It does not know that the suprasensible, situated as it is beyond space and time, is the concrete principle of the world, and consequently that it is also at the origin of that contingent and changeable coagulation we call "matter." A science that is called "exact" is in fact an "intelligence without wisdom," just as post-scholastic philosophy is inversely a "wisdom without intelligence"[32]

## IV. The Symbolism of Natural Forms and the Cosmological Sciences

In "Frost at Midnight" Coleridge addresses these lines to his baby son:

> But *thou*, my babe! shalt wander like a breeze
> By lakes and sandy shores, beneath the crags
> Of ancient mountain, and beneath the clouds,
> Which image in their bulk both lakes and shores
> And mountain crags: so shalt thou see and hear
> The lovely shapes and sounds intelligible
> of that eternal language, which thy God
> Utters, who from eternity doth teach
> Himself in all, and all things in himself.

The idea of the natural order as not only sacred but as a symbolic language strikes the modern mind as somewhat strange, perhaps as "poetic fancy." In reality it is the modern outlook which is idiosyncratic. Mircea Eliade has noted how, for *homo religiosus*, everything in nature is capable of revealing itself as a "cosmic sacrality," as a

---

32. Frithjof Schuon, *Light on the Ancient Worlds* (London, 1966), p.117.

hierophany. He also observes that for our secular age the cosmos has become "opaque, inert, mute; it transmits no message, it holds no cipher."[33] The traditional mind perceives the natural world as a hierophany, a theophany, a revelation—in short, as a teaching about the Divine Order. It is so by way of its analogical participation in the Divine qualities, which is to say that natural phenomena are themselves symbols of higher realities. A symbol, properly defined, is a reality of a lower order which participates analogically in a reality of a higher order of being. Therefore, a properly constituted symbolism rests on the inherent and objective qualities of phenomena and their relation to spiritual realities. The science of symbolism proceeds through a discernment of the qualitative significances of substances, colors, forms, spatial relationships and so on. As Schuon has observed,

> . . . we are not here dealing with subjective appreciations, for the cosmic qualities are ordered both in relation to being and according to a hierarchy which is more real than the individual; they are, then, independent of our tastes . . .[34]

This kind of symbolism is an altogether different matter from arbitrary sign systems and artificial representational vocabularies. Only when we understand the revelatory aspect of natural phenomena, their metaphysical transparency, can we fully appreciate the import of a claim such as this:

> Wild Nature is at one with holy poverty and also with spiritual childlikeness; she is an open book containing an inexhaustible teaching of truth and beauty. It is in the midst of his own artifices that man most easily becomes corrupted, it is they who make him covetous and impious; close to virgin Nature, who knows neither agitation nor falsehood, he had the hope of remaining contemplative like Nature herself.[35]

Or this, from the great 13th century Zen sage, Dogen:

33. Mircea Eliade, *The Sacred and the Profane* (New York, 1959), p.12-13, 178.
34. Frithjof Schuon, *Gnosis: Divine Wisdom* (London, 1979), p.110. The most magisterial explication of the science of symbols in recent times is to be found in René Guénon's *Fundamental Symbols* (Cambridge, 1995). For a brief but incisive discussion of symbolism-proper and its relation to intellectuality, see Ananda Coomaraswamy, "Primitive Mentality" in *Coomaraswamy 1: Selected Papers, Traditional Art and Symbolism*, ed., Roger Lipsey (Princeton, 1977), pp.286-307. See also Adrian Snodgrass, *The Symbolism of the Stupa* (Delhi, 1992), pp.1-10.
35. Frithjof Schuon, *Light on the Ancient Worlds* (London, 1965), p.84.

Harry Oldmeadow

They passed eons living alone in the mountains and forests; only then did they unite with the Way and use mountains and rivers for words, raise the wind and rain for a tongue, and explain the great void.[36]

Here are a few other formulations which signal the principle of the metaphysical transparency of the natural order:

The invisible things of him from the creation of the world are clearly seen, being understood by the things that are made.

(St Paul)[37]

If we look at the world . . . with the eyes of the spirit we shall discover that the simplest material object . . . is a symbol, a glyph of a higher reality and a deeper relationship of universal and individual forces . . .

(Anagarika Govinda)[38]

Stones, plants, animals, the earth, the sky, the stars, the elements, in fact everything in the universe reveals to us the knowledge, power and the will of its Originator.

(Al-Ghazali)[39]

The creatures are, as it were, traces of God's passing, wherein he reveals his might, power, wisdom and other divine qualities.

(St John of the Cross)[40]

The great, gashed, half-naked mountain is another of God's saints. There is no other like him. He is alone in his own character;

---

36. From Dogen's *Shobogenzo*, quoted in *Dharma Gaia: A Harvest of Essays on Buddhism and Ecology*, ed., Alan H. Badiner (Berkeley, 1990), p.xiii

37. St. Paul, *Romans* 1:20.

38. Anagarika Govinda, *Creative Meditation and Multi-Dimensional Consciousness* (Wheaton, 1976), p.102.

39. Al-Ghazali, quoted in T.C. McLuhan, *Cathedrals of the Spirit* (Toronto, 1996), p.107. For a study of the symbolism of animals within one particular spiritual economy, see Joseph Epes Brown, *Animals of the Soul: Sacred Animals of the Oglala Sioux* (Rockport, 1997).

40. *The Spiritual Canticle*, V:iii, quoted in Elizabeth Hamilton, *The Voice of the Spirit: The Spirituality of St John of the Cross* (London, 1976), p.89. Compare this with the well-known *hadith qudsi* (in which God Himself speaks): "I was a hidden treasure, I wanted to be known and I created the creatures"; or with St Thomas Aquinas: "Each creature is a witness to God's power and omnipotence; and its beauty is a witness to the divine wisdom . . . Every creature participates in some way in the likeness of the Divine Essence." Quoted in Matthew Fox, *The Coming of the Cosmic Christ* (Melbourne, 1989), p.75.

nothing else in the world ever did or ever will imitate God in quite the same way. That is his sanctity.

(*Thomas Merton*)[41]

Nature, then, is a *teaching*, a primordial Scripture. To "read" this Scripture, to take it to heart, is "to see God everywhere," to be aware of the transcendent dimension which is present in every cosmic situation, to see "the translucence of the Eternal through and in the temporal" (Coleridge).[42] The great Hindu saint and sage, Ramakrishna, who could fall into ecstasy at the sight of a lion, a bird, a dancing girl, exemplified this gift though in his case, Schuon adds, it was not a matter of deciphering the symbolism but of "tasting the essences."[43]

It is in the primal cultures (so often dismissed or patronized as "primitive" and "preliterate"), such as those of the Australian Aborigines, the African Bushmen, or the American Indians, that we find the most highly developed sense of the transparency of natural phenomena and the most profound understanding of the "eternal language." As Joseph Epes Brown has remarked of the Lakota experience, each form in the world around them bears such a host of precise values and meanings that taken all together they constitute what one would call their 'doctrine.'"[44] In the traditional world the natural order was never understood or studied as an autonomous and independent reality; on the contrary, the natural order was only to be understood within a larger context, drawing on theology and metaphysics as well as the cosmological sciences themselves. The material world was (and is) only intelligible through recourse to first principles which could not, and can not, be derived from empirical inquiry but from revelation, esoteric knowledge, gnosis, metaphysics:

41. Thomas Merton, *New Seeds of Contemplation* (New York, 1961), p.31.

42. Coleridge, quoted in Kathleen Raine, *Defending Ancient Springs* (Cambridge, 1985), p.109.

43. Frithjof Schuon, "Foundations of an Integral Aesthetics," in *Studies in Comparative Religion* 10:3 (1976), p.135n. See also Christopher Isherwood, *Ramakrishna and His Disciples* (Calcutta, 1974),p.61ff.

44. Joseph Epes Brown, *The Spiritual Legacy of the American Indians* (New York, 1982), p.37. Two works, comparatively free of the evolutionist and modernistic prejudices which color much of the "anthropological" literature, might be recommended as introductions to the Aboriginal and Bushmen cultures: James Cowan, *Mysteries of the Dreaming* (Bridport,1989), and Laurens van der Post, *The Heart of the Hunter* (Harmondsworth, 1965).

> The knowledge of the whole universe does not lie within the competence of science but of metaphysics. Moreover, the principles of metaphysics remain independent of the sciences and cannot in any way be disproved by them.[45]

No one has stated the crucial principle here better than the great Vedantin sage Shankara, who taught that the world of *Maya* (i.e., the world of appearances, of time-space relativities) is not inexplicable, it is only not self-explanatory.[46] To describe the futility of a purely materialistic science (such as we now have in the West), Shankara compares it to an attempt to explain night and day without reference to the Sun. In other words, the study of the natural world is not primarily an empirical business, although it does, of course, have an empirical dimension: matter does not exist independently and its nature cannot be understood in purely material terms. This is the great dividing line between the sacred sciences of the traditional worlds and the Promethean science of our own time.

## V. Beauty: Divine Rays

A few words on Beauty which we find everywhere in the natural order as well as in the human form itself, and in sacred art. Firstly, there is the intimate nexus between Truth, Goodness and Beauty. The inter-relationships of the three are more or less inexhaustible and there is no end to what might be said on this subject. Here we shall establish only a few general points, taking the nature of Beauty as our point of departure. Marsilio Ficino, the Renaissance Platonist, defined beauty as "that ray which parting from the visage of God, penetrates into all things."[47] Beauty, in most traditional canons, has this divine quality. Beauty is a manifestation of the Infinite on a finite plane and so introduces something of the Absolute into the world of relativities. Its sacred character "confers on perishable things a texture of eternity."[48] Schuon:

> The archetype of Beauty, or its Divine model, is the superabundance and equilibrium of the Divine qualities, and at the same

45. Seyyed Hossein Nasr, *Man and Nature: The Spiritual Crisis of Modern Man* (London, 1976), p.35.

46. See my article, "Sankara's Doctrine of Maya" in *Asian Philosophy* 2:2 (1992), pp.131-146.

47. Quoted in R.J. Clements, *Michelangelo's Theory of Art* (New York, 1971), p.5.

48. Frithjof Schuon, *Understanding Islam* (London, 1976), p.48.

time the overflowing of the existential potentialities in pure
Being . . . Thus beauty always manifests a reality of love, of deployment, of illimitation, of equilibrium, of beatitude, of generosity.[49]
It is distinct but not separate from Truth and Virtue. As Aquinas
armed, Beauty relates to the cognitive faculty and is thus connected with wisdom.[50] The rapport between Beauty and Virtue
allows one to say that they are but two faces of the one reality:
"goodness is internal beauty, and beauty is external goodness" or,
similarly, "virtue is the beauty of the soul as beauty is the virtue of
forms."[51] To put it another way, Oscar Wilde notwithstanding,
there are no beautiful vices just as there are no ugly virtues. The
inter-relationships of Beauty, Truth and Goodness explain why, in
the Oriental traditions, every *avatara* embodies a perfection of
Beauty. It is said of the Buddhas that they save not only by their
doctrine but by their superhuman Beauty.[52]

Schuon gathers together some of these principles in the following passage:

> . . . the earthly function of beauty is to actualize in the intelligent
> creature the Platonic recollection of the archetypes . . . there is a
> *distinguo* to make, in the sensing of the beautiful, between the aes-
> thetic sensation and the corresponding beauty of soul, namely
> such and such a virtue. Beyond every question of "sensible conso-
> lation" the message of beauty is both intellectual and moral: intel-
> lectual because it communicates to us, in the world of
> accidentality, aspects of Substance, without for all that having to
> address itself to abstract thought; and moral, because it reminds us
> of what we must love, and consequently be.[53]

Beauty, whether natural or man-made, can be either an open or a
closed door: when it is identified only with its earthly support it
leaves man vulnerable to idolatry and to mere aestheticism; it brings

49. Frithjof Schuon, *Logic and Transcendence* (New York, 1975), p.241.

50. See A.K. Coomaraswamy, "The Mediaeval Theory of Beauty" in *Selected
Papers 1: Traditional Art and Symbolism* (Princeton, 1977), pp.211-20, and two essays,
"Beauty and Truth" and "Why Exhibit Works of Art?" in *Christian and Oriental Phi-
losophy of Art* (New York, 1956), pp.7-22 (esp. 16-18), 102-109.

51. Frithjof Schuon, *Logic and Transcendence* (New York, 1975), pp.245-246. See
also Schuon, *Esoterism as Principle and as Way* (London, 1981), p.95.

52. As Schuon notes, "the name *Shunyamurti* (Manifestation of the Void)
applied to a Buddha is full of significance" (*Spiritual Perspectives and Human Facts*
[London, 1967], p.25n). See also Schuon, *In the Tracks of Buddhism* (London,
1968), p.121.

53. Frithjof Schuon, "Foundations of an Integral Aesthetics" in *Studies in Comparative Religion* 10:3 (1976), pp.131-132.

us closer to God when "we perceive in it the vibrations of Beatitude and Infinity, which emanate from Divine Beauty."[54]

## VI. The Western Desacralization of Nature

Western attitudes to nature, before the onslaughts of a materialistic scientism, had been influenced by archaic pagan ideas (derived principally from Greece and from Northern Europe), Platonism and Islam, and, pre-eminently, the Judeo-Christian tradition. Many contemporary environmentalists point the finger at the so-called "dominion ethic" apparently sanctioned by the *Genesis* account. There is no gainsaying the fact that Christian institutions have for centuries been accomplices in an appalling environmental vandalism; one readily understands the reasons why many environmentalists resort to a clutch of clichés about the destructive influence of Christianity. Like most clichés, those bandied about by anti-religious propagandists in the environmental debate have some truth in them. However, if we look a little more closely we will find that the story is rather more complicated than is often supposed.[55] Here I can do no more than offer a few fragmentary remarks. Like all cosmogonies, the *Genesis* myth deals with the relationship of the spiritual and material. The natural world is affirmed as God's handiwork. Throughout both Testaments of the Bible we are reminded that, "All things were made by him; and without him was not anything made that was made."[56] Furthermore, we are to understand the Creation itself as both a psalm of praise to its Creator and as a revelation of the divine qualities. As one contemporary Christian put it, "Creation is nothing less than a manifestation of God's hidden Being."[57] In the *Psalms* we have many affirmations of this kind: "The heavens declare the glory of God; and the firmament sheweth his handiwork." We find many similar passages in the Qur'an: "The seven heavens, and the earth, and all that is therein, magnify Him, and there is naught but magnifieth his praise; only ye

54. *Ibid.*, p.135.
55. See Wendell Berry's essay "Christianity and the Survival of Creation" in *Sex, Economy, Freedom & Community* (New York, 1993), pp.92-116.
56. *St John* 1:3.
57. Philip Sherrard, *Human Image, World Image: The Death and Resurrection of Sacred Cosmology* (Cambridge, 1992), p.152.

understand not their worship";[58] and "All that is in the heavens and the earth glorifieth Allah."[59] In fact we can find like passages in many of the great Scriptures from around the globe: thus in the *Bhagavad Gita*, to choose one example, the universe is celebrated as the raiment of Krishna who contains within himself all the worlds of time and space.[60]

In the *Genesis* account, the world of nature is *not* man's to do with as he pleases but rather a gift from God, one saturated with divine qualities, to be used for those purposes which sustain life and which give human life in particular, dignity, purpose and meaning. That this stewardship ethic could degenerate into a sanction for wholesale exploitation and criminal ruination is actually a betrayal of the lessons of *Genesis*. How did this come about? The cooperative factors at work in the Western desacralization of nature are complex but we may here mention a few of the more salient: Christianity's emergence in a world of decadent pagan idolatry which necessitated a somewhat unbalanced emphasis on God's transcendence and on "other-worldliness"; the consequent neglect of those sacred sciences which might later have formed a bulwark against the ravages of a materialistic scientism; the unholy alliance of an anti-traditional Protestantism with the emergent ideologies of a new and profane world-view.[61]

Various other ideas about and understandings of nature have circulated through the postmedieval world: nature as *chaos, disorder, wildness,* in contrast to "civilization," a threatening space which lay "outside" the social order (this motif has some pagan antecedents, especially in the Teutonic-Scandinavian religions rather than the Mediterranean and classical); nature as *matter* and as a *mechanistic system* governed by various "physical laws" amenable to investigation by a materialistic science (the legacy of the Scientific Revolution, of Newton, Bacon, Locke, Copernicus, Galileo, *et al.*); as *raw material,* an inexhaustible quarry to be plundered and, simultaneously, as "enemy" to be subdued, "tamed" or, even more ludicrously, "con-

---

58. Qur'an XVII.44.

59. Qur'an LVII.2.

60. Goethe had something of the sort in mind when he wrote, "Nature is the living, visible garment of God." Quoted in Victor Gollancz, *From Darkness to Light* (London, 1964), p.246.

61. The most authoritative analysis of this process is to be found in Nasr's *Man and Nature: The Spiritual Crisis of Modern Man* (London, 1976).

quered" (by industrialism, which provided a new field of applications for the "discoveries" of science); as an *Edenic paradise* peopled by "noble savages" (the romantic naturism of Rousseau and his many epigones); as uplifting *spectacle* (Wordsworth); as the *Darwinian jungle*, "red in tooth and claw"; as an *amenity*, a "resource" to be "managed" and protected for human recreation, tourism and the like; as *Gaia*, a single living organism ("deep ecology"); and as *"Wilderness"* (a pseudo-religious secularism, if one might so put it, which absolutizes "Nature" under a certain guise and thus becomes a form of idolatry—which is nothing other than the mistaking of the symbol for its higher referent). None of the post-medieval understandings in themselves offer any very real hope of providing a way out of our predicament. Clearly some contemporary developments and movements ("deep ecology," "eco-feminism," the new physics) yield some insights and can be helpful in dismantling the modern mind-set which has brought us to the current situation. But too often these well-intentioned gropings towards a more holistic understanding are bereft of any properly constituted metaphysical and cosmological framework. This is evident, for instance, in the fact that for all their radical aspirations the proponents of "a new ecological awareness" often fall prey to the materialistic and evolutionist assumptions which are at the root of the problem which they are trying to address. It must also be said that those who are properly skeptical about the pretensions of scientism are also often vulnerable to a kind of sentimental and warmed-over pantheism—sometimes on display in the effusions of the "New Age" enthusiasts. No, what is required is a reanimation of the principles and understandings which governed traditional understandings. The key, perhaps, is to be found in the word "sacramental"—and the catechistic formula is altogether precise and apposite: "an outward and visible sign of an inner and invisible grace."

One might schematize the contrast between traditional and modern world-views, and their respective "attitudes" to nature this way:

| Traditional Cultures: | Modern "Civilization": |
|---|---|
| mythological cosmogonies | the geological/historical "record" |
| primacy of the spiritual; spiritual worldview | primacy of the material; materialistic worldview |
| qualitative, synthetic and holistic sacred sciences | quantitative, analytic and fragmentary sciences |
| natural forms symbolic and transparent | natural forms mute and opaque |
| sacramental outlook | profane outlook |
| reciprocal, cooperative relationship with nature | exploitative, combative relationship with nature |
| ecological and "natural" economies | industrial and artificial economies |
| religious culture | secular culture |

Like all such schemas, this vastly oversimplifies the case—but it can perhaps serve as a signpost to those modes of understanding and of "being in the world" which we need to reawaken in the modern West. Before any such healing process can proceed (a healing of ourselves, of the earth, of our "relationship" with the whole cosmos and with what lies beyond it) we must accept that, at root, the "environmental crisis" is actually the symptom of a spiritual malaise. To return to health we must get to the seat of the disease rather that merely palliating the symptoms. As a contemporary Sufi, Abu Bakr Siraj Ed-Din, has so well expressed it:

> The state of the outer world does not merely correspond to the general state of men's souls; it also in a sense depends on that state, since man himself is the pontiff of the outer world. Thus the corruption of man must necessarily affect the whole . . .[62]

Similarly, Seyyed Hossein Nasr:

> The Earth is bleeding from wounds inflicted upon it by a humanity no longer in harmony with Heaven and therefore in constant strife with the terrestrial environment.[63]

In this context we might also feel the force of Emerson's claim that, "the views of nature held by any people determine all their institutions."[64]

We are not able here to detail the ways in which we might escape the tyrannical grip of a profane scientism and its various accomplices (industrialism, consumerism, "development," "economic

62. Abu Bakr Siraj Ed-Din, *The Book of Certainty* (New York, 1974), p.33.
63. Seyyed Hossein Nasr, *Religion and the Order of Nature* (New York, 1996), p.3.

growth" and other such shibboleths) and so begin to free ourselves and our world from the catastrophic consequences of a collective blindness and a quite monstrous *hubris* (the two, of course, being intimately related). We must relinquish our Luciferian ideas about "conquering" nature, and allow Mother Nature not only to heal herself but to heal us. As Kenneth Cragg has so properly observed,

> . . . nature is the first ground and constant test of the authentically religious temper—the temper which does not sacralize things in themselves nor desecrate them in soul-less using and consuming. Between the pagan and the secular, with their contrasted bondage and arrogance, lies the reverent ground of a right hallowing where things are well seen as being for men under God, seen for their poetry, mystery, order and serviceability in the cognizance of man, and for their quality in the glory of God.[65]

The way forward must also be a way back. Suffice it to say that all those concerned about the current "ecological crisis" would do well to ponder the implications of the following passage from Schuon:

> This dethronement of Nature, or this scission between man and the earth—a reflection of the scission between man and God—has borne such bitter fruits that it should not be difficult to admit that, in these days, the timeless message of Nature constitutes a spiritual viaticum of the first importance . . . It is not a matter of projecting a supersaturated and disillusioned individualism into a desecrated Nature—this would be a worldliness like any other—but, on the contrary, of rediscovering in Nature, on the basis of the traditional outlook, the divine substance which is inherent in it; in other words, to "see God everywhere". . .[66]

Here is the same truth expressed by Black Elk in the inimitable idiom of the Lakota Indians:

> Peace . . . comes within the souls of men when they realize their relationship, their oneness, with the universe and all its powers, and when they realize that at the center of the Universe dwells *Wakan-Tanka* [the Great Spirit] and that this center is really everywhere, it is within each of us.[67]

64. Quoted in T.C. McLuhan, *Cathedrals of the Spirit* (Toronto, 1996), p223.
65. Kenneth Cragg, *The Mind of the Qur'an* (London, 1973), p.148.
66. Frithjof Schuon, *The Feathered Sun* (Bloomington, 1990), p.13.
67. Joseph Epes Brown, *The Sacred Pipe* (Baltimore, 1971), p.115.

Thou eye of the Great God
Thou eye of the God of Glory
Thou eye of the King of Creation
Thou eye of the Light of the living
Pouring on us at each time
Pouring on us gently, generously
Glory to thee thou glorious sun
Glory to thee thou Face of the God of life.

— Ortha nan Gaidheal

## Chapter 4

# Christianity and the Survival of Creation

## Wendell Berry

## I

I confess that I have not invariably been comfortable in front of a pulpit; I have never been comfortable behind one. To be behind a pulpit is always a forcible reminder to me that I am an essayist and, in many ways, a dissenter. An essayist is, literally, a writer who attempts to tell the truth. Preachers must resign themselves to being either right or wrong; an essayist, when proved wrong, may claim to have been "just practicing." An essayist is privileged to speak without institutional authorization. A dissenter, of course, must speak without privilege.

I want to begin with a problem: namely, that the culpability of Christianity in the destruction of the natural world and the uselessness of Christianity in any effort to correct that destruction are now established clichés of the conservation movement. This is a problem for two reasons.

First, the indictment of Christianity by the anti-Christian conservationists is, in many respects, just. For instance, the complicity of Christian priests, preachers, and missionaries in the cultural destruction and the economic exploitation of the primary peoples of the Western Hemisphere, as of traditional cultures around the world, is notorious. Throughout the five hundred years since Columbus's first landfall in the Bahamas, the evangelist has walked beside the conqueror and the merchant, too often blandly assuming that their causes were the same. Christian organizations, to this day, remain largely indifferent to the rape and plunder of the

* Editor's Note: This essay was delivered as a lecture at the Southern Baptist Theological Seminary in Louisville, Kentucky.

world and of its traditional cultures. It is hardly too much to say that most Christian organizations are as happily indifferent to the ecological, cultural, and religious implications of industrial economics as are most industrial organizations. The certified Christian seems just as likely as anyone else to join the military-industrial conspiracy to murder Creation.

The conservationist indictment of Christianity is a problem, second, because, however just it may be, it does not come from an adequate understanding of the Bible and the cultural traditions that descend from the Bible. The anti-Christian conservationists characteristically deal with the Bible by waving it off. And this dismissal conceals, as such dismissals are apt to do, an ignorance that invalidates it. The Bible is an inspired book written by human hands; as such, it is certainly subject to criticism. But the anti-Christian environmentalists have not mastered the first rule of the criticism of books: you have to read them before you criticize them. Our predicament now, I believe, requires us to learn to read and understand the Bible in the light of the present fact of Creation. This would seem to be a requirement both for Christians and for everyone concerned, but it entails a long work of true criticism— that is, of careful and judicious study, not dismissal. It entails, furthermore, the making of very precise distinctions between biblical instruction and the behavior of those peoples supposed to have been biblically instructed.

I cannot pretend, obviously, to have made so meticulous a study; even if I were capable of it, I would not live long enough to do it. But I have attempted to read the Bible with these issues in mind, and I see some virtually catastrophic discrepancies between biblical instruction and Christian behavior. I don't mean disreputable Christian behavior, either. The discrepancies I see are between biblical instruction and allegedly respectable Christian behavior.

If because of these discrepancies Christianity were dismissible, there would, of course, be no problem. We could simply dismiss it, along with the twenty centuries of unsatisfactory history attached to it, and start setting things to rights. The problem emerges only when we ask, "Where then would we turn for instruction?" We might, let us suppose, turn to another religion—a recourse that is sometimes suggested by the anti-Christian conservationists. Buddhism, for example, is certainly a religion that could guide us toward a right respect for the natural world, our fellow humans, and our fellow creatures. I owe a considerable debt myself to Buddhism and Buddhists. But there are an enormous number of people—and I am one of them—whose native religion, for better or worse, is Christianity. We were born to it; we began to learn about it before we became conscious; it is, whatever we think of it, an intimate belonging of our being; it informs our consciousness, our language, and our dreams. We can turn away from it or against it, but that will only bind us tightly to a reduced version of it. A better possibility is that this, our native religion, should survive and renew itself so that it may become as largely and truly instructive as we need it to be. On such a survival and renewal of the Christian religion may depend the survival of the Creation that is its subject.

## II

If we read the Bible, keeping in mind the desirability of those two survivals—of Christianity and the Creation—we are apt to discover several things about which modern Christian organizations have kept remarkably quiet or to which they have paid little attention.

We will discover that we humans do not own the world or any part of it: "The earth is the Lord's, and the fullness thereof: the world and they that dwell therein."[1] There is in our human law, undeniably, the concept and right of "land ownership." But this, I think, is merely an expedient to safeguard the mutual belonging of people and places without which there can be no lasting and conserving human communities. This right of human ownership is limited by mortality and by natural constraints on human attention and responsibility; it quickly becomes abusive when used to justify large accumulations of "real estate," and perhaps for that reason such large accumulations are forbidden in the twenty-fifth chapter of Leviticus. In biblical terms, the "landowner" is the guest and steward of God: "The land is mine; for ye are strangers and sojourners with me."[2]

We will discover that God made not only the parts of Creation that we humans understand and approve but all of it: "All things were made by him; and without him was not anything made that was

1. Psalms 24:1. (All biblical quotations are from the King James version.)
2. Leviticus 25:23.

made."[3] And so we must credit God with the making of biting and stinging insects, poisonous serpents, weeds, poisonous weeds, dangerous beasts, and disease-causing microorganisms. That we may disapprove of these things does not mean that God is in error or that He ceded some of the work of Creation to Satan; it means that we are deficient in wholeness, harmony, and understanding, that is, we are "fallen."

We will discover that God found the world, as He made it, to be good, that He made it for His pleasure, and that He continues to love it and to find it worthy, despite its reduction and corruption by us. People who quote John 3:16 as an easy formula for getting to Heaven neglect to see the great difficulty implied in the statement that the advent of Christ was made possible by God's love for the world—not God's love for Heaven or for the world as it might be, but for the world as it was and is. Belief in Christ is thus dependent on prior belief in the inherent goodness—the lovability—of the world.

We will discover that the Creation is not in any sense independent of the Creator, the result of a primal creative act long over and done with, but is the continuous, constant participation of all creatures in the being of God. Elihu said to Job that if God "gather unto Himself his spirit and his breath, all flesh shall perish together."[4] And Psalm 104 says, "Thou sendest forth thy spirit, they are created." Creation is thus God's presence in creatures. The Greek Orthodox theologian Philip Sherrard has written that "Creation is nothing less than the manifestation of God's hidden Being."[5] This means that we and all other creatures live by a sanctity that is inexpressibly intimate, for to every creature, the gift of life is a portion of the breath and spirit of God. As the poet George Herbert put it:

> Thou art in small things great, not small in any . . .
> For thou art infinite in one and all.[6]

---

3. John 1:3.
4. Job 34:14-15.
5. Philip Sherrard, *Human Image: World Image* (Ipswich, Suffolk, England, Golgonooza Press, 1992), 152.
6. George Herbert, "Providence," lines 41 and 44, from *The Poems of George Herbert*, ed. by Helen Gardner (London: Oxford University Press, 1961), 54.

We will discover that for these reasons our destruction of nature is not just bad stewardship, or stupid economics, or a betrayal of family responsibility; it is the most horrid blasphemy. It is flinging God's gifts into His face, as if they were of no worth beyond that assigned to them by our destruction of them. To Dante, "despising Nature and her goodness" was a violence against God.[7] We have no entitlement from the Bible to exterminate or permanently destroy or hold in contempt anything on the earth or in the heavens above it or in the waters beneath it. We have the right to use the gifts of nature but not to ruin or waste them. We have the right to use what we need but no more, which is why the Bible forbids usury and great accumulations of property. The usurer, Dante said, "condemns Nature . . . for he puts his hope elsewhere."[8]

William Blake was biblically correct, then, when he said that "everything that lives is holy."[9] And Blake's great commentator Kathleen Raine was correct both biblically and historically when she said that "the sense of the holiness of life is the human norm."[10]

The Bible leaves no doubt at all about the sanctity of the act of world-making, or of the world that was made, or of creaturely or bodily life in this world. We are holy creatures living among other holy creatures in a world that is holy. Some people know this, and some do not. Nobody, of course, knows it all the time. But what keeps it from being far better known than it is? Why is it apparently unknown to millions of professed students of the Bible? How can modern Christianity have so solemnly folded its hands while so much of the work of God was and is being destroyed?

## III

Obviously, "the sense of the holiness of life" is not compatible with an exploitive economy. You cannot know that life is holy if you are content to live from economic practices that daily destroy life and

---

7. Dante Alighieri, *The Divine Comedy,* trans. by Charles S. Singleton, Bollingen Series LXXX, and *Inferno,* canto XI, lines 46-48 (Princeton, NJ: Princeton University Press, 1970).

8. Dante Alighieri, *Inferno,* canto XI, lines 109-11.

9. William Blake, *Complete Writings,* ed. by Geoffrey Keynes (London: Oxford University Press, 1966), 160.

10. Kathleen Raine, *Golgonooza: City of Imagination* (Ipswich, Suffolk, England: Golgonooza Press, 1991), 28.

diminish its possibility. And many if not most Christian organizations now appear to be perfectly at peace with the military-industrial economy and its "scientific" destruction of life. Surely, if we are to remain free and if we are to remain true to our religious inheritance, we must maintain a separation between church and state. But if we are to maintain any sense or coherence or meaning in our lives, we cannot tolerate the present utter disconnection between religion and economy. By "economy" I do not mean "economics," which is the study of money-making, but rather the ways of human housekeeping, the ways by which the human household is situated and maintained within the household of nature. To be uninterested in economy is to be uninterested in the practice of religion; it is to be uninterested in culture and in character.

Probably the most urgent question now faced by people who would adhere to the Bible is this: What sort of economy would be responsible to the holiness of life? What, for Christians, would be the economy, the practices and the restraints, of "right livelihood"? I do not believe that organized Christianity now has any idea. I think its idea of a Christian economy is no more nor less than the industrial economy—which is an economy firmly founded on the seven deadly sins and the breaking of all ten of the Ten Commandments. Obviously, if Christianity is going to survive as more than a respecter and comforter of profitable iniquities, then Christians, regardless of their organizations, are going to have to interest themselves in economy—which is to say, in nature and in work. They are going to have to give workable answers to those who say we cannot live without this economy that is destroying us and our world, who see the murder of Creation as the only way of life.

The holiness of life is obscured to modern Christians also by the idea that the only holy place is the built church. This idea may be more taken for granted than taught; nevertheless, Christians are encouraged from childhood to think of the church building as "God's house," and most of them could think of their houses or farms or shops or factories as holy places only with great effort and embarrassment. It is understandably difficult for modern Americans to think of their dwellings and workplaces as holy, because most of these are, in fact, places of desecration, deeply involved in the ruin of Creation.

The idea of the exclusive holiness of church buildings is, of course, wildly incompatible with the idea, which the churches also teach, that God is present in all places to hear prayers. It is incompatible with Scripture. The idea that a human artifact could contain or confine God was explicitly repudiated by Solomon in his prayer at the dedication of the Temple: "Behold, the heaven and the heaven of heavens cannot contain thee: how much less this house that I have builded?"[11] And these words of Solomon were remembered a thousand years later by Saint Paul, preaching at Athens:

> God that made the world and all things therein, seeing that he is lord of heaven and earth, dwelleth not in temples made with hands . . . For in him we live, and move, and have our being; as certain also of your own poets have said.[12]

Idolatry always reduces to the worship of something "made with hands," something confined within the terms of human work and human comprehension. Thus, Solomon and Saint Paul both insisted on the largeness and the at-largeness of God, setting Him free, so to speak, from ideas about Him. He is not to be fenced in, under human control, like some domestic creature; He is the wildest being in existence. The presence of His spirit in us is our wildness, our oneness with the wilderness of Creation. That is why subduing the things of nature to human purposes is so dangerous and why it so often results in evil, in separation and desecration. It is why the poets of our tradition so often have given nature the role not only of mother or grandmother but of the highest earthly teacher and judge, a figure of mystery and great power. Jesus' own specifications for his church have nothing at all to do with masonry and carpentry but only with people; his church is "where two or three are gathered together in my name."[13]

The Bible gives exhaustive (and sometimes exhausting) attention to the organization of religion: the building and rebuilding of the Temple; its furnishings; the orders, duties, and paraphernalia of the priesthood; the orders of rituals and ceremonies. But that does not disguise the fact that the most significant religious events recounted in the Bible do not occur in "temples made with hands." The most important religion in that book is unorganized and is sometimes profoundly disruptive of organization. From Abraham to Jesus, the most important people are not priests but shepherds, sol-

11. 1 Kings 8:27.
12. Acts 17-24 and 28.
13. Matthew 18:20.

diers, property owners, workers, housewives, queens and kings, man-servants and maidservants, fishermen, prisoners, whores, even bureaucrats. The great visionary encounters did not take place in temples but in sheep pastures, in the desert, in the wilderness, on mountains, on the shores of rivers and the sea, in the middle of the sea, in prisons. And however strenuously the divine voice prescribed rites and observances, it just as strenuously repudiated them when they were taken to be religion:

> Your new moons and your appointed feasts my soul hateth: they are a trouble unto me; I am weary to hear them.
> And when you spread forth your hands, I will hide mine eyes from you: yea, when you make many prayers, I will not hear: your hands are full of blood.
> Wash you, make you clean; put away the evil of your doings from before mine eyes; cease to do evil;
> Learn to do well; seek judgment, relieve the oppressed, judge the fatherless, plead for the widow.[14]

Religion, according to this view, is less to be celebrated in rituals than practiced in the world. I don't think it is enough appreciated how much an outdoor book the Bible is. It is a "hypaethral book," such as Thoreau talked about—a book open to the sky. It is best read and understood outdoors, and the farther outdoors the better. Or that has been my experience of it. Passages that within walls seem improbable or incredible, outdoors seem merely natural. This is because outdoors we are confronted everywhere with wonders; we see that the miraculous is not extraordinary but the common mode of existence. It is our daily bread. Whoever really has considered the lilies of the field or the birds of the air and pondered the improbability of their existence in this warm world within the cold and empty stellar distances will hardly balk at the turning of water into wine—which was, after all, a very small miracle. We forget the greater and still continuing miracle by which water (with soil and sunlight) is turned into grapes.

It is clearly impossible to assign holiness exclusively to the built church without denying holiness to the rest of Creation, which is then said to be "secular." The world, which God looked at and found entirely good, we find none too good to pollute entirely and destroy piecemeal. The church, then, becomes a kind of preserve of

14. Isaiah 1:13-17.

"holiness," from which certified lovers of God assault and plunder the "secular" earth.

Not only does this repudiate God's approval of His work; it refuses also to honor the Bible's explicit instruction to regard the works of the Creation as God's revelation of Himself. The assignation of holiness exclusively to the built church is therefore logically accompanied by the assignation of revelation exclusively to the Bible. But Psalm 19 begins, "The heavens declare the glory of God; and the firmament sheweth his handiwork." The word of God has been revealed in facts from the moment of the third verse of the first chapter of Genesis: "Let there be light: and there was light." And Saint Paul states the rule: "The invisible things of him from the creation of the world are clearly seen, being understood by the things that are made."[15] Yet from this free, generous, and sensible view of things, we come to the idolatry of the book: the idea that nothing is true that cannot be (and has not been already) written. The misuse of the Bible thus logically accompanies the abuse of nature: if you are going to destroy creatures without respect, you will want to reduce them to "materiality"; you will want to deny that there is spirit or truth in them, just as you will want to believe that the only holy creatures, the only creatures with souls, are humans— or even only Christian humans.

By denying spirit and truth to the nonhuman Creation, modern proponents of religion have legitimized a form of blasphemy without which the nature- and culture-destroying machinery of the industrial economy could not have been built—that is, they have legitimized bad work. Good human work honors God's work. Good work uses no thing without respect, both for what it is in itself and for its origin. It uses neither tool nor material that it does not respect and that it does not love. It honors nature as a great mystery and power, as an indispensable teacher, and as the inescapable judge of all work of human hands. It does not dissociate life and work, or pleasure and work, or love and work, or usefulness and beauty. To work without pleasure or affection, to make a product that is not both useful and beautiful, is to dishonor God, nature, the thing that is made, and whomever it is made for. This is blasphemy: to make shoddy work of the work of God. But such blasphemy is not

15. Romans 1:20.

possible when the entire Creation is understood as holy and when the works of God are understood as embodying and thus revealing His spirit.

In the Bible we find none of the industrialist's contempt or hatred for nature. We find, instead, a poetry of awe and reverence and profound cherishing, as in these verses from Moses' valedictory blessing of the twelve tribes:

> And of Joseph he said, Blessed of the Lord be his land, for the precious things of heaven, for the dew, and for the deep that croucheth beneath,
> And for the precious fruits brought forth by the sun, and for the precious things put forth by the moon,
> And for the chief things of the ancient mountains, and for the precious things of the lasting hills,
> And for the precious things of the earth and fullness thereof, and for the good will of him that dwelt in the bush.[16]

# IV

I have been talking, of course, about a dualism that manifests itself in several ways: as a cleavage, a radical discontinuity, between Creator and creature, spirit and matter, religion and nature, religion and economy, worship and work, and so on. This dualism, I think, is the most destructive disease that afflicts us. In its best known, its most dangerous, and perhaps its fundamental version, it is the dualism of body and soul. This is an issue as difficult as it is important, and so to deal with it we should start at the beginning.

The crucial test is probably Genesis 2:7, which gives the process by which Adam was created: "The Lord God formed man of the dust of the ground, and breathed into his nostrils the breath of life: and man became a living soul." My mind, like most people's, has been deeply influenced by dualism, and I can see how dualistic minds deal with this verse. They conclude that the formula for man-making is man = body + soul. But that conclusion cannot be derived, except by violence, from Genesis 2:7, which is not dualistic. The formula given in Genesis 2:7 is not man = body + soul; the formula there is soul = dust + breath. According to this verse, God did not make a body and put a soul into it, like a letter into an envelope.

16. Deuteronomy 33:13-16.

He formed man of dust; then, by breathing His breath into it, He made the dust live. The dust, formed as man and made to live, did not embody a soul; it became a soul. "Soul" here refers to the whole creature. Humanity is thus presented to us, in Adam, not as a creature of two discrete parts temporarily glued together but as a single mystery.

We can see how easy it is to fall into the dualism of body and soul when talking about the inescapable worldly dualities of good and evil or time and eternity. And we can see how easy it is, when Jesus asks, "For what is a man profited, if he shall gain the whole world, and lose his own soul?"[17] to assume that he is condemning the world and appreciating the disembodied soul. But if we give to "soul" here the sense that it has in Genesis 2:7, we see that he is doing no such thing. He is warning that in pursuit of so-called material possessions, we can lose our understanding of ourselves as "living souls"— that is, as creatures of God, members of the holy community of Creation. We can lose the possibility of the atonement of that membership. For we are free, if we choose, to make a duality of our one living soul by disowning the breath of God that is our fundamental bond with one another and with other creatures.

But we can make the same duality by disowning the dust. The breath of God is only one of the divine gifts that make us living souls; the other is the dust. Most of our modern troubles come from our misunderstanding and misvaluation of this dust. Forgetting that the dust, too, is a creature of the Creator, made by the sending forth of His spirit, we have presumed to decide that the dust is "low." We have presumed to say that we are made of two parts: a body and a soul, the body being "low" because made of dust, and the soul "high." By thus valuing these two supposed-to-be parts, we inevitably throw them into competition with each other, like two corporations. The "spiritual" view, of course, has been that the body, in Yeats's phrase, must be "bruised to pleasure soul." And the "secular" version of the same dualism has been that the body, along with the rest of the "material" world, must give way before the advance of the human mind. The dominant religious view, for a long time, has been that the body is a kind of scrip issued by the Great Company Store in the Sky, which can be cashed in to redeem the soul but is

17. Matthew 16:26.

otherwise worthless. And the predictable result has been a human creature able to appreciate or tolerate only the "spiritual" (or mental) part of Creation and full of semiconscious hatred of the "physical" or "natural" part, which it is ready and willing to destroy for "salvation," for profit, for "victory," or for fun. This madness constitutes the norm of modern humanity and of modern Christianity.

But to despise the body or mistreat it for the sake of the "soul" is not just to burn one's house for the insurance, nor is it just self-hatred of the most deep and dangerous sort. It is yet another blasphemy. It is to make nothing—and worse than nothing—of the great Something in which we live and move and have our being.

When we hate and abuse the body and its earthly life and joy for Heaven's sake, what do we expect? That out of this life that we have presumed to despise and this world that we have presumed to destroy, we would somehow salvage a soul capable of eternal bliss? And what do we expect when with equal and opposite ingratitude, we try to make of the finite body an infinite reservoir of dispirited and meaningless pleasures?

Times may come, of course, when the life of the body must be denied or sacrificed, times when the whole world must literally be lost for the sake of one's life as a "living soul." But such sacrifice, by people who truly respect and revere the life of the earth and its Creator, does not denounce or degrade the body but rather exalts it and acknowledges its holiness. Such sacrifice is a refusal to allow the body to serve what is unworthy of it.

# V

If we credit the Bible's description of the relationship between Creator and Creation, then we cannot deny the spiritual importance of our economic life. Then we must see how religious issues lead to issues of economy and how issues of economy lead to issues of art. By "art" I mean all the ways by which humans make the things they need. If we understand that no artist—no maker—can work except by reworking the works of Creation, then we see that by our work we reveal what we think of the works of God. How we take our lives from this world, how we work, what work we do, how well we use the materials we use, and what we do with them after we have used them—all these are questions of the highest and gravest religious significance. In answering them, we practice, or do not practice, our religion.

The significance—and ultimately the quality—of the work we do is determined by our understanding of the story in which we are taking part. If we think of ourselves as merely biological creatures, whose story is determined by genetics or environment or history or economics or technology, then, however pleasant or painful the part we play, it cannot matter much. Its significance is that of mere self-concern. "It is a tale / Told by an idiot, full of sound and fury, / Signifying nothing," as Macbeth says when he has "supp'd full with horrors" and is "aweary of the sun."[18]

If we think of ourselves as lofty souls trapped temporarily in lowly bodies in a dispirited, desperate, unlovable world that we must despise for Heaven's sake, then what have we done for this question of significance? If we divide reality into two parts, spiritual and material, and hold (as the Bible does not hold) that only the spiritual is good or desirable, then our relation to the material Creation becomes arbitrary, having only the quantitative or mercenary value that we have, in fact and for this reason, assigned to it. Thus, we become the judges and inevitably the destroyers of a world we did not make and that we are bidden to understand as a divine gift. It is impossible to see how good work might be accomplished by people who think that our life in this world either signifies nothing or has only a negative significance.

If, on the other hand, we believe that we are living souls, God's dust and God's breath, acting our parts among other creatures all made of the same dust and breath as ourselves; and if we understand that we are free, within the obvious limits of mortal human life, to do evil or good to ourselves and to the other creatures—then all our acts have a supreme significance. If it is true that we are living souls and morally free, then all of us are artists. All of us are makers, within mortal terms and limits, of our lives, of one another's lives, of things we need and use.

This, Ananda Coomaraswamy wrote, is "the normal view," which "assumes . . . not that the artist is a special kind of man, but that every man who is not a mere idler or parasite is necessarily some

18. William Shakespeare, *Macbeth*, ed. by Kenneth Muir (Cambridge, MA,: Harvard University Press, 1957), V,v, lines 13, 26-28, 49.

special kind of artist."[19] But since even mere idlers and parasites may be said to work inescapably, by proxy or influence, it might be better to say that everybody is an artist—either good or bad, responsible or irresponsible. Any life, by working or not working, by working well or poorly, inescapably changes other lives and so changes the world. This is why our division of the "fine arts" from "craftsmanship," and "craftsmanship" from "labor," is so arbitrary, meaningless, and destructive. As Walter Shewring rightly said, both "the plowman and the potter have a cosmic function."[20] And bad art in any trade dishonors and damages Creation.

If we think of ourselves as living souls, immortal creatures, living in the midst of a Creation that is mostly mysterious, and if we see that everything we make or do cannot help but have an everlasting significance for ourselves, for others, and for the world, then we see why some religious teachers have understood work as a form of prayer. We see why the old poets invoked the muse. And we know why George Herbert prayed, in his poem "Mattens":

> Teach me thy love to know;
> That this new light, which now I see,
> May both the work and workman show.[21]

Work connects us both to Creation and to eternity. This is the reason also for Mother Ann Lee's famous instruction: "Do all your work as though you had a thousand years to live on earth, and as you would if you knew you must die tomorrow."[22]

Explaining "the perfection, order, and illumination" of the artistry of Shaker furniture makers, Coomaraswamy wrote, "All tradition has seen in the Master Craftsman of the Universe the exemplar of the human artist or 'maker by art,' and we are told to be 'perfect, *even as* your Father in heaven is perfect.'" Searching out the lesson, for us, of the Shakers' humble, impersonal, perfect artistry, which refused the modern divorce of utility and beauty, he wrote:

19. Ananda K. Coomaraswamy, *Christian and Oriental Philosophy of Art* (New York: Dover, 1957), 98.

20. Walter Shewring, *Artist and Tradesmen* (Marlborough, MA: Paulinus Press, 1984), 19.

21. Herbert, *The Poems of George Herbert*, 54.

22. June Sprigg, *By Shaker Hands* (Hanover, NH: University Press of New England, 1990), 33.

Unfortunately, we do not desire to be such as the Shaker was; we do not propose to "work as though we had a thousand years to live, and as though we were to die tomorrow." Just as we desire peace but not the things that make for peace, so we desire art but not the things that make for art. . . . we have the art that we deserve. If the sight of it puts us to shame, it is with ourselves that the reformation must begin.[23]

Any genuine effort to "re-form" our arts, our ways of making, must take thought of "the things that make for art." We must see that no art begins in itself; it begins in other arts, in attitudes and ideas antecedent to any art, in nature, and in inspiration. If we look at the great artistic traditions, as it is necessary to do, we will see that they have never been divorced either from religion or from economy. The possibility of an entirely secular art and of works of art that are spiritless or ugly or useless is not a possibility that has been among us for very long. Traditionally, the arts have been ways of making that have placed a just value on their materials or subjects, on the uses and the users of the things made by art, and on the artists themselves. They have, that is, been ways of giving honor to the works of God. The great artistic traditions have had nothing to do with what we call "self-expression." They have not been destructive of privacy or exploitive of private life. Though they have certainly originated things and employed genius, they have no affinity with the modern cults of originality and genius. Coomaraswamy, a good guide as always, makes an indispensable distinction between genius in the modern sense and craftsmanship: "Genius inhabits a world of its own. The master craftsman lives in a world inhabited by other men; he has neighbors."[24] The arts, traditionally, belong to the neighborhood. They are the means by which the neighborhood lives, works, remembers, worships, and enjoys itself.

But most important of all, now, is to see that the artistic traditions understood every art primarily as a skill or craft and ultimately as a service to fellow creatures and to God. An artist's first duty, according to this view, is technical. It is assumed that one will have talents, materials, subjects—perhaps even genius or inspiration or

23. Ananda Ananda K. Coomaraswamy, *Selected Papers*, vol. 1 (Princeton, NJ: Princeton University Press, 1977), 255,259.
24. Coomaraswamy, *Christian and Oriental Philosophy of Art*, 99.

vision. But these are traditionally understood not as personal properties with which one may do as one chooses but as gifts of God or nature that must be honored in use. One does not dare to use these things without the skill to use them well. As Dante said of his own art, "far worse than in vain does he leave the shore . . . who fishes for the truth and has not the art."[25] To use gifts less than well is to dishonor them and their Giver. There is no material or subject in Creation that in using, we are excused from using well; there is no work in which we are excused from being able and responsible artists.

# VI

In denying the holiness of the body and of the so-called physical reality of the world—and in denying support to the good economy, the good work, by which alone the Creation can receive due honor—modern Christianity generally has cut itself off from both nature and culture. It has no serious or competent interest in biology or ecology. And it is equally uninterested in the arts by which humankind connects itself to nature. It manifests no awareness of the specifically Christian cultural lineages that connect us to our past. There is, for example, a splendid heritage of Christian poetry in English that most church members live and die without reading or hearing or hearing about. Most sermons are preached without any awareness at all that the making of sermons is an art that has at times been magnificent. Most modern churches look like they were built by robots without reference to the heritage of church architecture or respect for the place; they embody no awareness that work can be worship. Most religious music now attests to the general assumption that religion is no more than a vaguely pious (and vaguely romantic) emotion.

Modern Christianity, then, has become as specialized in its organizations as other modern organizations, wholly concentrated on the industrial shibboleths of "growth," counting its success in numbers, and on the very strange enterprise of "saving" the individual, isolated, and disembodied soul. Having witnessed and abetted the dismemberment of the households, both human and natural, by which we have our being as creatures of God, as living

25. Dante Dante, *Paradiso*, canto XIII, lines 121 and 123.

souls, and having made light of the great feast and festival of Creation to which we were bidden as living souls, the modern church presumes to be able to save the soul as an eternal piece of private property. It presumes moreover to save the souls of people in other countries and religious traditions, who are often saner and more religious than we are. And always the emphasis is on the individual soul. Some Christian spokespeople give the impression that the highest Christian bliss would be to get to Heaven and find that you are the only one there—that you were right and all the others wrong. Whatever its twentieth century dress, modern Christianity as I know it is still at bottom the religion of Miss Watson, intent on a dull and superstitious rigmarole by which supposedly we can avoid going to "the bad place" and instead go to "the good place." One can hardly help sympathizing with Huck Finn when he says, "I made up my mind I wouldn't try for it."[26]

Despite its protests to the contrary, modern Christianity has become willy-nilly the religion of the state and the economic status quo. Because it has been so exclusively dedicated to incanting anemic souls into Heaven, it has been made the tool of much earthly villainy. It has, for the most part, stood silently by while a predatory economy has ravaged the world, destroyed its natural beauty and health, divided and plundered its human communities and households. It has flown the flag and chanted the slogans of empire. It has assumed with the economists that "economic forces" automatically work for good and has assumed with the industrialists and militarists that technology determines history. It has assumed with almost everybody that "progress" is good, that it is good to be modern and up with the times. It has admired Caesar and comforted him in his depredations and defaults. But in its de facto alliance with Caesar, Christianity connives directly in the murder of Creation. For in these days, Caesar is no longer a mere destroyer of armies, cities, and nations. He is a contradicter of the fundamental miracle of life. A part of the normal practice of his power is his willingness to destroy the world. He prays, he says, and churches everywhere compliantly pray with him. But he is praying to a God whose works he is prepared at any moment to destroy. What could be more wicked than that, or more mad?

26. Mark Twain, *Adventures of Huckleberry Finn*, in *Mississippi Writings* (New York: Library of America, 1982), 626.

The religion of the Bible, on the contrary, is a religion of the state and the status quo only in brief moments. In practice, it is a religion for the correction equally of people and of kings. And Christ's life, from the manger to the cross, was an affront to the established powers of his time, just as it is to the established powers of our time. Much is made in churches of the "good news" of the Gospels. Less is said of the Gospels' bad news, which is that Jesus would have been horrified by just about every "Christian" government the world has ever seen. He would be horrified by our government and its works, and it would be horrified by him. Surely no sane and thoughtful person can imagine any government of our time sitting comfortably at the feet of Jesus while he is saying, "Love your enemies, bless them that curse you, do good to them that hate you, and pray for them that despitefully use you and persecute you."[27]

In fact, we know that one of the businesses of governments, "Christian" or not, has been to reenact the crucifixion. It has happened again and again and again. In *A Time for Trumpets*, his history of the Battle of the Bulge, Charles B. MacDonald tells how the SS Colonel Joachim Peiper was forced to withdraw from a bombarded château near the town of La Gleize, leaving behind a number of severely wounded soldiers of both armies. "Also left behind," MacDonald wrote, "on a whitewashed wall of one of the rooms in the basement was a charcoal drawing of Christ, thorns on his head, tears on his cheeks—whether drawn by a German or an American nobody would ever know."[28] This is not an image that belongs to history but rather one that judges it.

—1992

27. Matthew 5:44.
28. George MacDonald, *A Time for Trumpets* (New York: Bantam Books, 1984), 458.

### A Christmas Caroll

Dark and dull night, flie hence away,
And give the honor to this Day,
That sees December turn'd to May.
Why does the chilling Winters morne
Smile, like a field beset with corne?
Or smell, like a Meade new shorne,
Thus, on the sudden? —Come and see
The cause, why things thus fragrant be.

— Robert Herrick

*Chapter 5*

# The Spiritual and Religious Dimensions of the Environmental Crisis

## *Seyyed Hossein Nasr*

Considering the depth and breadth of the environmental crisis and the heedlessness of those who continue to pursue the very means and abet the very forces which have brought the crisis about, it might appear to be futile to speak about it again and again. But this crisis has a spiritual and religious dimension and is the result of the forgetting of certain perennial truths which need to be asserted and reasserted amidst the chaos in which we live. To express the truth is in fact the most important of all acts and one should take every opportunity to do so even if it seems to have no effect, at least none that is perceptible. Even if we are not able to perceive the effect, however, surely the expression of the truth bears its fruit; otherwise it would not have been considered as such a virtuous act in various traditions.

In any case there is nothing more timely to discuss than the question of the environmental crisis and the truths and falsehoods associated with this whole matter. It is not accidental that the word "crisis" is used in this context, for a veritable crisis it surely is, following upon the wake of that spiritual and intellectual crisis which is inseparable from the very world-view of the modern world. The earlier crisis which René Guénon had already discussed three quarters of a century ago in a number of works, including *Crisis of the Modern World*[1], was known to the few and ignored by the many. The environmental crisis, however, is too manifest to be ignored even by

---

\* Editor's Note: This paper was given under the auspices of the Religious Education & Environment Program (REEP) of the Friends of the Center, and the Temenos Academy, on 22 May 1998.

1. René Guénon, *The Crisis of the Modern World*, trans. Marco Pallis and Richard Nicholson (London: Luzac, 1962); originally published in 1927 as *La crise du monde moderne*.

the multitude. It is a crisis of the utmost gravity and urgency and anyone who neglects it is simply fooling himself or is daydreaming. It is, however, in our nature to try to evade confrontation with what requires of us the deepest transformation within ourselves.

The subject for my talk tonight has been chosen by my hosts. We have spent the whole day today here in London talking with some of the leading British theologians and scientists about this same question of the environmental crisis and some of them are in the audience tonight. Probably they are tired of it being discussed again, but because of the urgent nature of the subject, I am always glad, though saddened, to speak about it and to repeat certain basic theses. The situation today reminds one sometimes of the last few hours of the Titanic when people were playing music while their ship was sinking. We are obliged to turn again and again to these matters since, unfortunately, the negative forces which are bringing chaos upon our world continue unabated. In fact, it is necessary to repeat the theme of the environmental crisis even if it seems that no one is listening because, as already mentioned, the very assertion of the truth on any level is itself the most positive of all acts. Even if outwardly it seems to have no effect, in reality it does. Even if one person were to change his or her view that might mean a great deal.

It may be our nature to try to evade an imminent danger unless we really face it, but we do not want to face it for the very reason that it is a danger. The grave picture that is painted by serious scholars and honest scientists who are interested in the future of humanity can often be counteracted by having a film company send a camera into the woods to photograph a few birds flying around with the pretense of showing how "normal" the environmental situation of the earth is, even in urban areas. The truth is, however, otherwise. There is a major crisis at hand and it must be taken completely seriously. Moreover, one must also realize that the environmental crisis cannot be solved by good engineering (or better engineering); cannot be solved by economic planning; cannot even be solved by cosmetic changes in our conception of development and change. It requires a very radical transformation in our consciousness, and this means not discovering a completely new state of consciousness, but returning to the state of consciousness which traditional humanity always had. It means to rediscover the traditional way of looking at the world of nature as sacred presence.

For the title of my lecture, as you can see, I have chosen both the words "spiritual" and "religious." That was done on purpose, because the present usage of the word "religion" in many quarters often leaves out precisely the spiritual element. Those people who are looking for the inner dimension of religious experience and of religious truth, are seeking another word to supplement the word "religion." It is tragic that this is so but it is nevertheless a fact. The word "spirituality" in its current sense, and not the Latin term from which it derives, is a modern term. As far as my own research has shown, the term spirituality as it is used today began to be employed by French Catholic theologians in the mid-nineteenth century and then crept into English. We do not find the use of this term as we now understand it earlier than the last century. Today it denotes for many people precisely those elements of religion which have been forgotten in the West and which therefore have come to be identified wrongly with spirituality as distinct from religion. From my point of view, which is always of course a traditional one, there is no spirituality without religion. There is no way of reaching the spirit without choosing a path which God has chosen for us, and that means religion (*religio*). Therefore, the reason I am using both words is not for the sake of expediency, but to emphasize that I mean to include a reality which encompasses both spirituality and religion, in the current understanding of these terms, although traditionally the term religion would suffice since in its full sense it includes all that is understood by spirituality today.

It is important we remember that all of us on the globe share in destroying our natural environment, although the reasons for this are different in different parts of the globe. In the modern world the environment is destroyed by following the dominating philosophy, while in what remains of the traditional world it is done in spite of the prevailing world-view and most often as a result of external coercion as well as temptation, whether it be direct or indirect. I have repeated this truth in many places and have caused some people to become angry, but the fact is that the only action in which nearly everybody participates at the present moment of human history, from communist to socialist, to capitalist, from Hindu and Muslim to atheist, from Christian to Shinto, is in living and acting in such a way as to cause the destruction of the natural environment. This fact must seep fully into our consciousness while at the same time we remember the differences in motive and perspective among religious and secularized sectors of humanity. Obviously, for those for whom religion is still a reality, it is much easier to appeal to religion and the religious view of nature to discover the means through which a solution would be found for the crisis from which we all suffer.

We often forget that the vast majority of the people in the world still live by religion. And yet most Western intellectuals think about environmental issues as if everyone were an agnostic following a secular philosophy cultivated at Oxford, Cambridge or Harvard and so they seek to develop a rationalist, environmental ethics based on agnosticism, as if this would have any major effect whatsoever upon the environmental crisis. It is important to consider in a real way the world in which we live. If we do so then we must realize why in fact religion is so significant both in the understanding and in the solution of the environmental crisis. Let us not forget, I repeat, that the vast majority of the people in the world live according to religion. The statistic that is often given, saying that only half of humanity does so, is totally false because it is claimed that in addition to the West one billion two hundred million Chinese are atheists or non-religious. This is not at all the case. Confucianism is not a philosophy, but a religion based upon ritual—I shall come back to that in a few moments. There are at most a few hundred million agnostics and atheists spread mostly in the Western world, with extensions into a few big cities in Asia and Africa. But this group forms a small minority of the people of the world. Those who live on the other continents, as well as many people in Europe and America, still live essentially in a religious world. Although in the West the religious view of nature has been lost, even here it is still religion to which most ordinary people listen, while the number is much greater in other parts of the globe. That is why any secularist ideology that tries to replace religion always tries also to play the role of religion itself. This has happened with the ideology of modern science in the West which for many people is now accepted as a "religion." That is why the people who try to sell you many kinds of goods on television do so as "scientists"—as agents of "authority"—and always wear a white robe, not a black robe of traditional priests. They are trying to look like members of the new "priesthood." They function as the "priesthood" of a pseudo-religion. Their whole enterprise is made to appear not as simply ordinary science but as something that replaces religion. For people who accept this thesis it would be feasible to accept a rationalistic ethics related to science, but the vast majority of the people in the world still heed authentic religion. Consequently, for them, no ethics would have efficacy unless it was religious ethics.

In the West, for four hundred years, philosophers influenced by scientism have been trying to develop secular ethics and, sure enough, there are many atheists who are very ethical in their life. But by what norm are they to be considered as ethical? By no other than the very norms which religion instilled in the minds of people in the West. If somebody murders his neighbor we think it is unethical. But why is it unethical? What is wrong with that? The television programs you watch on nature in Africa show that animals are eating each other all the time. If we are just animals, then what is wrong if we kill one another? The fact that everybody says "no" to such an act is precisely because there are certain religious values instilled even into the secular atmosphere of the modern West which speaks of so-called secular ethics. The values of this ethics really have their roots in religion. In any case no secular ethics could speak with authority except to those who would accept the philosophical premises of such ethics.

The fact remains that the vast majority of the people in the world do not accept any ethics which does not have a religious foundation. This means in practical terms that if a religious figure, let us say, a *mulla* or a *brahmin* in India or Pakistan, goes to a village and tells the villagers that from the point of view of the *Sharî'ah* (Islamic Law) or the Law of Manu (Hindu law) they are forbidden to cut this tree, many people would accept. But if some graduate from the University of Delhi or Karachi, who is a government official comes and says, for rational reasons, philosophical and scientific reasons, that it is better not to cut this tree, few would heed his advice. So from a practical point of view the only ethics which can be acceptable to the vast majority, at the present moment in the history of the world, is still a religious ethics. The very strong prejudice against religious ethics in certain circles in the West, which have now become concerned with the environmental crisis, is itself one of the greatest impediments to the solution of the environmental crisis itself. This fact cannot be doubted in any way.

There is a second reason why religion is so important in the solution of the environmental crisis. There are many elements involved here but as this is only a one-hour lecture I have to summarize. We all know and even if we are not personally concerned with the metaphysical, spiritual and cosmological roots of the environmental crisis, we are none the less aware of the fact that outwardly (I do not say inwardly) this crisis is driven by the modern economic system appealing to human passions, especially the passion of greed intensified by the creation of false needs, which are not really needs but wants. This is in opposition to the view which religions have espoused over the millennia, that is, the practice of the virtue of contentment, of being content with what one has. The modern outlook is based on fanning the fire of greed and covetousness, on trying to do everything possible to attach the soul more and more to the world and on making a vice out of what for religion has always been a virtue, that is, to keep a certain distance and detachment from the world; in other words, a certain amount of asceticism. There is a famous German proverb, "there is no culture without asceticism"; and this is true of every civilization.

We are living in the first period in human history in the West in which, except for a few small islands here and there of Orthodox or Catholic or Anglican monasticism, and a few people who try to practice austerity, asceticism is considered to be a vice, not a virtue. It is not taught in our schools as a virtue; it is taught as a vice, preventing us from realizing ourselves, as if our "selves" were simply the extension of our physicality. This idea of self-realization is, of course, central to oriental and certain occidental traditions. But it has become debased in the worst way possible and transformed into the basis for modern consumerism, which can be seen in its most virulent form in America—now fast conquering Europe, and doing a good job of reaching India, China, Indonesia, etc. (within the next decade we will have several billion new consumers in such countries thirsting for artificial things which they have lived without for the last few thousand years). And what this will do to the earth God alone knows. It is beyond belief and conjecture what will happen if present trends continue. So what is it that can rein in the passions, either gradually or suddenly? Nothing but religion for the vast majority of people who, believing in God and the afterlife, still fear the consequences of their evil actions in their lives in this world. If it were to be told to them that pollution and destruction of the environment is a sin in the theological sense of the term they would think twice before indulging in it. For the ordinary believer the wrath of God and fear of punishment in the afterlife is the most powerful force against the negative tendencies of the passionate soul. For nearly all people on the earth who continue to pollute the air and the water, and whose life-style entails the destruction of the natural environment, what is it that is going to act as a break against the ever-growing power of the passions except religion? The religions have had thousands of years to deal with the slaying of the passionate ego, this inner dragon, to use the symbol mentioned in so many traditions. St. Michael's slaying of the dragon with his lance has many meanings, one of which is, of course, that the lance of the Spirit alone is able to kill that dragon; or what in Sufism is called *nafs*, that is the passionate soul, the lower soul within us. We rarely think of that issue today. But where is St. Michael with his lance? How are we going to stop people from wanting more and more if not through the power of the Spirit made accessible through religion? And once you have opened up the Pandora's box of the appetites, how are you going to put the genie back into the box? How are you going to be able, with no more than rational arguments, to tell people to use less, to be less covetous, not to be greedy, and so forth? No force in the world today, except religion, has the power to do that unless it be sheer physical coercion.

For the vast majority of people there is no other way to control the great passions within us which have now been fanned by, first of all, the weakening of religion and, secondly, the substitution of another set of values derived from a kind of pseudo-religion whose new gods are such idols as "development" and "progress." But such notions do not have the power to help us control our passions. On the contrary they only fan the fire of those passions. We have been witness during the last generation alone to the ever greater debunking of the traditional religious attitudes towards the world, especially what we call in Arabic *ridâ*, that is contentment with our state of being, a virtue which is the very opposite of the sin of covetousness. Of course, the Muslims have been criticized by the West for a long time for simply being fatalistic in the face of events, of being too content with their lot. This same de-bunking has also been directed towards similar Christian values. But that is because of a deep misunderstanding. Where, in the current educational system in the West, is attention being paid to these traditional virtues? Even from a purely empirical, scientific point of view, these virtues must be seen as being of great value seeing that they have made it possible for human beings to live for thousands of years in the world without destroying the natural environment as we are currently doing. These traditional virtues that allowed countless generations to live in equilibrium with the world around them were at the same time conceived as ways of perfecting the soul, as steps in the perfection of human existence. These virtues provided the means for living at peace with the environment. They also allowed man to experience what it means to be human and to fulfill his destiny here on earth, which is always bound to try to inculcate such virtues within oneself.

Another cardinal and central role of religion in the solution of the environmental crisis, one that goes to its very root, is much more difficult to understand within the context of the modern mind-set. This role is related to the significance of religious rituals as a means of establishing cosmic harmony. Now, this idea is meaningless in the context of modern thought, where ritual seems to have no relation or correspondence with the nature of physical reality. In the modern world-view, rituals are at best personal, individual, subjective elements that create happiness in the individual or establish a relationship between him or her and God. That much at least some modern people accept. But how could rites establish cosmic harmony? From the modern scientific point of view such an assertion seems to make no sense at all. But it is not nonsense; it is a very subtle truth that has to be brought out and emphasized. From both the spiritual and the religious perspective, the physical world is related to God by levels of reality which transcend the physical world itself and which constitute the various stages of the cosmic hierarchy. It is impossible to have harmony in nature, or harmony of man with nature without this vertical harmony with the higher states of being. Once nature is conceived as being purely material, even if we accept that it was created by God conceived as a clockmaker, this cosmic relationship can no longer even be conceived much less be realized. Once we cut nature off from the immediate principles of nature —which are the psychic and spiritual or angelic levels of reality—then nature has already lost its balance as far as our relation to it is concerned.

Now rituals, from the point of view of religion, are God-made. I am not using the term ritual as seen from the secular point of view, as if one were putting on one's gown and going to some commencement exercise or some other humanly created action, often called a "ritual" in everyday discourse today. I am using it in the religious sense. According to all traditional religions, rituals descend from Heaven. A ritual is an enactment or rather re-enactment here on earth of a divine prototype. In the Abrahamic world, that means that rituals have been revealed to the prophets by God and taught by them to man. The "repetition" of the Last Supper of Christ in the Eucharist, or the daily prayers of Muslims, where do they come from? According to the followers of those religions, they all come from Heaven. In Hinduism and Buddhism one observes the same reality. The differences are of context and world-view, but the fundamentals are the same. There is no Hindu rite which was invented by someone walking along the Ganges who suddenly thought it up. For the Hindus they are of divine origin. The Muslim daily prayers, which we have all seen in pictures, were given by the Prophet to Muslims on the basis of instructions received from God. Even the Prophet did not invent them. The Eucharist "re-enacts" the Last Supper which, as the central rite of Christianity, was first celebrated by Christ himself.

Now, these rites, by virtue of their re-enactment on earth, link the earth with the higher levels of reality. A rite always links us with the vertical axis of existence, and by virtue of that, links us also with the principles of nature. This truth holds not only for the primal religions, where certain acts are carried out in nature itself—let us say the African religions or the Aboriginal religion of Australia, or the religions of the Native American Indians—but also in the Abrahamic world, in the Hindu world, and in the Iranian religions. Whether one is using particular natural forms such as a tree or a rock or a cave or something like that, or man-made objects of sacred and liturgical art related to rites carried out inside a church, synagogue, mosque or Hindu temple, it does not make any difference. The same truth is to be found in all these cases. From a metaphysical point of view a ritual always re-establishes balance with the cosmic order.

In the deepest mystical sense, nature is hungry for our prayers, in the sense that we are like a window of the house of nature through which the light and air of the spiritual world penetrate into the natural world. Once that window becomes opaque, the house of nature becomes dark. That is exactly what we are experiencing today. Once we have shut our hearts to God, darkness spreads over the whole of the world. This, of course, is something very difficult to explain to an agnostic mentality. But from a practical, expedient point of view at least it should be taken into consideration even by those who do not take rites seriously, seeing what has happened to nature at the hands of those sectors of humanity who no longer perform traditional rites. All religious people who believe in the efficacy of rites and perform them have a way of looking at the natural world and their place in it which is very different from the secularist way that has itself led us to the environmental crisis. You have all read or heard about examples of various religious rituals and their relation to nature, even in lesser-known religions. Perhaps the best known, as far as displaying the direct relation between rituals and the natural world is concerned, is the rain-dance of the Native Americans, about which skeptics make jokes. But some people take it very seriously and go to Native American medicine men, the shamans, to try to help them to help bring rain. Of course, such a thing is laughed at by official science, but that does not matter for such a science neglects the *sympathaeia* which exists between man and cosmic realities.

We have similar rituals all over the Islamic world, the Hindu world, the Buddhist world and in the traditional Christian world. But in the modern Western world it has now become more or less eclipsed, although it is has not disappeared completely. In Greece, once you go out of big cities, you still see it and in Italy, in the villages, when there is news of an earthquake, people recite the beginning of the Gospel of John in Latin, which many still know by heart. The faithful recite it in a ritual sense to help recreate balance and harmony with the natural world by calling upon Divine Mercy. I can hardly overemphasize the significance of this aspect of religion because it is impossible for a human collectivity to live in harmony with nature without this ritualized relationship with the natural world and harmony with God and the higher levels of cosmic hierarchy. If we do not have this relationship, nature is reduced to an "it," to a pure fact, to a material lump, not in itself, of course, but for us and we must bear all the consequences which such a view entails.

Along with providing a sound basis for ethics, perhaps the most important role of religion in the understanding of the roots of the environmental crisis (and here I would include especially the spiritual element of religion because it is the spiritual, metaphysical, and esoteric dimension of religion which emphasizes this element), is that religion possesses an extensive doctrine about the nature of the world in which we live. That is, religion, when it was integral and not truncated as it has become today in the West, provided not only a doctrine about God, not only a doctrine about the human state, but also a doctrine about the world of nature. And here, by doctrine, I mean knowledge (*doctrina*), not only opinion, but authentic knowledge which is not in any way negated by the scientific knowledge of the world. Every religion provides not only teachings pertaining to the emotional and sentimental realm, not only principles for ethical action, but also knowledge, knowledge in the deepest sense of the term of God, of the human state, and also of nature. There is no major religion whose integral tradition does not provide such a knowledge. Some religions emphasize one element, some religions another. Certain religions, such as Confucianism, do not speak about cosmogony and eschatology, but they have a vast cosmology. Of other religions, the reverse is true. But these three types of knowledge, that is, knowledge of God or the Ultimate Principle, of the human state and of nature, have to exist in all integral religions.

Now, one does not need to look very far to see what has happened in the modern world. Gradually, from the seventeenth century onwards, first in the West then spreading in recent decades to other parts of the world, the legitimacy of the religious knowledge of nature has been rejected. Most people who study the views of an Eriugena or a St. Thomas Aquinas on nature do so as historians. But their views are not accepted by the mainstream of modern Western society as legitimate knowledge of the world. What has been lost is a way of studying nature religiously, not simply as "poetry," as this term is used today in a trivializing sense and not of course in a positive one. True poetry possesses a great message as far as nature is concerned, a message which itself is usually religious. In any case modern society has disassociated knowledge of nature from religion as well as sapiential poetry itself, and relegates the religious attitude and knowledge of nature to sentiment or "simply" to poetic sensibility.

We have wonderful examples of nature poetry in the great poetry produced in the nineteenth century in this country. The Romantic poets produced beautiful poetry about nature. But what effect did it have on the physics departments of the universities? Absolutely none precisely because the science that developed in the seventeenth century, through very complicated processes which I cannot go into now, began to exclude from its world-view the possibility of a religious or metaphysical form of knowledge of nature. This science even excluded the poetic view of nature in so far as it claimed any intellectual legitimacy and sought to be more than what some would call "mere poetry." Modern science has clung to that monopoly very hard, even in this pluralistic age of ours, in which everything other than science is relativized. Post-modernists usually deconstruct everything except modern science because if this were to be done the whole world-view of modernism along with post-modernism would collapse. So you have a kind of scientific exclusivity and monopoly which has been created and accepted by most although not all people in the modern world. Goethe, the supreme German poet as well as a scientist, rebelled very strongly against this monopolistic claim of modern science. There were also certain scientists, such as Oswald, who was a reputable chemist who rejected scientific mechanism; and one can name others. But these are exceptions to the rule. The rule became that there is no other knowledge of nature except what is called scientific knowledge. And if someone claims that there is a religious knowledge of nature then it is usually claimed that it is based on sentiment, on emotions, or in other words on subjective factors. If, for example, you see a dove flying and you think of the Holy Spirit, that is simply a subjective correlation between your perception of the dove and your own sentiments. There is no objectivity accorded to the reality of nature as perceived though religious knowledge. That is why even symbolism has become subjectivized—it is claimed to be "merely" psychological, à la Jung. The symbols which traditional man saw in the world of nature as being objective and as being part of the ontological reality of nature, have been all cast aside by this type of mentality which no longer takes the religious knowledge of nature seriously.

During the last thirty years, when the thirst for a more holistic approach to nature made itself felt, something even worse occurred because neither mainstream religion nor modern science showed any interest whatsoever in the religious and symbolic knowledge of nature and the holistic approach to it. The water sought for this thirst seeped under the structures of Western culture and came out in the form of New Age movements, nearly all of which are very much interested in the science of the cosmos. But what they claim is really a New Age pseudo-science of the cosmos. It is not an authentic traditional science because a traditional science of the cosmos always has to be related to a traditional religious structure.

In this New Age climate the word "cosmic" has gained a great deal of currency precisely because of the dearth of an authentic religious knowledge of the cosmos in the present-day world. Somehow the thirst had to be satisfied. So we have had both excavation of the earlier Western esoteric teachings about nature—usually presented in distorted fashion—or borrowings from oriental religions and their teachings about nature, often distorted. Even the famous and influential book of Frithjof Capra, *The Tao of Physics,* does not really speak of Hindu cosmology or Chinese physics, but only mentions certain comparisons between modern physics and Hindu and Taoist metaphysical ideas.

To be sure there are many profound correlations and concordances to be found between certain aspects of biology, astronomy and quantum mechanics on the one hand and oriental doctrines of nature, of the cosmos, on the other. I would be the last person to doubt that truth. But what has occurred for the most part is not the kind of profound comparison we have in mind, but its parody, a kind of popularized version of a religious knowledge of nature, usually involving some kind of occultism or even some kind of an existing cult. The great interest shown today in Shamanism in America, in the whole phenomena of the Native American tradition (which is one of the great and beautiful primal traditions that still survives to some extent), with weekend Shamanic sessions, is precisely because such teachings appeal to a kind of mentality that seeks some sort of knowledge of nature of a spiritual and holistic character other than what modern science provides. This phenomenon is one of the paradoxes of our day which has not helped the environmental crisis in any appreciable way. Indeed, it has created a certain confusion in the domain of religion and created a breach between the mainstream religious organizations which still survive in the West—whether they be Catholic, Protestant or Orthodox— and these pseudo-movements and the New Age phenomenon which they rightly oppose. The fact that these pseudo-religious movements are very pro-environment, yet in an ineffectual manner, has caused many people in the mainstream to take a stand against the very positions which they should be defending. So we have the paradoxical situation in America today where the most conservative Christian groups are those which are least interested in the environment. This phenomenon was not originally caused by the rise of the New Age religions but is certainly related to it and strengthened by it.

It is now necessary to say something about what constitutes the religious view of nature. It is important for us to understand that ordinary human beings in all civilizations deal with religion to the extent that it concerns their everyday life. Only the sages, the seers and the saints, are able to reach the heart of religion, but they always bring something from the heart and disseminate it throughout the whole body of the religious community. Now in the Western world (the Christian world), and the Islamic world which is a religion which is a cousin of Christianity and Judaism (Judaism, of course, sharing something of both worlds), the religious science of nature was not part and parcel of the everyday teaching of religion as far as ethics were concerned. On the everyday level these religions teach that one should be good, one should love one's neighbor, which includes beings other than man, one should give tithe and alms, one should say one's prayers, etc. But, the fact is that in the traditional ambience there was also always present this inner spiritual message and knowledge concerning nature which was accessible to those in these civilizations who sought such a knowledge. It was this message that first became eclipsed in the West before the onslaught of a secular science took hold of the predominant world-view. It was not that first a secular science took hold in the West and then the spiritual understanding of nature was eclipsed, but the other way around. The loss of the Christian sapiential view of the cosmos during the Renaissance left a vacuum which after two centuries came to be filled by a secular science which could not see in nature anything other than quantity and motion, as Galileo asserted.

One can now ask what is this religious view of nature? The religious view, as understood by the ordinary sense of the believer, is that this world is created and sustained by God; it is His creation; or one could in the non-Abrahamic context say that it is the manifestation of the Principle, of let us say the Tao of the Far Eastern traditions. The Origin does not have to be identified in name as the Abrahamic God, but it is always the Divine Principle which is none other than God. On the deeper level the religions teach that there is something spiritual and ultimately meaningful in nature. On this deeper level it is this meaning which has to be deciphered and understood. This deeper meaning is not, however, like the exoteric teachings of the religion which are meant for one and all. We are talking here about a type of knowledge that is not accessible to everyone, but only to those few capable of metaphysical intuition and who are willing to master the language in which the Divine Message is written upon the leaves of the cosmic book. Knowledge is not evenly and democratically distributed in any domain. You only have a few great mathematicians in Great Britain and the other 54 million people have only a rudimentary grasp of mathematics. It is like that in every field. With metaphysics it is the same; there are only a few who can grasp its teachings: here it is certainly not quantity that is important.

There is a fine book by William Chittick on the cosmology of Ibn 'Arabi which is called *The Self-Disclosure of God*. It is the most extensive book on Sufi cosmology in English, one which brings out clearly this esoteric and metaphysical knowledge of nature in its Sufi context.[2] This type of knowledge was always reserved for the few but is now made available publicly to all those endowed with the necessary qualifications to understand such doctrines. God self-discloses Himself. It is not only a question of creation of the world by God, but there is also creation in God. Creation first takes place *in divinis* and then is manifested externally. Therefore, although creation is not God, it is not completely divorced from its Divine Origin. We might say the cat is also God's creation, and so, at best, we should not molest the cat in the street. The truth, however, is much more profound than that. The cat is ultimately a manifestation of some aspect of the Divine Reality itself. Therefore the essential reality of the cat is in the Divine Reality—the cat in the street. God has knowledge of this cat, and that knowledge of God which involves the archetype of the cat *in divinis* is inseparable from the Divine Reality in the ultimate sense. All of nature is the self-disclosure of God Himself to Himself, without which it would be literally nothing.

I do not want to go into these complicated philosophical concepts of archetypes, Platonic ideas and so on which we find in different languages in all of the traditions. I am speaking in simple language for the purposes of this discourse. Put simply one can say that everything in the world is a divine presence and witness to God. The Quran is very specific about this: *kullu shay in yusabbihu*

2. William C. Chittick, *The Self-Disclosure of God: Principles of Ibn al-Àrabî's Cosmology* (Albany: State University New York, 1998).

*bihamdihi* (that is, "everything in the universe sings the praise of Him," [sings the praise of God]. [3] So every time we destroy a species, we are destroying a prayerful being. It is like murdering someone while he is praying. It is as abominable as that. In the time I am delivering this lecture we will have destroyed several species. It is amazing what we are doing. They say that 30 per cent perhaps of all the species in the world will have been destroyed in the next twenty years. This horrendous fact is directly the result of a type of knowledge of nature having been lost, a knowledge which is based on the nexus between all creatures and their Divine Source. If I make such a statement, one might think that I am talking as a dreamy Persian philosopher or poet, and what I say has nothing to do with real knowledge. Knowledge of the cat is the size of its tail, the structure of its bones and so forth and so on. To be sure that is all part of the knowledge of the cat. But the knowledge of the cat is not exhausted by our knowledge of its physical aspect. What we learn about the physical aspect of the cat is in itself remarkable. The structure of the cat, as with any other creature, is amazing enough, consisting, as it does, of the smallest units of life, which have not evolved from simplicity to complexity but appeared on the natural scene with remarkable complexity. But the religious view neither limits itself to this external knowledge nor does it deny such knowledge. It deals with the very being of a creature as locus of Divine Presence. The result of such knowledge is that we must live with the creatures of the world, not only by necessity, but also because of our own spiritual welfare. The destruction of nature is ultimately the destruction of our own inner being and finally our external life as well. Of course, from the point of view of cause and effect, it is the reverse; it is the pollution of our inner being that has caused the pollution of the natural environment. It is our inner darkness that has now extended outward into the world of nature. The chaos of the outward reflects like a mirror what has happened within ourselves.

Without resuscitation of this religious and metaphysical view of nature, everything else we say about the environmental crisis is just cosmetics and politics. We have to experience the profound rebirth of our conception of the world as *temenos*, a sacred precinct, as the Greek word signifies. It is not only the mosque, the temple or the

---

3. Quran 17:44.

church that is a sacred precinct; it is not only human beings, but the whole world, everything in creation that bears testimony to the Divine Presence and which is therefore *temenos*. As this verse of the Quran, which I cited for you, asserts, it is not only human beings who sing the praise of God. Everything has it own tongue with which it praises Him. Everything sings the praise of God by virtue of its very existence. We might not understand the language, but the song of praise is there. It is very significant that so many of the great saints of the Abrahamic world who were sensitive to nature claimed to have some kind of communion with nature beyond human language. I mean such figures as St. Francis of Assisi who spoke to the birds; we have examples of that in Islam and in fact in all religions, not only the Abrahamic ones. The religious view of nature requires of us a complete re-understanding of what nature is, and who we are as human beings who act upon nature, because it is impossible to discuss nature without discussing the image that we have of ourselves.

The fact that in our religions it has been told to us that all of nature praises God presupposes that God wants us to know this reality, that He has bestowed us with the means to understand such a message. That itself is enough to prove to those with eyes to see and ears to hear that in the deepest sense we are God's viceregents here on earth. We have a viceregal and pontifical function in this world. Of course, many of us have now abdicated that function. Modern man has not only destroyed most of the monarchies in the world, but has also tried to destroy the king or the queen within. There is a regal function which the human being has, what I have called a pontifical function, the function of being a bridge between Heaven and earth. The *pontifex* originally meant "bridge." We all have this function, the pontifical function, or the regal function within us which we have now cast aside. The religious point of view means that our relation to nature, the very fact that we accept that nature is the locus of God's Presence, imposes upon us the necessity to fulfill that viceregal function.

Now God is not only the creator of nature but also its sustainer and nourisher. To fulfill that caliphal function (*khalîfah* or viceregent is an Islamic term; I could equally use terms drawn from other religions), therefore means not only that we must be able to make use of nature but also that we are required to sustain and protect nature. The idea that nature is out there only for our use is not only un-Islamic, it is also not a traditional Christian idea. It has been foisted upon Christianity by certain later interpretations and also by certain modern critics of the environmental crisis trying to blame Christianity (and also Judaism) for the crisis which is much more the consequence of the secularization of nature and what I call the absolutization of the human state, beginning with Renaissance humanism and all that came after it. In the religious perspective, even religions which accord a very special position to human beings, the human being is never absolutized. For example, in Christianity people have certain rights, but the rights of God come before everything else.

Ours is the only time in history in which human beings claim for themselves absolute human rights with disrespect for the rights of either God or the rest of His creation. There is nothing that is more dangerous for the environment than this view of human rights. It is going to kill us all. If we continue our foolish ways, our great grand-children will have only one right and that is to die. Meanwhile, in the name of the rights of human beings, we are destroying the web of life on the planet. This absolutization of human rights and claims is one of the most dangerous ideas that has come out of modern civilization, no matter what the newspapers and politicians say. Its dangers are much greater than its benefits, albeit there are certain benefits. There is hardly anything that is completely black or white in history. Something completely black would not exist; something completely white would be celestial. Everything in this world is a mélange of the two. I am not saying there are no contingent benefits to this way of conceiving of our rights here on earth. But from the point of view of the natural environment, what I call the abolutization of the human state, that is taking God's rights and nature's rights away and giving them all to man, is at the very heart of the environmental crisis. It is this dangerous possibility that the religious view of man and nature always avoided. No matter what the Quran or the Bible say about man's right to make use of the world of nature, they also emphasize man's responsibility towards nature. The existing situation in which we always shout about rights without mentioning our responsibilities, is a trait of modernism. Ours is the first period in human history in which irresponsible people believe that they have absolute rights with which they are born. People are brought up to believe that even if they do not fulfill their responsibility, they have rights. This certainly is not the traditional point of view.

If one could resuscitate the religious view of nature and of man, one would be able once again to relativize our importance and our so-called needs, which is the only way that would allow us to survive. What is absolute in the human being is not his animal needs: it is his spiritual essence. It is the manifestation of the Absolute Itself in each being. What we have done in the modern world is to transform that spiritual reality into a purely earthly one, thereby endangering the earth. I must repeat here what I have said before, that one could understand the whole tragedy of the environmental crisis by realizing that modern man has taken the notion of God as Infinite and horizontalized it, trying to realize the Infinite in a finite world, that is, substituting ever-changing things, ever-changing objects, going from one thing to another, to satiate her or his thirst for the Infinite in the physical domain which is by definition finite. But our thirst for the infinite can only be satisfied vertically. The fact that we are never satisfied with earthly needs derives from a profound metaphysical truth, from the truth that our soul was not made for the finite. We are made for the Infinite. But the fact that this thirst is now horizontalized and is turned to never-ending material needs causes us to be always unhappy about what we have. That we continue to dream that the next object we acquire is going to make us happier is precisely the result of forgetting who we are, that essential nature of the human state emphasized by all religions.

The religious view of man and nature which has been lost, a loss which is the root cause of the environmental crisis, is also based on a very important principle which may be difficult for us to grasp but whose loss is, I think, also one of the root causes of the separation of man from nature. That principle is the idea of law or order in the religious sense in the world of nature, an idea which is to be found in one way or another in all the sacred traditions. From *Tao* to *dharma*, to *rta* to *Shari'ah*, to *nomos*, whatever term is used to designate this reality in different traditions, whatever the difference of emphasis, none the less the essential content of these terms remains the same. They all demonstrate that there is an order that governs man as well as nature, from which comes our modern word "cosmos." The Greek word *cosmos* means both order and beauty, which is extremely significant: the idea of order as beauty. All of these cardinal concepts possess a religious as well as a cosmic sense.

For example, *nomos* in Greek meant not only the laws by which the planets move, but also the laws which govern human life, laws by which the wise man should live. In Islam the Greek word has come into Arabic as *nâmûs,* and we use the term *nâmûs* as being almost equivalent to the *Sharî'ah,* the Divine Law (which is a Quranic term), but also we use it for laws of nature. The very word *sunnah* in Arabic, which means both tradition and the wonts of the Prophet, is used in the Quran as also *sunnât-Allâh.* We have not only the *sunnah* of the Prophet, but also the *sunnah* of God, which is precisely the laws and principles governing the existence of all creatures. *Sunnât-Allâh* is ultimately the laws and norms which govern religion as well as God's creation, the principles by which the world functions, what we observe as the laws of nature. The same holds true for *dharma* even if this term is not associated with the personal God of monotheism. Nearly all contemporary Buddhist thinking about the environment rotates around this single concept of *dharma.* The word *dharma* (translated sometimes as duty, law or principle) is at the fore of discussions in this matter because *dharma* is not only related to the correct way of living, but also to the principles according to which things are what they are. In fact everything in turn has its *dharma.* The streams, the flowers and the mountains have their own *dharma;* that is why this term is so difficult to translate into English. The same holds true of the Hindu term *rta,* which is not only the law for human beings but also for the cosmos. The religious world-view points to a kind of mystery— because it is really a mystery from a purely human point of view— the mystery of the relationship between laws that should govern us morally and spiritually and the laws that govern the universe.

There is a profound relation between the two. There are currently some attempts by a number of scientists to try and rebuild this bridge from the other side. Professor Wilson, the famous evolutionary biologist from Harvard, has just published two essays which have been the cause of much discussion in the American intellectual establishment. He begins by saying that the humanities and science should come together and overcome the separation that now exists between them. He further proposes that they should do so by developing the humanities on the basis of biology. He proposes that one should develop ethical and social laws for society on the basis of what people like him have discovered in the biological world. This is not what the religious view has in mind at all, because none of us wants to live under one form or another of social Darwinism, applying what people wrongly call the "laws of the jungle" or some other so-called biological law to human society. In fact the image we have of the "law of the jungle" is itself a prejudice, because if it were the only law involved all the animals would already have eaten each other. In truth we find that an incredible harmony pervades the jungle and the relation between living and non-living beings, a harmony to which little attention is paid by many scientists.

This kind of idea of law pertaining to both society and the cosmos is not what I am talking about. Rather, I am saying that traditional man believed that his way of living—whether a particular individual chose to follow God's laws (or the *Tao*, or the Principles of things—you can be non-theistic and talk about these terms as well)—was related to how the world functioned. This principle was the basis of the hieratic function of the priest-kings in various traditional civilizations. For example, the Chinese emperor was the bridge between Heaven and earth and performed certain rituals which were related to the harmony of the cosmos. The same principle can be observed in the function of the pharaohs of ancient Egypt, Melchizedek in the Hebrew tradition, Saoshyant in Zoroastrianism and many, many others. We can also see examples of it in historical times in the three monotheistic religions.

Now it is not possible to recreate those institutions until the return of Melchizedek or the Mahdi, but it is possible to bring back the idea that there must be some kind of relationship between our ethical norms and the way we deal with the world of nature. We cannot have the world of nature as simply a pure "it," an object totally bereft of value in the classical Galilean and Cartesian sense of the term, with an island populated by ethical beings with ethical concerns which are irrelevant to the rest of creation. The whole debate that is now going on about the question of animal rights versus human rights, how we should deal with the animal world, these are very complex questions and related to this link between ethical laws and cosmic laws. Thank God such debates have come to the fore at this late hour. If we had thought about them when we were beginning to destroy the forests in Africa and America a few centuries ago, we would not probably have been in such a dire situation. In modern times nobody even thought of these matters until now when we are made aware that if we continue in our present course, having killed off all the big animals we will be left with only a few small creatures. Our neighbors will be just a few species of small creatures which we cannot destroy so quickly.

My time is running out but I want, in the last part of this lecture, to say a few words about the complicated process by which the loss of the religious view of the environment took place in different parts of the world and especially in Western Christianity; not the whole of Christianity, for Greek Orthodox and Russian Orthodox Christianity have pursued a different path, at least until recently. Also in this matter other religions and civilizations of the world have followed other historical lines of development which are very different from that of the modern West. Although the fruits of modern science and technology, in the form of Boeing jets, go to all of the continents of the world, and the political heirs of Mahatma Gandhi have atomic bombs, in other religions and civilizations there did not occur this long process whereby gradually the world of nature was secularized with the effect that a respected thinker from the modern West can hardly think in religious terms about the world of nature. The process which took place in the West did not occur in other parts of the world even in Eastern Christianity and Oriental Judaism. The question of distinguishing between various views of nature is not, therefore, just one of religion but also of geography, of a particular development of religion and type of culture and civilization that came into being in Western—mostly North Western—Europe, in modern times and then spread to America and elsewhere.

In order to understand the present environmental crisis, it is important to grasp this point, especially if one is looking seriously for a solution. Non-Western people in general do not understand the process by which the secularization of nature took place in the West. They rarely grasp the significance of the fact that modern science is not simply an "objective" knowledge of nature but is based on a particular philosophy and also on the idea of domination over nature. This is especially so in physics and chemistry where one aims at a controlled situation in the laboratory in order to analyze a part of the physical world under the complete control of the experimenter and thereby gain the means to better dominate the physical world. This pursuit of controlled power has succeeded and thereby allowed Western science, as applied in various technologies, to gain remarkable domination over nature during the last two hundred years. It is this "method" along with certain philosophical presumptions concerning the nature of reality that has landed us in our current predicament. Although not aware of the philosophical background of the rise of modern science and the idea of domination over a segmented nature "coerced" into situations of controlled experiment, non-Western people are none the less fully aware of the relation between the applications of modern Western science and power. They also think that this science can help them gain power and domination over their own affairs, but without thinking of its consequences whether they be ethical, spiritual, or environmental. That is why, in the non-Western world, all forms of government, from the left to the right, from the religious to the antireligious, subscribe to the applications of modern science in the form of modern technology and espouse the cause of industrialization with as great a rapidity as possible. This fact in itself is quite amazing given the survival of the religious view of nature among their people. I give you the following example, which is annoying but true.

For several years in the 1970s I was the president of Iran's most important scientific and technological university. The reason I accepted this task was to be able to create intellectual and cultural responses which could protect Persian culture in the face of the powerful onslaught of Western science and technology. Now, our university was building a plant for nuclear energy in the port of Bushehr in the Persian Gulf. The students in the university who were opposed to this project would come out nearly every day with pronouncements of how terrible it was to carry out this project and were turning the issue into a political one against the government. I was happy to agree on this issue and said at the time to the authorities that in this question the students are right and I tried several times to stop the plant's development, as I believed that from an environmental point of view it was dangerous and not really needed. But my voice was not heard and the plan went ahead. As soon as the Islamic Revolution of 1979 took place, the further building of the plant was stopped. Nineteen years later, however, with the expense of several billion extra dollars, the plant is now being completed. It is a telling fact that, whether one has the royal regime or the Islamic Republic in Iran, the monarchy of Saudi Arabia or the secular Baa'th party of Iraq, the Hindu Nationalist Party the BJP, or Communist China, or the very different political systems of Malaysia or Indonesia, no matter where one looks, one sees that the attitude towards modern Western science and technology is in each case nearly the same. The reason is the misunderstanding of non-Western people of what is really involved; of the dangers which threaten their religion and also endanger the whole earth; of the impossibility of repeating the errors of the industrialized West in every corner of the globe in the name of gaining independence from the domination of the West. This is the reason why interest in the whole environmental issue has started so late in the non-Western world.

In the West, however, one has had a very different process. Gradually, step by step, the religious view of nature was lost and the mechanistic point of view replaced it. And now, after three or four hundred years (really since the trial of Galileo) the religious establishment in the West is trying, one way or another, to reformulate a theology of nature. For that very reason I think that the Western thinkers who are dealing with this issue have a very grave responsibility, not only for the Christian or the Jewish world, but globally. Quite obviously they, who having gone through all of these battles, are much more aware of all the issues involved than many people in the non-Western world who are only now turning to this question. From the other side, the thinkers of other religions have the advantage that amidst their co-religionists the sense of the sacred in nature and the legitimacy of a religious knowledge of nature has not been lost to the degree one sees in the West.

Let me conclude by giving a few practical suggestions. What can be done at this late hour to try to reverse the critical environmental situation? I am certainly not opposed to individual or group efforts to try to clean up the Thames, or to prevent a particular tree from being cut; thank God for that. Such actions can only delay but cannot prevent our mass suicide. The fact that we are murdering creation is what has to stop. The only action for the preservation of the environment which is likely to be effective must be based first of all on the thesis that we are responsible for our actions: we cannot sit down and do nothing with the pretext that this has been destined by God or is inevitable because of the march of modern technology. God holds us responsible for what we do and what we do not do but could and should do. When we accept and acknowledge the freedom given to us to not only destroy nature but also to live in harmony with it and then ponder freely all the possibilities this may give rise to, we see that our only possible action is not even action in the ordinary sense but a change in our state of being and consciousness.

There is no other way than to change our whole world-view. That means, bluntly, that we are faced with the stark choice of either the death of the modern world or the death of humanity. There is no third choice. By the death of the modern world I do not mean the death of all human beings living in the modern world. I mean the death of the point of view which we call modernism, which is based on the severing of the relationship between man and the Divine and between man and nature as spiritual reality. This severance has to be repaired, which means that the current modern world-view must be discarded. There is no other way. All compromises at this stage of history are the worst kind of treason. It is much better not to compromise at a time when compromise simply destroys the opportunity for us to do something serious. We have had too many compromises with the truth in the modern world. I always say jokingly that the modern world is characterized by somebody getting up in the morning and saying two and two is six. Then they debate all day long and some nice, liberal pacifist comes along and says, do not argue, do not fight, we will make it five and settle the count. The world has gone on day after day, year after year in this manner and can no longer afford to do so. When we come to the question of the environment, I believe that like any other basic matter involving truth and falsehood one has to be categorical and no longer compromise in any way any principle that is involved. I do not see how the modern world, with its presumptions, can survive. No less can humanity survive while holding to a world-view, which is false in its very foundations. How can we keep the word "development," as currently understood in our vocabulary, and elect people who believe in continuous material development, without committing suicide? I would be glad to be proven wrong. I am not only a philosopher, but have also studied the sciences and if somebody can show me on the basis of serious scientific evidence that my assessment of the environmental crisis is wrong, then I shall accept and thank God for it. But I do not see that if you extrapolate all the present trends, as scientists tend to do all the time, how it will be possible in the future for the earth to sustain human life, not to speak of life with quality.

It is in light of this situation that the religious view of nature becomes so significant. The resuscitation of the religious view of nature implies, of course, a very radical step. First of all it implies that religion must challenge not what science says within its own legitimate domain but the monopolistic claims of science. Science is a view of the natural world, and if its applications in the form of technology had not become wedded to greed, had it not caused such overpopulation, etc., it would have been an exceptional achievement, which in a sense it is despite its philosophical short-comings and negative consequences. But that is another question. As far as the natural environment is concerned, however, there must be a space within the mind of modern man for a view of nature other than the modern scientific one.

There must also exist profound criticisms of all views which would try to negate and gloss over the traditional understanding of the relationship between man and the world. We must overcome this hypnotic trance which causes us to make all kinds of false asser-tions and deny age-old truths by claiming that we are now in the space age or something like that, as if there were not still beautiful donkeys in Cyprus and therefore, logically, we could call our age the donkey age. What is it that makes the metaphor of the space age so important for us at the expense of so much else that still exists in our world? We must ask this question and wake up from this trance. Our problem is not solved by talking of the space age. Our problem is what we are currently doing here on earth, to ourselves, to our families, to our greater family of living creatures, to the non-living creatures of the earth and to the skies that we are also polluting.

There must be a re-assertion of the religious view of the world without compromise, without being intellectually embarrassed, as one sees so often among Western theologians. There is nothing intellectually embarrassing about the religious view of nature if one were only to understand it in depth. If one were to understand the metaphysics that stands behind it, one would realize that it is in fact based on intellectual knowledge of the highest order. My dear friend, Dr Martin Lings, apparently spoke about metaphysics and the perennial philosophy to some of you a couple of weeks ago. That kind of metaphysics which lies at the heart of all authentic reli-gions, if fully understood, is not something embarrassing, to say the least. One can present it to the most acutely aware and rational minds among the philosophers or scientists of our day without the least amount of inferiority complex.

It should be remembered, however, that one can never build something unless one has cleared the ground. That is, there is a need first of all for an in-depth criticism of all the errors of the modern world in light of the truth of traditional teachings. Often I, and people like me, are told why do you keep criticizing things, why can you not just state your ideas? But it is impossible to be indifferent in the face of error. Knowledge always implies both truth and falsehood. We live in a world in which outside of science the word truth is very unfashionable. Few in official academic life talk about the truth anymore; it is the last word one talks about in fashionable intellectual circles in the West today. Consequently, one also does not need to speak of falsehood, which in the domain of religion has to do with heresy (a term that few even in the churches talk about or use; today's culture prefers to speak of "alternative lifestyle"). Truth is no longer a significant category. But from the point of authentic knowledge, knowledge cannot exist without truth. In physics, chemistry or biology, if someone comes up with a new theory about something we cannot say, all right, you keep your view and I shall keep my view and we will be friends. This is because from the point of view of science you have to test things out and either one theory or the other is true as the term truth is defined in the particular science in question. In the same way when we come to the sapiential dimension of religion, we cannot remain impervious, even in the name of charity, not to say indifference or intellectual laziness, to what negates the truth, and we must be critical of any world-view which would do violence to our nature, to our destiny, to our relationship to the world, to the animals and the plants, and ultimately, of course, to God. The ultimate question for us, the ultimate challenge, is: who are we? What are we doing here? And the response has always been that we are here first of all to remember who we are; we are here to remember what the world is in its spiritual reality; and above all we are here to remember God who is the source of both the world and ourselves. Only through this remembrance can we regain the vision necessary to live at peace with God, with ourselves and with His creation, with all of His creation both animate and inanimate, that by His Mercy sustains and nourishes us even if in our ignorance we are unworthy of all His blessings. The attainment of this peace alone can ameliorate the critical condition of the world about us by establishing order again within ourselves and by opening our eyes to the vision of the natural world as the theatre of His endless theophanies.

*Hidden under all forms of thought,*
*Under the form of all created things:*
*Look where I may, still nothing I discern*
*But Thee throughout this universe . . .*

*Erase the words "this" and "that": duality*
*Denotes estrangement and repugnancy:*
*In all this fair and faultless universe*
*Naught but one Substance and one Essence see.*

*— Jami*

*Chapter 6*

# Our Mother Earth

## *Oren Lyons*

A thousand years ago a man came from the west. And he came across the water, and he brought a great message of peace. He came across the water, the great lake that you now call Ontario; he stopped on the shores, and he visited the various nations who were at war and who had forgotten how to live together. He came with a great message of peace; and he gathered the strongest and the fiercest of leaders in the Great Council. And it took many years; but with the help of Hiawentah, whom you call Hiawatha, together they created the Houdenosaunee, the great league of peace—one thousand years ago. And the principles were set down, at that time, of how to conduct ourselves, of how to raise the chiefs, how to raise the clan mothers; and how to set men in council, so that they could first perform the ceremonies as the spiritual being, the center, of the nation. The ceremonies were the first obligation of the chiefs, and the faith keepers, and the clan mothers. And then they were to sit in council for the welfare of the people.

A thousand years ago we were given this message by the Creator; we were given a government by the Creator. This government was not manufactured from the minds of men, it was given to us; and we were to cherish it. And each generation was to raise its chiefs and to look out for the welfare of the seventh generation to come. We were to understand the principles of living together; we were to protect the life that surrounds us; and we were to give what we had to the elders and to the children. The men were to provide; and the women were to care for the family, and be the center, the heart, of the home. And so our nation was built on the spiritual family, and we were given clans: the turtle-the eagle-the deer-the beaver-the wolf-the bear-the snipe-the hawk: symbols of freedom. We were given an understanding of how free people live. And we were told to protect the freedom of every individual; we were told that sovereignty began with the individual, and you protect that. And so a free nation stood, and a great peace prevailed.

Many years later there landed, on our shores to the east, our white brother. And he brought with him things that we could not contend with. We were told at an earlier time that the name Ga-nya-di-yo, whom you call Handsome Lake, would be important; and so it came to pass that in the year 1800 we were given a third and final message of how to deal with the things that were brought across the water—when our men were drunk; when our home fires were out; when the dogs walked in the ashes; and the children and the women hid in the woods because of what the whisky and the liquor did to our men. And we were given a message at that time; and this message told us about Ga-nya-di-yo; and again the Creator took pity on us, He felt sorry for us, and He gave the third message of how to deal with the whisky and with gambling, how to deal with the Bible and the missionaries. We were told at that time what would happen to this earth. And as Ga-nya-di-yo walked with the Four Beings, the Four Protectors, who had been sent by the Creator to look out for mankind, they pointed out to him, here and there, "What do you see?" "I see a woman, so fat that she can't rise, yet she continues to stuff her mouth, she continues to eat like a glutton." And they never said whether that was right or wrong; they asked him, what did he see? And so they went, and he was given this opportunity to see, and to be told that one day the water would not be fit to drink, that indeed the water would burn, that the trees would begin to die from the tops down; that the chief of all trees, the maple, would signal to us the time of the deterioration of life, when the end would be near. He told us, and pointed out the variety of events that would occur: the sickness of our children and of the elders, and of what money would do—the greatest sickness of all.

Now we are faced with these things, as leaders of our people, as people given a great responsibility; we in this generation must deal with all of these elements.

When the Creator gave His Great Law and planted the great tree of peace, He uprooted it, and He threw under it all the weapons of war. He said: You are now a nation of peace; and I will give you *oyankgwa-oohway*, the sacred tobacco; and that will be your strength. That will be what you depend on, the spiritual power of prayer, a belief: the belief of your people. And if you have one mind, and you consider this again, it is the power that you have. So it happens when you burn the tobacco and use the sacred cornmeal that all of the animals stop and they listen; they turn, and they listen to these words.

Our brothers, the bears and the wolves and the eagles, are Indians. They are Natives, as we are. At one time we spoke their language; at one time we conversed, a long time ago. The two-leggeds have fallen from grace. Those animals and those wingeds, they live in a state of absolute grace; they can do no wrong. It is only we who have been given a choice, so clearly pointed out by the Four Beings: this is the way it is, they said, and what do you see here? They did not tell him: Do this or do that; they said, This is the way it is: what you do will be up to you. And that is what the Creator gave to us, the choice: a great gift, the mentality that we have. And among us there are even people with other gifts—a gift of art, or a gift of speech, or a gift of a smile that can make everyone laugh. Whatever it is, each of us was born with a mission. We were born with a mission, and we must know what it is and develop it and do it. And that's a choice— that is your choice.

We went to Geneva—the Six Nations, and the great Lakota nation—as representatives of the indigenous people of the Western Hemisphere. We went to Geneva, and we spoke in the forum of the United Nations. For a short time we stood equal among the people and the nations of the world. And what was the message that we gave? There is a hue and cry for human rights—human rights, they said, for all people. And the indigenous people said: What of the rights of the natural world? Where is the seat for the buffalo or the eagle? Who is representing them here in this forum? Who is speaking for the waters of the earth? Who is speaking for the trees and the forests? Who is speaking for the fish—for the whales, for the beavers, for our children? We said: Given this opportunity to speak in this international forum, then it is our duty to say that we must stand for these people, and the natural world and its rights; and also for the generations to come. We would not fulfill our duty if we did not say that. It becomes important because without the water, without the trees, there is no life.

New York City—you live here; you can't get a clean drink of water here. The water you drink is filthy. You don't know what clear spring water is like, because you have to drink what comes out of the tap. And eventually it will kill you. Eventually, you will not be able to clean that water; nor your children, nor your grandfather, nor your grandmother. . . . You think about it. . . . When you are sick and when your children are sick, you remember what the Indian said to you about water.

We are indigenous people to this land. We are like a conscience. We are small, but we are not a minority. We are the landholders, we are the land keepers; we are not a minority. For our brothers are all the natural world, and by that we are by far the majority. We want you to understand the opportunity now. It is no time to be afraid— there is no time for fear. It is only time to be strong, only a time to think of the future, and to challenge the destruction of your grand-children, and to move away from the four-year cycle of living that this country goes through, from one election to another, and think about the coming generations.

We spoke about human rights and we spoke in defense of all people and of all children. But remember that as long as we are burning tobacco, as long as the Indian nations exist, so will you. But when we are gone, you too will go.

*Dahnato (now I am finished).*

*Tewa: Song of the Sky Loom*

*Oh our Mother the Earth oh our Father the Sky*
*Your children are we*
    *with tired backs we bring you the gifts you love*

*So weave for us a garment of brightness*

*May the warp be the white light of the morning*
*May the weft be the red light of evening*
*May the fringes be the falling rain*
*May the border be the standing rainbow*

*Weave for us this bright garment*
*that we may walk where birds sing*
    *where grass is green*

*Oh our Mother the Earth oh our Father the Sky*

## Chapter 7

# The Desanctification of Nature

## *Philip Sherrard*

By the phrase, "the desanctification of nature," I refer to that process whereby the spiritual significance and understanding of the created world has been virtually banished from our minds, and we have come to look upon things and creatures as though they possessed no sacred or numinous quality. It is a process which has accustomed us to regard the created world as composed of so many blind forces, essentially devoid of meaning, personality and grace, which may be investigated, used, manipulated and consumed for our own scientific or economic interest. In short, it has led us to see the world only as so much secularized or desacralized material, with the consequence that we have ruptured the organic links and spiritual equilibrium between man and nature, and have restricted religion more and more to the privacy of the individual conscience or to concern for the beyond of a transcendent God or of an individual salvation after earthly existence is over.

This does not mean of course that people have stopped finding a charm or a beauty in nature, or an outlet from the artificial and suffocating atmosphere of our over-industrialized cities. On the contrary, from the eighteenth century onwards our history has been characterized by periodic "back to nature" movements, as if nature was a kind of unspoilt paradise ready with ever-open arms to compensate man for all the other losses he has suffered. But what this so often represents is the romantic or sentimental reaction of an exhausted and disillusioned individualism, containing in it very little that may be described as spiritual. In fact, it can very well go, and very often has gone, with an entirely "atheist" outlook. What is in question here is not this kind of naturalism, but a loss of the sense of the divine in nature—a loss of the sense that the very stuff of the universe has a sacred quality. In what follows I shall try to say something of how this situation has come about and what it means.

There has been a growing tendency within the post-mediaeval Christian world to look upon creation as the artifact of a Maker who as it were has produced it from without. This has provided us with a picture of a God in heaven who, having set the cosmic process in motion and having left it to run more or less on its own and according to its own laws, now interferes directly on but rare occasions and then only in the form of special and "abnormal" acts operated upon the world from without. The result is that the relation between God and creation tends to be seen predominantly as one of cause and effect: God is a world cause, a supreme or first cause or principle of being; and the world and its laws are what He has produced.

On this account, it may be possible to speak of some analogy between God and creation. It may be possible to say that creation is a "moving image of eternity," a kind of projection in corruptible terms of its unmoved perfection, or even that signs and indications of God may be discerned in visible phenomena. But what is difficult to envisage in this perspective is the idea that creation actually participates in the divine, and is an actual mode of existence or embodiment of the living, ever-present God.

I would call this idea that creation is the embodiment of the divine—with its rider that all nature has therefore an intrinsically sacred character—the sacramental idea of creation. This would appear appropriate because what is implied in this idea is that the Christian understanding of sacrament, which is usually applied only to the specific rites that go by the name of sacraments in the institutional Church, is applied to the realm of nature as a whole.

A sacrament, it must be remembered, demands a material expression. In fact, the archetype of all sacramental activity is the Incarnation of Christ Himself. In the Incarnation, the Logos becomes flesh: there is an intimate meeting and inextricable intertwining of the spiritual and the material. What is defended or affirmed in the great Christological discussions which resulted in the pronouncements of Nicaea and Chalcedon is that the two natures in Christ—the divine and the human, the uncreated and the created—are not merely juxtaposed in the person of Christ. There is not simply an assumption by the divine of the human. These ways of regarding the mystery of the two natures in Christ are felt to be inadequate and to fail to do justice to its reality. What is defended or affirmed is the actual union of the two natures—a union "without confusion, without change, without division, without separation," as the formula of the Council of Chalcedon puts it. In other words, it is maintained that however vast and fundamental the difference between the uncreated and the created may appear, there is ultimately no radical dichotomy between them. If God is God, and if God is manifest in Christ, then creation must be capable of becoming one with the uncreated and it must be possible to transcend the apparent ontological gap between them.

This is why when the Greek Fathers speak of the Eucharist, which is the image of the Incarnation—and it must be remembered that for the Greek Fathers the only difference between image and archetype is that the image as such is not the archetype as such— they insist that the material sign of the sacrament is not simply something to which the Spirit is attached, as if the Spirit were an extraneous element added to the matter, or one that "transubstantiates" the matter through His presence. On the contrary, they insist that there is a total integration of the material and the spiritual, so that the elements of bread and wine are an actual mode of existence of the divine and there is a complete union between them.

In other words, the sacrament presupposes an actual incarnation of divine power and life; and what is communicated to man in the sacrament is this divine power and life. As St Cyril of Alexandria puts it: "For the Son is in us on the one hand bodily, as man, united and mixed by means of the Eucharist (mystical blessing); and also spiritually, as God, by the energy and grace of His own Spirit renewing the spirit that is in us for the renewal of life and making us participants in His divinity."[1]

It is now possible to see the consequence of applying the Christian understanding of the sacrament to the realm of nature as a whole. It means that nature is regarded not as something upon which God acts from without. It is regarded as something through which God expresses Himself from within. Nature, or creation (the terms are interchangeable in this context), is perceived as the self-expression of the divine, and the divine as totally present within it. It is not a case of complete absorption of the one in the other, or of subservience on the one side and detachment on the other. Moreover, the created depends for its existence on the uncreated, while

---

1. Cyril of Alexandria, P.G. 74, 564.

the uncreated does not depend in the least for its existence on the created. But each finds its own identity in the other, and each at the same time keeps its own identity in the other.

In creating what is created, it is Himself that God creates, in another mode. In creation He becomes His own image, in such a way that He enters into it from within. He is its within. Creation is the realm in which God's dynamic, pulsating energies are made manifest. Its apparent stability is simply the flux of these energies, its solidity the result of their ceaseless flow. In this respect the difference between the activity of the Spirit in nature and the activity of the Spirit outside nature is one of degree only, not of kind: it is a difference of the mode in which the Spirit operates while the energies through which He operates remain always divine and uncreated.

Like the Eucharist, nature is a revelation not merely of the truth about God but of God Himself. The created world is God's sacrament of Himself to Himself in His creatures: it is the means whereby He is what He is. Were there no creation, then God would be other than He is; and if creation were not sacramental, then God would not be its creator and there would be no question of a sacrament anywhere. If God is not present in a grain of sand then He is not present in heaven either.

It is, then, this sacramental idea of nature which has been eliminated from our minds in order to permit that process of desanctification about which I have spoken. I say "from our minds" advisedly, because the fact that we do not "see God in all things" and sense His presence everywhere does not mean that He is not in all things and is not present everywhere. Reality is what it is, and so is revelation. That we fail to perceive them as what they are means that we have lost sight of them, not that the structure of reality has changed. The secular has its origin in man's loss of spiritual vision or—what is the same thing—in the hardening of his heart; and the contraction of the world of nature to a self-contained entity, which is what happens when we ignore its sacred aspect, represents not so much a closing off of nature itself as a closing of our own eyes. We always have to remember that how we see the world about us is but a reflection of the state of our own inner world. Ultimately it is because we see ourselves as existing apart from God that we also see nature as existing apart from God.

This last statement is to the point here because what the modern scientific outlook and the building of our modern technological and economic order demonstrate is the triumph of precisely the view in which the world is seen as a self-contained entity, existing in its own right, apart from God, and consequently as something that man is quite entitled to explore, organize and exploit without any reference to the divine. The modern secular world owes its immediate origin not so much to the Renaissance and Reformation or to Copernicus and Galileo as to the scientific revolution of the seventeenth century, with its "New Philosophy," as the scientists of the seventeenth century themselves called it.

In its turn, this revolution may be said to have two main characteristics, which are closely interconnected. The first is that it assumed that knowledge must be based on the observation of external phenomena: it must be based on sense-data without reference to the divine or indeed to any preconceived *a priori* ideas. The second is that it concluded that in order to reduce the data obtained from the observation of external phenomena to a coherent and reliable system of knowledge they must be submitted to the discipline of mathematics. A recapitulation and further elaboration of the theories of two of the leading exponents of this revolution, Francis Bacon and René Descartes, will illustrate what is implied in this.

Bacon's intention was to provide a frame of reference for the whole range of physical phenomena, if not for all knowledge. All possible knowledge must be coordinated, he wrote, into "a single systematic treatise, a Natural History such as may supply an orderly foundation for philosophy and include material reliable, abundant and well-arranged for the task of interpretation."[2] But in order for such a task to be carried out there must be a complete separation of religion from "philosophy": they must not be "commixed together,"[3] because while philosophy follows the light of nature (that is to say, is based upon experiment and observation) religion "is grounded upon the Word and Oracle of God."[4] Not only must

---

2. Francis Bacon, Preface to *Parasceve*, in *The Works of Francis Bacon*, ed. J. Spedding, R.L. Ellis, D.D. Heath (London, 1889), p.393.
3. Francis Bacon, *Advancement of Learning*, ed. W.A. Wright (Oxford, 1900), II,6,i.
4. *Ibid.*, II,24,3.

no metaphysical or theological ideas provide the criteria for assessing the significance of what is observed, but also what is observed must not be thought to provide any evidence or support for metaphysical or theological ideas: "out of the contemplation of nature, to induce any verity or persuasion concerning the points of faith is in my judgment not safe."[5] The divorce between religion and philosophy is absolute: concern for the spiritual is banished from the study of physical phenomena and all scientific knowledge must be derived from the observation of a natural world regarded as a self-subsistent entity.

Descartes comes in a somewhat different way to much the same conclusion, but with him the emphasis that the knowledge of nature is ultimately a mathematical knowledge is more explicit. This is not the place to retrace the steps by which Descartes arrived at his conclusion, "I think, therefore I am"—a purely artificial conclusion, because one cannot think without thinking about something; or to retrace the steps by which, having established this initial certainty of self as the basis of thought, he went on to distinguish between ideas that were vague and confused and others that were clear and distinct and to accept the latter as being true apprehensions of and truly applicable to the real world. In this context I wish only to recall that Descartes was a great mathematician and that it was therefore perhaps inevitable that among these clear and distinct ideas which he accepted as true he regarded mathematical ideas as the most important. Mathematical ideas were true in a supreme sense, and it was they that could be taken as providing real knowledge.

This idealizing attitude towards mathematics as providing real knowledge, or a knowledge of the real, was not of course new. It was the attitude, for instance, of the Greeks of the Pythagorean-Platonic tradition. But here it is important to make a distinction. Greek mathematics had no point of contact with sense-data. On the contrary it was held in high esteem precisely because it was thought to provide a way of escape from the physical world. It was seen as a way through which we could learn to leave the world of sense-data behind. In fact, it was because the phenomenal and historical world did not correspond to the ideal of mathematical knowledge that it came to be regarded as more or less unreal. What was real was the

5. *Ibid.*, II,6,i.

realm of entities which could be apprehended by the mind without the interposition of sense; and this realm of reality was changeless and timeless in the sense of having no reference to the world of change and time at all. Moreover, the geometrical figures in which it could be expressed were related to one another not physically but only intelligibly or logically. Hence in the Greek thought of this tradition there is a sharp divide between Being—which is the real world of the basically mathematical entities that constitute true knowledge—and Becoming, which is the phenomenal world of change and about which there can be no true knowledge but only opinion.

For Bacon and for Descartes on the other hand it was precisely this phenomenal world—the world of nature—that was the center of interest. It was this world which by now was being regarded as virtually the real world, and as the basis of all knowledge—something that Descartes makes completely clear in the third of his four precepts of Logic, where he resolves "to conduct my thoughts in such order that, by commencing with objects the simplest and easiest to know, I might ascend, little by little and, as it were, step by step, to the knowledge of the more complex."[6] And if this more complex knowledge was assumed to have pre-eminently a mathematical character, so that mathematical knowledge was held to be the most perfect form of knowledge, this was for a reason more or less opposite to that for which it had been held in such high esteem by the Greeks of the Pythagorean-Platonic tradition: it was valued by the Cartesians precisely because it was thought that it corresponded to or was correlated with the phenomenal world of change and time, the world of sense-data.

In fact it was now believed that mathematics, and mathematics alone, could provide the most adequate account of the physical world. What this meant was that the experimental method, originally devised in order to assist in the discovery of the efficient causes of observed effects, now became a method of constructing mathematical descriptions of them which are thought to be true in their own right. The mathematical entities contained in the theories used to describe the "appearances" are taken to be identical with the substance itself of the real world. They are given an onto-

---

6. Descartes, *Discourse on Method*, 2, trans. J. Veitch, *The Method, Meditations and Selections from the Principles of Descartes* (London, 1899), p.19.

logical value in their own right. For Descartes and his successors, mathematics was not only the study of the world extended in time and space. It was also held to provide a real knowledge of this world. And mathematics, whether concerned with measurement or enumeration, is the application of the science of quantity.

Hence as a result of the scientific revolution of the seventeenth century it came to be thought not only that the world of nature is a self-contained entity, but also that those aspects of its reality which can be known in a true sense and which therefore alone have significance are those susceptible to mathematical or quantitative study and treatment. They are those aspects which can be weighed and measured and numbered—aspects which to all intents and purposes are claimed to constitute the whole of the natural order. It is this conclusion that gives Cartesian and post-Cartesian science its particular character and explains why the realm of nature apart from the divine has in the end become identified with the realm of science, and why science itself has been identified with the techniques of weight and enumeration and measurement.

It is in the light of these developments that we can see more clearly how and in what sense the building of our modern secular world has involved the desanctification of nature. First, in order for modern science to come into existence nature had to be regarded as an object divorced from all ontological roots or participation in the non-physical realm of the divine. What was known as formal causation disappears and what is left is the purely mechanistic interpretation of matter, according to which matter contains in itself the efficient causes of its own observable processes.

Second, the attribution of value and significance solely to those aspects of the natural order which are susceptible to quantitative study means that what was identified as nature was the realm of matter deprived of all qualitative elements, for the simple reason first that no non-observable qualities were to be taken into account and second that in any case no qualitative elements are susceptible to the kind of observation and analysis which science has adopted and which is, in an inexplicably exclusive manner, called scientific. Hence all spiritual qualities are *ipso facto* excluded from the objects science investigates, and at the same time it is tacitly assumed that there is nothing else to know about these objects except what can be observed by the so-called scientific method.

Physical phenomena are to be accounted for in physical categories alone, and that is all there is to be accounted for in them. The idea that every natural effect has a spiritual cause is completely neglected, and the fact that the neglect amounts to a kind of spiritual castration of the natural order seems to be of little or no concern. It is as if one examined and analyzed the Eucharist according to the scientific method and because one could not discern any trace of the divine in it declared that it was simply composed of its material elements. Having adopted a method of investigation which in its nature precludes the perception of spiritual qualities, it is gratuitous, to say the least, to pronounce that the object one investigates is to be explained in non-spiritual categories alone.

Yet it is the conclusions achieved by this kind of circulatory reasoning which for the last three hundred years or more have been regarded as constituting knowledge in a virtually exclusive sense and which moreover have been termed scientific. It is precisely the fact that these conclusions or what are called scientific theories are the product of this kind of circulatory reasoning, and not of experiment and observation, which makes the claim that they are objective so spurious. Having restricted the scope of scientific investigation to the rationally observable and purely quantitative aspects of what is changing and impermanent, and having adopted more or less exclusively a view of causality that takes into account merely efficient causes and ignores formal or spiritual causes, scientists are literally condemned to trying to explain things in terms of those meager interpretative possibilities which are all they can now envisage. In other words, their theories or hypotheses do no more than reflect the limitations within which they operate and have no greater objectivity than the arbitrary and illusory assumptions which underlie them.

Modern science, then, ignoring the sacred aspect of nature as a condition of its own genesis and development, tries to fill the vacuum it has created by producing mathematical schemes whose only function is to help us to manipulate and "dominate" matter on its own plane, which is that of quantity alone.[7] The physical world, regarded as so much dead stuff, becomes the scene of man's uncurbed exploitation for purely practical, utilitarian or acquisitive

---

7. T. Burckhardt, "Cosmology and Modern Science," *Tomorrow* (London, Summer 1964), p.186.

ends. It is treated as a de-incarnate world of phenomena that are without interest except in so far as they subserve statistics or fill test-tubes in order to satisfy the curiosity of the scientific mind, or are materially useful to man considered as a two-legged animal with no destiny beyond his earthly existence.

This is why the application of science—which is not really the application of science at all but the application of an unbelievable ignorance—has produced such disequilibrium, ugliness and even destruction not only in the natural world but in human life as well. Paradoxical as it may seem, through our attempt to achieve a knowledge of the world based on the observation of the physical phenomena of this world, we have reduced ourselves to a chronic state of blindness. We have lost our capacity to see not only the reality of the world about us but even of what was to have been the main purpose of our investigation to start with—the reality of our own presence within the world. If man thinks and acts as if God does not exist and is not present in all things, he thinks and acts a lie; and the result of this is that he reduces his own life to a falsity, which is the same thing as unreality.

This dehumanization of man is an inevitable consequence of man's attempt to live as though he were only human. Man can be truly human only when he is mindful of his theomorphic nature. When he ignores the divine in himself and in other existences he becomes sub-human. And when this happens not merely in the case of a single individual but in the case of society as a whole, then that society disintegrates through the sheer rootlessness of its own structure or through the proliferation of psychic maladies which it is powerless to heal because it has deprived itself of the one medicine capable of healing them.[8]

Moreover, it must be said that many scientists themselves are now aware of it. They have begun to realize that by restricting science to the quantitative study of things they are imposing purely artificial limits on it and that so long as this is the case there can never be any understanding of the true nature of the objects they study: science under these conditions is forced to remain within the world of "pointer-readings" and mathematical concepts which are no more than mere hypotheses, or which indeed may not have any

8. Seyyed Hossein Nasr, *The Encounter of Man and Nature* (London, 1968), *passim*.

reference to the real at all. They are fully aware too that since qualitative or spiritual elements are not subject to verification by the senses, no amount of experimental research can either prove or disprove their presence in the physical world. But it has seemed worthwhile to recall, however briefly, the main characteristics of Cartesian and post-Cartesian science for two reasons, the one connected indirectly and the other directly with our theme. The first reason is that while many scientists themselves have become aware of the impasse into which they have been led by science as conceived and practiced in the post-Cartesian period, and so have also become conscious that perhaps therefore the assumptions on which that science is based need re-examination, Christian—as well as non-Christian—theologians often seem strangely unaware of all this. Indeed, we have developed, really in imitation of scientific practice, such disciplines as Biblical criticism or the historical method, and we are ready to "de-mythologize" religion in the same imitative spirit; but we have singularly failed (with the exception of representatives of the Neo-Thomist school and one or two others) to provide any adequate criticism of modern science itself and of the assumptions on which it is based.

In fact, the contrary is more nearly the case: theologians and even human intelligence itself have capitulated to science. To understand the truth of this statement one has only to take into account the degree to which theologians accept the hypothesis of evolution, for instance, as axiomatic, and treat it as a kind of imperative condition to which everything, including theology itself, must accommodate itself. Teilhard de Chardin may be an extreme example of the capitulation of the religious consciousness to this hypothesis, but he is not alone by any means. Some even go so far as to regard the scientific method as a means which can be used in order to get a better understanding of the wisdom of God and the wonder of creation. In this view, the physicist who observes new patterns in the natural order and the technologist who applies these discoveries for practical purposes are both, whatever their attitude, fulfilling a "high priestly" function, revealing and extending God's glory in the universe.

Indeed, nearly all attempts to reconcile religion and science have been made by theologians, not by scientists (who appear to be more perceptive in this respect). What such a reconciliation generally involves is an attempt to adapt the principles of religion—transcendent and immutable—to the latest findings of science, and so to make religion "reasonable" or in keeping with the "spirit of the age" by appearing "scientific." Naturally, the particular scientific hypotheses in the name of which this adaptation is carried out are often discarded by scientists themselves by the time the theologians have completed their task. There can be no greater disservice done to the Christian religion than to tie it up with scientific views which in their very nature are merely temporary.[9] Far from religion and science mutually supporting each other it may be said that the more one is involved with science and its methods the more likely is one to become impervious to the experience of those realities which give religion its meaning. This is one reason why it has seemed worthwhile to point once again to the grounds which justify such a statement.

More important in this context is the second reason for indicating the main characteristics of post-Cartesian science and the manner in which it has so devastatingly contributed to the desanctification of the natural order. It is that these characteristics and their consequences are implicit in certain forms of the Christian theological tradition itself. An alleged connection between Christianity and modern science has often been affirmed. "I am convinced," wrote Berdiaev,[10] "that Christianity alone made possible both positive science and technics." Behind this kind of assumption is the idea that because the central proposition of Christianity is that "The Logos was made flesh" it tends to be the most materialistic of all the great religions and so somehow the progenitor of the natural and materialist sciences.

This is as it may be, and in any case begs many questions. But whether there is some truth in it or not, it surely cannot be said that the aim of any religion is to produce a world from which nearly every non-material consideration is excluded, in which everything is seen as independent of God and in which it is claimed that things may be understood virtually as though God does not exist. One wonders whether the greatest deceit of the devil may not lie in his pretence to an independence of this kind. Yet it is precisely such an independent world—one in which the sacramental quality of things has been almost totally obscured—that has grown out of the

9. E. Mascall, *Christian Theology and Natural Science* (London, 1956), p.166.
10. N. Berdiaev, *The Meaning of History* (London, 1935), p.113.

western Christian matrix. This may be in some part due to the character of Christianity itself and to the historical conditions in which it appeared. One might, for instance, in this connection point to the early Christian reaction against paganism, against the cosmic religion and the naturalism of the Hellenistic world, with its tendency to divinize the natural and human orders in their own right: a reaction expressed in Colossians[11] where the entire cosmos is described as controlled by "the elemental spirits of the universe" opposed to Christ, although "created through him and for him." It has even been said that one of the most characteristic novelties of Christianity was that it demystified or, if you wish, secularized the cosmos: the idea that God abides in the elements, in water, in springs, in stars, in the emperor, was from the beginning totally rejected by the Apostolic Church;[12] and a legacy of this attitude is still evident in the horrified cry of "pantheism" which tends to greet every suggestion that God does live in His creation. It may in this connection be relevant to point out here that what distinguishes the sacramental view of nature from a point of view which tends to divinize the natural order in its own right, is that while in the first nature is sought and known in the light of God, in the second it is God who is sought and identified in the elements of nature themselves.

Then in addition to this is the fact that Christianity is a religion without a sacred law. Unlike Judaism or Islam or Hinduism it possesses no *corpus* of concrete laws inseparable from its revelation and theoretically applicable to all aspects of human life and human society. It came as a spiritual way without such a *corpus*, so that when it became the religion of a civilization it was forced to incorporate Roman and even common law into its structure—law for which, in spite of the efforts of St Thomas and others, it was difficult to claim the authority of the will of God or the divine sanction possessed by the teachings of Christ which are concerned with direct spiritual principles. This has meant that it has always been more easy to detach, so to speak, the political, social and economic sphere of human life from the framework of the Christian revelation and so to leave it exposed to domination by purely secular interests and

11. Col. 1:16; 2:8.
12. J. Meyendorff, "Orthodox Theology Today," *Sobornost*, series 6, 1 (London, 1970), p.16.

influences, than has been the case in the context of the civilizations of other great religions possessing a sacred law supported by the authority of revelation itself.

This being said, however, it still remains true that there is a direct causal connection between the process of desanctification of the natural order and certain developments within Christian theology itself. It is not possible here to do more than indicate the character of these developments. But if it is remembered that a recognition of the sacramental principle depends upon an understanding that in the sacrament there is an actual participation of the material in the spiritual, the created in the uncreated, so that the apparent ontological disparity between them is somehow transcended, then it follows that a failure to perceive the sacramental quality of the natural order must go with a failure to grasp this participation in all its fullness. It must go, in other words, with a sense that there is a virtually unbridgeable ontological gap between the spiritual and the material, the uncreated and the created. This would indicate that the theological developments in question would be those that tend to emphasize the disparity between the uncreated and the created realms and so lead to the one being regarded as independent of the other in the manner indicated.

The attempt to discern these developments may well begin with St Augustine. Here it must be said that what St Augustine in the first instance understands by nature is not the physical world as we now perceive it by means of the senses. Nature signifies for him first of all the original and uncontaminated state of things as they issued "in the beginning" from God through the act of divine creation: the world before the Fall, before it became warped and depraved through human defection. But even here, in his conception of the creation of this pre-fallen world, and moreover in his conception of the creation of its highest and most perfect beings, the angels, St Augustine already inserts the thin end of the wedge which, driven further in, produces the sense of dichotomy between the uncreated and the created to which I have referred.

The quality of grace, St Augustine asserts—the quality of spiritual illumination—is not something intrinsic to the created nature of angels as such. It is not their natural element. It is something added to them as a gift. This giving presupposes the existence of a recipient. It presupposes the existence of a creature existing in a state other than that of grace. In other words, in the Augustinian perspective one is invited to envisage a historical phase in which the creature exists in a state of pure nature without participation in divine grace; and this is so even though both the creation of a being capable of receiving the gift of grace and the giving of the gift that is to be received are gratuitous acts on the part of God.

Moreover, according to St Augustine all created beings—angels and all beneath the angels—are first made (though not created) in the eternal uttering of their ideas in the Logos of God. But these ideas of things as they are in God's mind—these "principial forms or stable and unchangeable essences of things," as St Augustine calls them[13]—in the light of which all things are created, again in Augustinian thought are not regarded as intrinsic to those things when they are created. They remain extrinsic to their being. They cannot become the core itself of that being, a ray of divine light within the creature. In themselves, created things must always remain distinct and separate from God ontologically. Rational creatures—angels and men—may apprehend themselves through intellection as ideas in God's mind. These ideas can be the standards for what each thing ought to be. But they can never become the reality itself of each thing, its own proper subject. The being of each thing in itself is and must remain exterior to the divine idea in the light of which it is created. It can never participate in the inner life of this idea.

The separation between Creator and created here appears as radical—a separation not to be bridged by any process of human thought or imagination or by any act of human will: any aspirations towards "deification" in the traditional Christian sense are by definition chimerical, as is any attempt to see and know the divine through sharing in the life of the divine itself. What man can see or know of God are merely the *vestigia Dei* or traces of the divine visible in creation or impressed on the human mind by the source of divine light which itself must always remain exterior to it.[14]

This, as I said, is the state of affairs in the pre-fallen world. In the fallen world as seen by St Augustine—the world in which we actually live—things are far worse, and this separation between the uncreated and the created is now truly abysmal. Through the Fall man

---

13. St Augustine, *De Diversis Quaestionibus*, 83, 46, 1-2; P.L. 40, 29-30.
14. See E. TeSelle, "Nature and Grace in Augustine's Expositions of Genesis 1, 1-5," *Recherches augustiniennes*, V (Paris, 1968), pp.95-137.

and the rest of the natural order are deprived of even that extrinsic participation in grace which they possessed in their pre-fallen state. Their original and true nature is now vitiated, totally corrupt and doomed to destruction. It is a lump of damnation.

As for the communication of grace, through which alone man and the world may be redeemed from depravity, this, it was thought by St Augustine and his mediaeval successors, was confined to the visible Church and depended on the performance of certain rites, like baptism, confirmation, ordination and so on, which it was the privilege of the ecclesiastical hierarchy to administer to a submissive and obedient laity. The magnificent scope of the Logos doctrine with its whole "cosmic" dimension—the idea of God incarnate in all human and created existence—which from the time of the Alexandrians and Cappadocians down to the present day has been one of the major themes of Orthodox Christian theology, was tacitly but radically constricted in Western thinking. Spontaneous personal participation "in Christ" became identified with membership of a juristic corporational institution which claimed to be the unique sphere of the Spirit's manifestation, the judge of His presence, and the manipulator of His activity.

In these conditions to say that everything in the created order by virtue of the simple fact of its existence possesses, even if unaware of it and so in a potential state, an intrinsically sacramental quality which unites it to the divine, would have been tantamount to blasphemy. Instead, there was a radical separation of the sacred from the secular: everything inside the Church (understood as an earthly society) was sacred; outside the formal limits of the Church, or in nature, the activity of the Spirit was denied: everything outside these limits was secular, deprived of grace, incurably corrupt and doomed to disintegration.

From St Augustine we may turn to the other major representative of western mediaeval theology, St Thomas Aquinas; and it is against this background of the radical disparity in St Augustine's thought between the world and the Church, nature and grace, or nature and what is now regarded as the supernatural, that the efforts of St Thomas to "save" the natural world must be viewed. Unless it is viewed against this background the fact that his thought helped to consolidate the rift between the world of nature and the divine and so contributed to the process of desanctification we are tracing may seem inexplicable.

It must be remembered that by the time St Thomas set out upon his attempt to reconcile all views, however contradictory they might appear, in an all-embracing synthesis, the idea of the separation between the natural (understood now in the non-Augustinian, Aristotelian sense as a physical reality) and the supernatural was so deeply embedded in Latin thought that it was impossible to establish any genuine ontological link between them. The only way therefore by which the natural world could be freed from the opprobrium attached to it in Augustinian thought and could be accorded a positive status in its own right was, paradoxical as it may sound, to dissociate it altogether from the sphere of theology, to make it independent of theological control, and to substitute for any genuine relationship between the sphere of nature and the sphere of theology the principle of analogy.

It was to this end that St Thomas made his suggestion that there are two levels on which things are viewable, the natural and the supernatural level. The latter is the state in which grace is paramount, and it corresponds to the sphere of theology. But where the efficacy of nature itself is concerned, no grace is necessary, because nature follows its own inherent laws which have nothing to do with grace.[15] All grace does in relation to the natural world is to bring to perfection the operations in nature which have begun without its intervention and exist quite independently of it: grace does not destroy nature but perfects it,[16] and this is to imply that although nature is better with the addition of grace it can exist quite adequately without it.

The immediate conclusion is that there must be different principles appertaining to the natural and the supernatural spheres. There must be, as St Thomas put it,[17] a double order in things. This means that nature itself—the natural as such—is now accorded a status of its own, to all intents and purposes independent of the divine; and the Augustinian dichotomy between nature and grace is replaced by a dualism between the natural and the supernatural. Assuredly, God is still regarded as the author of nature, but essentially nature works according to its own laws, and it is quite sufficient

15. St Thomas Aquinas, *Summa Theologica*, I-II, qu. 10, art. 1.
16. *Ibid.*, I,i, qu. 8, ad. 2.
17. *Ibid.*, I, qu. 21, art. 1 ad. 3.

to take account only of these laws in order to discover how nature does work.

Moreover, these laws are thought to be characterized by reasonableness or rationality; and man, defined now as a rational animal, shares in the laws of nature to the fullest extent because he can recognize them through his reasoning faculties. This natural reasoning capacity with which man is endowed operates without any revelation or grace and may pursue its investigations without any reference to the articles of faith. Indeed, the only knowledge which man as a rational creature could effectively obtain was said to be that which he could derive from the observation of phenomena through the senses[18]—a proposition which is at the very basis of the later scientific attitude to knowledge.

It is true that St Thomas was constrained to state that the conclusions of natural reason could not affect, and must ultimately conform to, the conclusions of faith. But he was constrained to state this because God Himself—and this is the lynch-pin of the whole system—was now regarded as to the fullest degree a rational being, so that unless something had gone very wrong somewhere there could hardly be any ultimate contradiction between the principles of God's rationality and the laws of nature which He had established to operate on purely rational lines. By means of this kind of argument St Thomas was able to preserve a delicate and correspondingly precarious synthesis between the idea that nature was an integral part of the divine order and the idea that essentially it existed in its own right, autonomous and independent within its own terms of reference, operating according to its own laws, premises and purposes.

Analytical Thomist methodology, with its supposition that man is dependent on sense-data for the acquisition of knowledge and that he can apprehend spiritual realities only in so far as he discerns in the natural world evidence of their transcendent and unknowable perfections,[19] effectively promotes the idea that there is an uncrossable boundary between God and man, between the divine and the human. Implicit in it is a failure to grasp the full significance of the unity of the two natures in one person; and the imme-

18. St Thomas Aquinas, *De Veritate*, ii, 3, obj. 19 et ad 19; *Summa Theologica*, 1a, 12, 12.
19. St Thomas Aquinas, *Contra Gentiles*, 1, 3.

diate consequence of this was to be the neglect of the possibility of man's personal participation in the divine and a growth in the conviction that he may know the truth concerning God only indirectly by means of his rational faculty operating within the one sphere accessible to it, that of the natural world. And here again what is implicit is not man's supra-rational and personal participation in the inner meaning, the indwelling logos of this world, or his disclosure of God's self-expression within it, but a belief that he may decipher, articulate and eventually dominate it as a self-sufficient entity by the use of his individual reason in disregard of, if not in contradiction to, the truths of the Christian revelation.

The result could only be that in the following centuries philosophers (like for instance William of Ockham or Marsiglio of Padua) less endowed than St Thomas with a capacity for maintaining his subtle balance between nature and revelation, would break the now tenuous link between nature and the divine, would assert the autonomy of reason, divorce philosophy completely from religion, and claim an unlimited charter to pursue their own methods of inquiry into nature without any reference to metaphysical or theological principles, not because God did not exist or had not created nature but because in practical terms He was no longer present as an immanent, ever-working principle and energy in the natural world.

The scene was set for the scientific revolution of the seventeenth century and the emergence of the mechanistic and materialist science of the modern world; and it is not without justice that in a famous passage Alfred North Whitehead traces the origin of the modern scientific movement directly back to the scholastic insistence on the rationality of God and to the concomitant insistence, reached in the way we have described, on the belief that every detailed occurrence in the physical world can be correlated with its antecedents in a perfectly definite and rational manner.[20]

That in trying to rescue nature from the pit of perdition to which it had been consigned by St Augustine, St Thomas should have contributed in this way directly to the formation of the secular mentality and secular approach to nature does, as I said, become understandable when it is remembered that he accepted as virtually

20. A.N. Whitehead, *Science and the Modern World* (New York, 1926), p.18.

axiomatic the conception of a God who by definition cannot be ontologically present in the activities of the world which He has created. But the question remains as to why the presence of God is thought to be limited in this way, and it is in answering this question that it may be possible to specify the limitations of the Augustinian-Thomist tradition more precisely. I would venture to suggest that the answer to this question is related to two interconnected themes, the one metaphysical and the other theological.

The metaphysical theme is connected with a conception of form and matter, basically Aristotelian in character but accepted by both St Augustine and St Thomas, according to which God is identified with the formal and active principle and matter is regarded as the principle of formlessness and potentiality. This latter principle, although not opposed explicitly to God, is said to have an absolutely minimal degree of being, and is to such an extent identified with non-being in a purely privative or deficient sense that it can be described as that which is not.[21] In fact, its capacity to be is limited to a capacity to receive form, which comes solely from God, while in itself it tends always, by its formlessness, towards nothingness and non-existence.[22] In short, it is the abyss of disintegration over which every created being is suspended, and as such it is linked with evil, which in its turn may be equated with a disruption of form or a perversity of order, a lapse into nonbeing.[23]

Moreover, this material principle of formlessness is said to lie at the basis of all formal creation: everything created is regarded as a mixture or composition of matter with form, of an indeterminate substratum with the determination acquired from God. Hence no finite being can ever be "like" God, still less be "deified," because by definition all finite beings share in the material substratum with its intrinsic deficiency and "godlessness." God—the formal principle and the principle of Being—is pure actuality and there is no potentiality in Him. The material principle on the other hand, which is a formless or deficient cause, coincides with potentiality. Since natural existence also shares in the character of potentiality it can never be a sacramental reality in the full sense of the word unless it becomes other than it is or is, in other words, transubstantiated.

21. St Augustine, *Confessions*, XII, 6, 6.
22. St Augustine, *De Genesi ad litteram*, 1, 4, 9.
23. See E. TeSelle, *Augustine the Theologian* (London, 1970), pp.143-4.

One of the limitations in the Augustinian-Thomist tradition which would appear to make it difficult, if not impossible, to envisage a full and reciprocal union between God and nature, the uncreated and the created, is therefore that God is conceived solely as the principle of pure actuality, with the consequence that potentiality is regarded as implying a certain lack of being in a negative or deficient sense and so in this respect as outside God; and the same must apply to whatever shares in potentiality.

The theological theme in which a certain limitation in this same tradition is expressed is connected with the doctrine of the Trinity. Here perhaps we reach what is really the crux of the matter. The sacramental understanding of nature depends, as we have seen, upon the recognition of the actual immanence of nature in the divine, the sense that the creative energies of God did not merely produce the created world from without like a builder or an engineer, but are the ever-present, indwelling and spontaneous causes of every manifestation of life within it, whatever form this may take. It depends, in other words, upon the recognition of the continuing, vitalizing activity of the Holy Spirit in the world, animating these energies—luminous uncreated radiations of the divine—in the very heart of every existing thing. In its essence therefore the absence of this sacramental understanding must signify a deficiency in the doctrine of the Holy Spirit.

In effect, the doctrine of the Holy Spirit was not fully affirmed in Latin Christendom. The "cosmic" significance of Pentecost, in which the revelation of the Father and Son is consummated in that of the Spirit, was attenuated, and the full deployment of the doctrine of the Trinity was correspondingly arrested and frozen.[24] The Son was conceived pre-eminently in the unity of His being with that of the Father; and this emphasis on the transcendent unity and simplicity of the Trinity, confirmed and sealed by the *filioque*, meant that the Spirit was regarded as in ontological dependence on the Son. This in its turn, combined with a failure to distinguish adequately between God's essence and His existence or, in the case of St Thomas, with a conception that actually identifies God's essence with His existence, prevented it from being possible to understand how God, in the Spirit, "goes out" of Himself and enters with His

24. On this theme, see my *Church, Papacy and Schism* (London, 1978), pp.96-114.

129

uncreated "existential" energies into creation without either disrupting His unity and simplicity or abandoning His transcendence.

Under these conditions it was of course impossible to visualize any real activity of the Spirit in nature or, conversely, any real participation of nature in the divine. Instead nature, in the way we have seen, is accorded a status of its own, independent of the divine. And the same status is accorded to man, because man, defined as a rational animal, shares in all the characteristics and attributes of nature. It only remained for the now tenuously-conceived link between the divine and nature, the divine and the human, to be broken—not by denying that God created both nature and man but by saying that for all practical purposes the divine cannot be taken into account as an operational principle—and the way was open for that process of dehumanization and desanctification to which our contemporary world bears such powerful witness.

*O Man,*
*Regard thyself,*
*Thou hast within thyself*
*Heaven and Earth*

        *— Hildegard of Bingen*

## Chapter 8

# O Hanami: Flower Viewing

## *Hari Prasad Shastri*

Through the wild cherry-blossoms that snow
Yamato's hills with petals fair,
The shining morning sun-rays glow:
Will you not come and see them there?

*A Japanese Verse*

It was a fine day. The cherry-blossoms were swinging on the branches over the green grass on the slope of a hill overlooking a tranquil lake. Children of all ages, dressed in multi-colored *kimonos*, were playing about the trees, some chasing the butterflies, others collecting the daisies and yellow buttercups, with no purpose in view. Lao-tzu says purpose destroys the spirit of an act and robs it of spontaneity. Love, when aimless and purposeless, exalts the soul, but when married to a plan, it becomes a commerce, something soulless. Is there any beauty or rest to the soul in learning book-keeping? To learn a language just for the love of its beauty and poetry is so very different from learning practical chemistry to invent a new face powder.

Love is adoration of beauty; an exercise of the spiritual principle of our soul which gives the mind an entry into the palace of Truth.

Today the schools and offices of Yokohama have a holiday to allow the people to view the cherry-blossoms. The Japanese call it *O Hanami*. Men and women, children with their nurses and old folks, are in the country to view the beauty of the blossoms which come, nobody knows from where, for two days. They do not die on the branches; their color does not fade. When they have delivered their message of the love of Buddha and taught a lesson in detachment, they leave the branches in small petals and dance in the wind, as if saying a good-bye to the trees and the wind, and cover mother earth with their purity and beauty. The wind is in love with their high spirit and lifts the petals from the earth to embrace them; but they

*133*

must go to the Land of Truth, the Platonic Region of Eternal Ideas, the Paradise of the holy Buddha.

"We must cultivate beauty of character in daily life," declare the cherry-blossoms. Live to diffuse beauty, seeing the eternal, immutable Truth, in the passing and the changing and leave the world like them, smiling, beautifying and peace-giving.

Passions are wrong because they cloud our reason, narrow the scope of our heart and localize our soul. Prejudices—that is, unreasoned, uncritical opinions, like fanatical patriotism and race-worship—darken our reason. Love tainted by a desire for possession and personal gratification is like an over-ripe persimmon, full of color but insipid in taste.

The Japanese do not cry when the cherry-blossoms are gone; they do not pray for their continuance when they are over.

"For enjoyment of the cherry-blossoms," the monk Basho says, "you must approach them with a vacant mind, free from business worries or domestic cares." Why? They narrow the soul and do not let the impressions of beauty impregnate it with Truth. Silence, inner and outer, is essential for the enjoyment of beauty. It is in complete silence that the Japanese view the cherry-blossoms. When they sit for a picnic under the cherry trees, they are silent; but they can sing if the soul prompts them to do so. Music is silence of the soul, objectified into sound vibrations. Love needs silence. If the din of desires agitates the heart, there is only the shadow of Love. "I love you" is a vulgar expression which means nothing.

> I approached her with my protestations of love
>      and she closed her doors.
> A horseman came and stood in silence, just in adoration.
>      She went with him.

The cherry-blossoms, *Sakura,* are the compassion of the holy Buddha. They belong to him. No Japanese will pluck them for his neighbor's daughter. They are to be enjoyed where they are and as they are.

The Empress Yukio of the Nara period, after her worship of the Buddha, came out early in the morning and saw her palace garden full of cherry-blossoms. She stood in an attitude of prayer and dedicated them to the Bodhisattvas of the past and the future. This is the attitude of a Yogi to the world.

King Shivaji founded the Mahratta Empire after long and painful campaigns against the Mohammedans. He offered the crown and the sword to his Guru Shri Ram Das, saying: "Under your orders I have founded this vast empire. It is yours. Just let me live with you as your personal servant." This is the Karma Yoga of the Gita.

Late in the evening I returned from Yokohama to Tokyo. Miss Yaeko, my landlady's cultured daughter, welcomed me with cherry-like smiles and said, "Teacher, I see you are returning from a temple. You look so peaceful."

"Yes, dear, I am back from the temple of nature, having listened to the silent sermons of the cherry blossoms—on the evanescence of the world and the reality of Beauty."

Beneath the autumn sky
Some blossoms grow, which never see
A bird or butterfly.

— Basho

*Chapter 9*

# Creation According to Ibn 'Arabî

*Toshihiko Izutsu*

## I. The Meaning of Creation

"Creation" (*khalq*) is unquestionably one of the concepts upon which stands the Islamic world-view. It plays a prominent role in all aspects of the religious thought of Islam. In theology, for example, it constitutes the very starting-point of all discussions in the form of the opposition between the "temporality" (*hudûth*) and "eternity *a parte ante*" (*qidam*). The world is an "originated" (or "temporally produced") thing because it is the result of Divine creation. And this conception of the world's being "originated" (*muhdath*) forms the basis of the entire system of Islamic theology.

In the world-view of Ibn 'Arabî, too, "creation" plays an important part as one of the key-concepts. The creative word of God, "Be!" (*kun*) has a decisive meaning in the coming-into-being of all beings. However, the most basic concept of Ibn 'Arabî's ontology is self-manifestation, and the world of Being is after all nothing but the self-manifestation of the Absolute, and no event whatsoever occurs in the world except self-manifestation. In this sense, "creation" which means the coming-into-being of the world is naturally identical with self-manifestation.

But we would make a gross mistake if we imagine that since the ontology of Ibn 'Arabî is based on self-manifestation and since there is nothing but self-manifestation, "creation" is after all, for him, a metaphor. To think that Ibn 'Arabî used the term "creation" making a concession to the established pattern of Islamic thought, and that he merely described self-manifestation in a more traditional terminology, is to overlook the multilateral nature of his thought.

One of the characteristic features of Ibn 'Arabî's thought is its manifoldness. In the presence of one important problem, he usually develops his thought in various directions and in various forms with the help of rich imagery. This, I think, is due largely to the unusual profundity and fecundity of his experience which always underlies his thinking. The depth and richness of mystical experience demands, in his case, multiplicity of expression.

The theory of "creation" which we are going to examine is not to be considered as a mere religious metaphor, or some esoteric teaching disguised in traditional theological terminology. "Creation" is to him as real as "self-manifestation." Or we might say that one and the same fundamental fact existing in his consciousness has two different aspects, one "creation," and the other "self-manifestation."

The first thing which attracts our attention about his theory of "creation" is the important part played by the concept of "triad" or "triplicity," *thalâthîyah*. This marks it off from the theory of "self-manifestation."

The starting-point is as usual the Absolute. The ontological ground of existence is the One-Absolute. But the One, if considered in its phenomenal aspect, presents three different aspects. They are: (1) the Essence (not *qua* Essence in its absoluteness, but in its self-revealing aspect), (2) the Will or *irâdah* (here the Absolute is a "Willer," *murîd*), and (3) the Command or *amr*[1] (here the Absolute is a "Commander," *âmir*).

These three aspects in the order given here represent the whole process of "creation." The process may be briefly described as follows. First, there arises in the One-Absolute self-consciousness—or Knowledge (*'ilm*)—and the permanent archetypes appear in the Divine Consciousness. This marks the birth of the possible Many. And thereby the Presence of the Essence (i.e., the ontological level of the Absolute *qua* Absolute) descends to the Presence of Divinity (*ilâhîyah*, "being God").

Then, in the second place, there arises the Will based on this Knowledge to bring out the archetypes from the state of nonexistence into the state of existence. Then, on the basis of this Will, the Command—"Be!" (*kun*)—is issued, and thus the world is "created."

Having these preliminary remarks in mind, let us read the passage in which Ibn 'Arabî describes the process.[2]

1. It is also called Word (*qawl*).
2. *Fusûs al-Hikam*, pp.139-140/ 115-116. In quoting from the *Fusûs al-Hikam* (*Fus.*), I shall always give two paginations: (1) that of the Cairo edition of 1321

Know—may God assist you in doing so!—that the whole matter (i.e., "creation") in itself has its basis in the "singleness" (*fardîyah*). But this "singleness" has a triple structure (tathlîth). For the "singleness" starts to appear only from "three." In fact "three" is the first single (i.e., odd) number.

What Ibn 'Arabî wants to convey through these laconic expressions may be made clear if we explain it in the following way. He begins by saying that the very root of "creation" is the "singleness" of the Absolute. It is important to remark that he refers here to the Absolute as "single" (*fard*), not as "One." In other words, he is not speaking of the Absolute as Absolute in its essential absoluteness. We are here at a lower stage at which the Absolute has selfconsciousness or Knowledge.

According to Ibn 'Arabî, "one" is not a number at all; it is the principle and "birth-place" of all numbers from "two" onwards, but it is not itself a number. "One" is absolutely above all relations; it is naturally above the concept itself of number.

"Single" is not like that. Outwardly it is "one," but in its inner structure it is not "one," because the concept of singleness contains in itself the concept of "other." It is "one" in so far as it is other than others. In this sense, "single" is internally divisible and divided, because we cannot represent it without at the same time representing—negatively, to be sure—the idea of otherness. In this sense it is "one" composed of more than one unit. And "three" is the smallest, i.e., first, "single" number in the infinitely extending series of numbers—which makes it particularly appropriate for functioning as the starting-point of the Divine act of creation.

And from this Presence of Divinity (i.e., the ontological plane where the Absolute is no longer One but Single, endowed with an inner triplicity) the world has come into existence. To this God refers when He says: "Whenever We decide (lit. "will" the existence of) something, We only say to it, 'Be!,' and it comes into existence" (XVI, 40). Thus we see (the triplicity of) the Essence, the Will, and the Word.[3] Anything would not come into existence if it were not for (1) the Essence and (2) its Will—the Will which is the drive with which the Essence turns towards bringing something in particular into existence—and then (3) the Word "Be!" uttered to that

A.H., containing al-Qâshânî's commentary, and (2) that of Affîfî's critical edition, Cairo, 1946 (1365 A.H.).

   3. Reading: *hâdhihi dhât wa-irâdah wa-qawl.*

particular thing at the very moment when the Will turns the Essence in that direction.[4]

The passage just quoted describes the structure of the triplicity on the side of the Agent, i.e., the Absolute. But the triplicity on the part of the Creator alone does not produce any effect. In order that the creative activity of the Absolute be really effective, there must be a corresponding triplicity also on the part of the "receiver" (*qâbil*), i.e., the thing to be created. Creation is actualized only when the active triplicity perfectly coincided with the passive triplicity.

(The moment the creative Word of God is uttered) there arises in the thing to be created, too, a singleness having a triplicity. And by this triplicity alone does the thing, on its part, become capable of being produced and being qualified with existence. The triplicity in the object consists of (1) its thing-ness (*shay'iyyah*), (2) its hearing (*samâ'*), and (3) its obeying (*imtithâl*) the Command of the Creator concerning its creation. So that the (creaturely) triad corresponds with the (Divine) triad.

The first (1) is the permanent archetypal essence of the thing in the state of non-existence, which corresponds to the Essence of its Creator. The second (2) is the hearing of the Command by the thing, which corresponds to the Will of its Creator. And the third (3) is its obedient acceptance of what it has been commanded concerning its coming into existence, which corresponds to the (Creator's) Word "Be!" Upon this, the thing actually comes into being.

Thus the "bringing-into-being" (*takwîn*, or "production") is to be attributed to the thing (created). For if the thing had not in itself the power of coming into being when the Word ("Be!") is uttered, it would never come into existence. In this sense it is the thing itself that brings it into existence from the state of non-existence.[5]

It is remarkable that a special emphasis is laid here in the process of creation on the "power" (*quwwah*) of the thing to be created. A thing is not created in a purely passive way, that is, mechanically and powerlessly, but it participates positively in its own creation.

When God decides to bring something into existence, He simply says to it "Be!" And the thing, in response, comes into existence. In this process, the coming-into-being (*takawwun*) itself is an

---

4. *Fus.*, pp.139-140/ 115-116.
5. *Fus.*,p.140/ 115-116.

act of that thing, not an act of God. This conception is explained by al-Qâshânî in the following terms:[6]

> The coming-into-being, that is, the thing's obeying the Command, pertains to nothing else than the thing itself, for it (i.e., coming-into-being) is (as Ibn 'Arabî says) in the power of the thing; that is to say, it is contained potentially in the thing, concealed. This is why God (in the above-quoted Qoranic verse) ascribes it (i.e., coming-into-being) to the thing, by saying, "and it comes into existence."[7] This sentence means that the thing (upon hearing the Word) immediately obeys the order and comes into existence. And the thing is capable of doing so simply because it is already existent in the Unseen (i.e., potentially), for the archetypal subsistence is nothing other than a concealed inner mode of existence. Everything that is "inward" has in itself the power to come out into "outward" existence. This is due to the fact that the Essence (designated by the) Name "Inward" (*bâtin*) is the same Essence (designated by the) Name "Outward" (*zâhir*), and because the "receiver" (*qâbil*) is (ultimately) the same as the "Agent" (*fâ'il*).

Such is the original theory of "creation" put forward by Ibn 'Arabî. He affirms very emphatically that the "production" (*takwîn*) is to be ascribed to the thing produced, not to the Absolute. Such a position will surely be criticized by ordinary believers as considering God "powerless" (*'âjiz*). But, this position is not at all blasphemous in the eyes of those who really know the structure of Ibn 'Arabî's world-view. Surely, in this world-view, the things (creatures) are described as being so positively powerful that they leave but a limited space for the direct activity of the Absolute. On a deeper level, however, those things that are provisionally considered as independently existent are nothing but so many particularized, delimited forms of the Absolute, and all are involved in an ontological drama within the Absolute itself; all are a magnificent Divina Commedia.

The idea of "production" (the last stage of the "creation") being ascribable to the things and not to the Absolute is further explained by Ibn 'Arabî in the following way:[8]

> God states categorically that the "production" pertains to the (created) thing itself, and not to God. What pertains to God in

6. p.140.
7. The point is that God does not say in this verse *fa-yukawwin* ("and *He* brings it into existence") but says *fa-yakûn* ("and *it* comes into existence"), the subject of the sentence being the thing itself.
8. *Fus.*, p.140/ 115-116.

this matter is only His Command. He makes His part (in the creative process) clear by saying: "Whenever We decide (the existence of) something, We only say to it 'Be!', and it comes into existence" (XVI, 40). Thus the "production" is ascribed to the thing though, to be sure, the latter acts only in obedience to the Command of God. And (we must accept this statement as it is because) God is truthful in whatever He says. Besides, this (i.e., the ascription of the "production" to the thing) is something quite reasonable, objectively speaking.

(This may be illustrated by an example.) Suppose a master who is feared by everybody and whom nobody dares to disobey commands his slave to stand up by saying to him, "Stand up!" (*qum*); the slave will surely stand up in obedience to the command of the master. To the master pertains in the process of the slave's standing up only his commanding him to do so, while the act of standing up itself pertains to the slave; it is not an act of the master.

Thus it is clear that the "production" stands on the basis of triplicity; in other words, three elements are involved on both sides, on the part of the Absolute as well as on the part of the creatures.

It will be evident, then, that in Ibn 'Arabî's thought, the principle of *creatio ex nihilo* holds true. But what makes his thesis fundamentally different from the ordinary Islamic *creatio ex nihilo* is that the *nihil*, for Ibn 'Arabî, is not a total unconditional "non-existence," but "non-existence" in the particular sense of something being as yet non-existent as an empirical or phenomenal thing. What he regards as *nihil* is "existence" on the level of the intelligibles, or—which comes to the same thing—in the Consciousness of God. Ontologically, his *nihil* is the "possible" (*mumkin*), i.e., something that has the power (or possibility) to exist. The ordinary view which makes "creation" a sort of Divine monodrama has its origin in the ignorance of the positive power to be attributed to the "possibles." All things, in Ibn 'Arabî's view, have enough power to come out from the concealment into the field of existence in response to the ontological Command of God. Thus the creaturely world is possessed of "efficiency" (*fâ'ilîyah*). And the things that constitute this would participate actively and positively in the creation of themselves.

Looking at an artisan who is engaged in molding things out of clay, one might make a superficial observation that the clay has no positive "efficiency" of its own, and that it lets itself be molded into whatever form the artisan likes. In the view of such a man, the clay in the hands of an artisan is sheer passivity, sheer non-action. He overlooks the important fact that, in reality, the clay, on its part, positively determines the activity of the artisan. Surely, the artisan can make quite a considerable variety of things out of clay, but whatever he may do, he cannot go beyond the narrow limits set by the very nature of the clay. Otherwise expressed, the nature of the clay itself determines the possible forms in which it may be actualized. Somewhat similar to this is the positive nature of a thing in the process of "creation."

The same observation, however, clearly shows that, although the things do possess "efficiency," the latter is after all secondary, not primary. Herein lies the fundamental difference between God and the world. "As women are by nature a degree lower than men," the creatures are a degree lower than the Absolute. The things, with all their positive powers and capacities, have no essential priority.

> As women are a degree lower than men according to God's saying: "and men are a degree above them (i.e., women)" (II, 228), the things that have been created in the image (of God) are naturally a degree lower than the One who has brought them into being in His image, in spite of the fact that their forms are God's Form itself.

> And by that very degree which separates God from the world, God is completely independent (i.e., has absolutely no need) of the whole world, and is the primary Agent. As for the "form," it is but a secondary agent and has no essential priority which pertains only to the Absolute.[9]

## II. The Feminine Element in the Creation of the World

In the last part of the preceding section reference has incidentally been made to the idea that women are by nature a degree lower than men. This, however, should not be taken to mean that Ibn 'Arabî considers the role played by the feminine in the process of world creation quite secondary, let alone unimportant. On the contrary, the entire creative process, in his view, is governed by the principle of femininity.

The starting-point of his thinking on this problem is furnished by a famous Tradition which runs: "Of all the things of your world,

9. *Fus.*, p.273/ 219.

three things have been made particularly dear to me, women, per-
fumes, and the ritual prayer, this last being the 'cooling of my eye'
(i.e., a source of my highest joy)." In this Tradition, Ibn 'Arabî
observes, the number "three"—triplicity again!—is put in the feminine form (*thalâth*), in spite of the fact that one of the three things
here enumerated (*tîb*, "perfume") is a masculine noun. Ordinarily,
in Arabic grammar, the rule is that, if there happens to be even one
masculine noun among the things enumerated, one treats the
whole as grammatically masculine, and uses the numeral in the masculine form (*thalâthah*, for example, instead of *thalâth*, meaning
"three").

Now in this Tradition, the Prophet intentionally—so thinks Ibn
'Arabî—uses the feminine form, *thalâth*, and this, in his view, has a
very deep symbolic meaning. It suggests that all the basic factors
that participate in creation are feminine, and that the whole process
of creation is governed by the principle of femininity (*ta'nîth*). Ibn
'Arabî draws attention to the process by which a man (male) comes
into being:[10]

> The man finds himself situated between an essence (i.e., the
> Divine Essence) which is his (ontological) source and a woman
> (i.e., his own mother) who is his (physical) source. Thus he is
> placed between two feminine nouns, that is to say, between the
> femininity of essence and the real (i.e., physical) femininity.

The Essence (*dhât*), which is the original ground of all Being, is
a feminine noun. The immediate ontological ground of the forms
of all beings, i.e., the Divine Attributes, *sifât* (sg. *sifah*), is a feminine
noun. The creative power of God, *qudrah* is a feminine noun. Thus,
from whatever aspect one approaches the process of creation, one
runs into a feminine noun. The Philosophers (*falâsifah*) who blindly
follow Greek philosophy assert that God is the "cause" (*'illah*) of the
existence of the world. This is a mistaken view, and yet it is significant, Ibn 'Arabî adds, that even in this wrong opinion about creation, a feminine noun, *'illah*, is used to denote the ultimate ground
of the creation of the world.

The whole problem is dealt with by al-Qâshânî in a far more
scholastic way as follows:[11]

10. *Fus.*, p.274/ 220.
11. pp.274-275.

The ultimate ground (or origin) of everything is called Mother (*umm*), because the mother is the (stem) from which all branches go out. Do you not see how God describes the matter when He says: "And He created from it (i.e., the first soul, meaning Adam) its mate, and out of the two He spread innumerable men and women" (IV, 1). As you see, the "wife" (of Adam) was feminine. Moreover, the first unique "soul" from which she was created was itself feminine.[12] Just in the same way, the Origin of all origins over which there is nothing is designated by a (feminine noun), haqîqah or "Reality" . . . Likewise the words designating the Divine Essence, 'ayn and dhât, are feminine.

Thus his (i.e., Muhammad's) intention in making (the femininity) overcome (the masculinity)[13] is to draw attention to the special importance of the femininity which is the very origin and source of everything that spreads out from it. And this is true not merely of the world of Nature but even of Reality itself.

In fact, Reality is the Father (*ab*) of everything in that it is the absolute Agent (i.e., the absolutely Active, *fâ'il*). But Reality is also the Mother (because of its passivity). It gathers together in itself both "activity" (*fi'l*) and "passivity" (*infi'âl*), for Reality is "passive" (*munfa'il*) in so far as it manifests itself in the form of a "passive" thing, while in the form of the "active" (Agent) it is "active." The very nature of Reality requires this unification of the "determination" (*ta'ayyun*) and "non-determination" (*lâta'ayyun*).[14] Thus Reality is "determined" by all determinations, masculine and feminine, on the one hand. But on the other, it stands high above all determinations.

And Reality, when it becomes determined by the first determination,[15] is One Essence requiring a perfect balance and equilibrium between "activity" and "passivity," between the exterior self-manifestation (*zuhûr*) and the interior self-concealment (*butûn*).[16] And

---

12. Although Adam is a man, he is, as a soul (*nafs*), feminine.

13. The reference is to the above-quoted Tradition, in which the Prophet uses the feminine numeral *thalâth* in spite of the presence of a masculine noun among the three things enumerated.

14. "Determination" (or more strictly "being determined") refers to the passive side of the Absolute, i.e., the Absolute as manifesting itself in a concrete (determined) thing. "Non-determination" refers to the active side of the Absolute, i.e., the Absolute as the absolute Agent.

15. The "first determination" (*al-ta'ayyun al-awwal*) means the self-manifestation of the Absolute to itself as a unifying point of all the Divine Names. The Absolute is here the "one" (*wâhid*), and the ontological stage the *wâhidîyah*, "Oneness."

16. The Absolute *qua* One is potentially all beings but it is in actuality still one. So it is neither in the state of pure exterior self-manifestation nor in that of pure

in so far as it is the "Inward" (*bâtin*) residing in every form, it is "active," but in so far as it is the "Outward" (*zâhir*), it is "passive" . . . The first determination, which occurs by (the Absolute's) manifesting itself to itself, attests to the fact that the Essence is absolute and non-determined, for its self-determination (*ta'ayyun bi-dhâti-hi*) must necessarily be preceded by non-determination (*lâ-ta'ayyun*). Likewise when Reality *qua* Reality is actualized in every determined (i.e., concretely delimited) existent, its determination (also) requires that it be preceded by non-determination. Nay, rather, every determined existent, considered in its reality apart from all consideration of its actual delimitations, is an absolute (i.e., every determined existent is in its ontological core an absolute—which is nothing but the Absolute itself). A determined existent, in this sense, depends upon the Absolute (which is inherent in it) and is sustained by it. So everything is "passive" in relation to that absolute (ontological) ground, and is a locus of self-manifestation for it, while that ground is "active" and remains concealed in the thing.

Thus everything is "passive" considered from the point of view of its being determined, but "active" in itself,[17] considered from the point of view of its being absolute. But the thing itself is essentially one . . . So Reality, wherever it goes and in whatever way it appears, has (two different aspects; namely), "activity" and "passivity," or "fatherhood" (*ubuwwah*) and "motherhood" (*umûmah*). And this justifies the (Prophet's having used) the feminine form.

The Absolute, which is the ultimate and real origin of "creation," has something feminine in it, as indicated by the feminine form of the word "Essence" (dhât). Furthermore, if we consider analytically the ontological structure of the creative process, we find, even at its first stage, the "first determination," a feminine principle, the "motherhood," co-operating with a masculine principle, the "fatherhood." The Divine Essence, in brief, is the Mother of everything in the sense that it represents the "passive" element which is inherent in all forms of Being.

## III. Perpetual Creation

We turn now to one of the most interesting features of the theory of creation peculiar to Ibn 'Arabî. This part of his theory is histori-

interior concealment, but it keeps, so to speak, a perfect balance between these two terms.

17. I read: [*wa-fâ'il*] *min nafsi-hi*, etc.

cally of primary importance because it is a critique of the atomistic philosophy of the Ash'arite theologians.[18]

In Ibn 'Arabî's world-view, the self-manifestation of the Absolute is a perpetual process whose major stages—(1) the "most holy emanation," (2) the "holy emanation," and then (3) the appearance of concrete individual things—go on being actualized one after another like successive, recurrent waves. This ontological process repeats itself indefinitely and endlessly. At every moment, and moment after moment, the same eternal process of annihilation and re-creation is repeated. At this very moment, an infinite number of things and properties come into being, and at the next moment they are annihilated to be replaced by another infinity of things and properties.

Thus we cannot experience the same world twice at two different moments. The world we actually experience is in perpetual flow. It changes from moment to moment. But this continual and perpetual change occurs in such an orderly way according to such definite patterns that we, superficial observers, imagine that the same one world is there around us.

Describing this perpetual flow of things in terms of the concept of "creation", Ibn 'Arabî says that the world goes on being created anew at every single moment. This he calls "new creation" (*al-khalq al-jadîd*). The expression must not be taken in the sense of a "new" creation to be contrasted with the "old," i.e., the earlier, creation of the world. The word "new" (*jadîd*) in this context means "ever new" or "which is renewed from moment to moment." The "new creation" means, in short, the process of everlasting and ever new act of creation.

Man, being endowed with self-consciousness, can have a real living feel of this "new creation" both inside and outside himself, i.e., both in his mind and in his body, by becoming conscious of "himself," which goes on changing from moment to moment without ever stopping as long as he lives. However, ordinary people

18. The idea presents a very important and interesting problem from the viewpoint of comparative Oriental philosophy. See my "The Concept of Perpetual Creation in Islamic Mysticism and Zen Buddhism" (in *Mélanges offerts à Henry Corbin*, ed. Seyyed Hossein Nasr [Tehran, 1977], pp. 115-148). [This same article appears in a more recent compendium of essays by the author, entitled *Creation and the Timeless Order of Things* (Ashland, Oregon: White Cloud Press, 1994), pp.141-173. *Ed.*]

are not aware of the process of "new creation" even with regard to themselves.

Ibn 'Arabî describes this process also as a "perpetual ascent" (*taraqqî dâ'im*). This is a very important point at which we can look into the very basis of his idea of the "new creation."

> The wonder of all wonders is that man (and consequently, every-thing) is in a perpetual process of ascending. And yet (ordinarily) he is not aware of this because of the extreme thinness and fine-ness of the veil[19] or because of the extreme similarity between (the successive forms).[20]

That everything is involved in the process of the ever-new creation means primarily that the Absolute is continually manifesting itself in the infinity of "possible" things. This is done by the ontological "descent" (*nuzûl*) of the Absolute towards the lower levels of Being, first to the archetypes and then to the "possible." But the same process of perpetual "descent" is, when it is looked at from the side of the "possible," turns out to be a perpetual process of ontological "ascent." Everything, in this sense, is perpetually "ascending" towards the Absolute by the very same "descending" of the latter.

The "ascent" (*taraqqî*) of the things, in other words, is nothing but the reverse side of the "descent" of the Absolute towards them. The things in the state of non-existence receiving the mercy of the Absolute and obtaining thereby existence, produces, from the standpoint of these things, the image of their "ascending" toward the original source of existence. Al-Qâshânî paraphrases the above-quoted passage in the following way:[21]

> One of the most miraculous things about man is that he is in a per-petual state of ascent with regard to the modes of the "prepared-ness" of his own archetypal essence. For all the modes of the archetypes are things that have been known to God (from eter-nity), permanently fixed in potentiality, and God brings them out to actuality incessantly and perpetually. And so He goes on trans-forming the possibilities (*isti 'dâdât*, lit. "preparednesses") that have been there from the beginningless past and that are (there-

---

19. When you look at something through an extremely fine and transparent fabric you do not become aware of the existence of the veil between you and the thing. The "veil" here refers to the outward form shown by the act of "ascending."
20. *Fus.*, p.151-152/124.
21. p.152.

fore) essentially uncreated, into infinite possibilities that are actually created.

Thus everything is in the state of ascending at this very moment because it is perpetually receiving the endlessly renewed ontological (*wujûdîyah*) Divine self-manifestations, and at every self-manifestation the thing goes on increasing in its receptivity for another (i.e., the next) self-manifestation.

Man, however, may not be conscious of this because of his eyes being veiled, or rather because of the veil being extremely thin and fine. But he may also become conscious of it when the self-manifestations take on the forms of intellectual, intuitive, imaginative, or mystical experiences.

The concept of "new creation," thus comprising the ontological "descent" and "ascent," is a point which discloses most clearly the dynamic nature of the world-view of Ibn ʿArabî. In this world-view, nothing remains static; the world in its entirety is in fervent movement. The world transforms itself kaleidoscopically from moment to moment, and yet all these movements of self-development are the "ascending" movements of the things toward the Absolute-One, precisely because they are the "descending" self-expressions of the Absolute-One. The One is the Manifold and the Manifold is the One. In fact the "descent" and "ascent" describe exactly the same thing.

(As a result of the "new creation," we are constantly faced with similar forms, but of any two similar forms) one is not the same thing as the other. For in the eyes of one who recognizes them to be two similar things, they are different from one another. Thus a truly perspicacious man discerns Many in the One, while knowing at the same time that the Divine Names, in spite of their essential diversity and multiplicity, point to one single Reality, for the Names are nothing but multiplicity posited by the reason in Something which is essentially and really one.

Thus it comes about that in the process of self-manifestation the Many becomes discernible in one single Essence. This may be compared to the Prime Matter which is mentioned in the definition of every form. The forms are many and divergent, but they all go back in reality to one single substance which is their Prime Matter.[22]

In this passage, Ibn ʿArabî seems to be speaking of the horizontal similarity-relationship between the concrete beings. He emphasizes

22. *Fus.*, p.152/ 124-125.

the particular aspect of the "new creation" in which the concretely existent things in the phenomenal world are after all infinitely various forms of the Divine self-manifestation, and are ultimately reducible to the One. But the same applies also to the vertical, i.e., temporal, relation between the ever new creations. In what is seemingly one and the same thing the "new creation" is taking place at every moment, so that the "one and the same thing," considered at two successive moments, is in reality not one and the same, but two "similar" things. And yet, despite all this, the thing maintains and never loses its original unity and identity, because all the new and similar states that occur to it successively are eternally determined by its own archetype.

These two aspects of the "new creation," horizontal and vertical, are brought to light by al-Qâshânî in his commentary on the passage just quoted.[23]

A truly perspicacious man discerns a multiplicity of self-determinations in the one single Essence which appears in an infinite number of "similar" forms. All the Divine Names like the Omnipotent, the Omniscient, the Creator, the Sustainer, etc., point in reality to one single Essence, God, despite the fact that each of them has a different meaning from the rest. This shows that the divergence of the meanings of the Names is merely an intelligible and mental multiplicity existing in what is called the "essentially One," that they are not a really and concretely existent multiplicity. Thus the self-manifestation in the forms of all the Names is but a multiplicity discernible within one single Essence. The same is true also of the events that take place successively (in "one and the same thing"). All the successive self-manifestations that are similar to each other are one in reality, but many if taken as individual self-determinations. (The Master) illustrates this with the example of the Prime Matter (*hayûlâ*). You mention the Prime Matter in defining any substantial Form. You say, for example, "Body (*jism*) is a substance having quantity," "Plant (*nabât*) is a body that grows up," "Stone (*hajar*) is a body, inorganic, heavy, and voiceless," "animal (*hayawân*) is a body that grows up, has sense perception, and moves with will," "Man (*insân*) is a rational animal." In this way, you mention "substance" as the definition of "body," and you mention "body"—which is "substance" (by definition)—in the definitions of all the rest. Thus all are traced back to the one single reality which is "substance."

23. p.152-153.

This fact can be known only by mystical vision, and is never disclosed to those who understand everything through rational thinking. Thus it comes about that the majority of men, including the Philosophers, are not aware of the phenomenon of the "new creation." They do not see the infinitely beautiful scene of this kaleidoscopic transformation of things.

> How splendid are God's words concerning the world and its perpetual renewal with each Divine breath which constitutes an "ever new creation" in one single reality. (But this is not perceived except by a few), as He says in reference to a certain group of people—indeed, this applies to the majority of men—"Nay, they are in utter confusion with regard to the new creation." (L, 15).[24] These people (are in confusion with regard to it) because they do not know the (perpetual) renewal of the things with each Divine breath.[25]

Al-Qâshânî describes the scene of this perpetual renewal of the things as he sees it in his philosophico-mystical intuition in the following terms:[26]

> The world in its entirety is perpetually changing. And every thing (in the world) is changing in itself from moment to moment. Thus every thing becomes determined at every moment with a new determination which is different from that with which it was determined a moment ago. And yet the one single reality which is attained by all these successive changes remains forever unchanged. This is due to the fact that the "one single reality" is nothing but the reality itself of the Absolute as it has taken on the "first determination," and all the forms (i.e., the successive determinations) are accidents that occur to it successively, changing and being renewed at every moment.

> But (ordinary) people do not know the reality of this phenomenon and are therefore "in utter confusion" regarding this perpetual process of transformation which is going on in the universe. Thus the Absolute reveals itself perpetually in these successive self-manifestations, while the world is perpetually being lost due to its

24. Ibn 'Arabî, as he often does, is giving quite an arbitrary meaning to the Qoranic verse. The actual context makes it clear beyond any doubt that God is here speaking of Resurrection after death, which is conceived of as a "new creation." The "new creation" does not certainly mean in this verse the ever new process of creation which is Ibn 'Arabî's thesis.

25. *Fus.*, p.153/ 125.

26. p.153.

annihilation at every moment and its renewed birth at the next moment.

Al-Qâshânî goes a step further and asserts that this perpetual "new creation" not only governs the concrete existents of the world, but that even the permanent archetypes are under its sway. The archetypes in the Divine Consciousness appear and disappear and then appear again, repeating the same process endlessly as innumerable lamp-lights that go on being turned on and put out in every successive moment. He says:[27]

> The ontological emanation (*al-fayd al-wujûdiy*) and the Breath of the Merciful are perpetually flowing through the beings of the world as water running in a river, forever being renewed continuously. In a similar way, the determinations of the Absolute-Existence in the form of the permanent archetypes in the eternal Knowledge (i.e., Divine Consciousness) never cease to be renewed from moment to moment. (And this happens in the following way). Thus, as soon as the first ontological determination leaves an archetype in a place, at the next moment the next determination is attached to it in a different place. This is nothing other than the appearance of an archetype belonging in the sphere of Divine Knowledge in the second place following its disappearance in the first place, while that archetype itself remains forever the same in the Knowledge and in the world of the Unseen.

It is as if you saw millions of lights flickering against the background of an unfathomable darkness. If you concentrate your sight on any one of these illumined spots, you will see its light disappearing in the very next moment and appearing again in a different spot in the following moment. And the Divine Consciousness is imagined as a complicated meshwork formed by all these spots in which light goes on being turned on and extinguished at every moment endlessly. This is indeed an exceedingly beautiful and impressive image. But Ibn 'Arabî himself in his *Fusûs* does not seem to describe the permanent archetypes in this way in terms of the "new creation." The "new creation" he speaks of concerns the concrete things of the sensible world.

Let us return to Ibn 'Arabî and analyze his concept of "new creation" as he develops it in relation to his atomistic philosophy. He finds in the Qoranic account of the miracle of Bilqîs, Queen of

27. pp.195-196.

Sheba, an admirable illustration of this incessant annihilation and re-creation which is going on in the world of Being. The account is found in the Qoran, XXVII, 38-40.

Once Solomon asked those who were there in his presence, jinn and human beings, whether any of them could bring him the throne of the Queen. Thereupon one of the jinn said "I will bring it to thee before thou risest from thy place!" But a man "who had knowledge of the Scripture"[28] said, "I will bring it to thee before thy gaze returns to thee (i.e., in the twinkling of an eye)." And he did bring the throne on the spot from the far-off country in South Arabia and set it in front of Solomon.

How could he accomplish this miracle? Ibn 'Arabî says that the man simply took advantage of the "new creation." The throne of the Queen was not transported locally from Sheba to the presence of Solomon. Nobody, in fact, can carry any material object from one place to a distant place in the twinkling of an eye. Nor did Solomon and his people see the throne in hallucination. Rather the throne which had been with Bilqîs was annihilated and, instead of being re-created in the same place, was made to appear in the presence of Solomon. This is, indeed, a miraculous event, in the sense that a thing disappeared and in the next moment appeared in a different place. From the viewpoint of the "new creation," however, such an event is not at all an impossibility. For, after all, it is nothing but a new throne being created in an entirely different place.

> The superiority of the human sage over the sage of the jinn consists in the (deeper knowledge possessed by the former concerning) the secrets of the free disposal of anything at will and the particular natures of things. And this superiority can be known by the amount of time needed. For the "return of the gaze" towards the man who looks is faster than the standing up of a man who stands up from his seat . . . For the time in which the gaze moves to an object is exactly the amount of time in which the gaze gets hold of the object however great the distance may be between the man who looks and the object looked. At the very moment the eye is opened, its gaze reaches the sphere of the fixed stars. And at the very moment the perception stops, the gaze returns to the man. The standing up of a man from his seat cannot be done so quickly.

28. The Qoran does not give his name. Commentators assert that the man was a sage whose name was Âsaf b. Barakhiyâ.

Thus Âsaf b. Barakhiyâ was superior to the jinn in his action. For the moment Âsaf spoke, he accomplished his work. And Solomon saw at the same moment the throne of Bilqîs. The throne was actually placed in his presence in order that no one should imagine that Solomon perceived (from afar) the throne in its original place without its being transferred.

In my opinion, however, there can be no local transference in one single moment. There occurred (in Solomon's case) simply a simultaneous annihilation and re-creation in such a manner that no one could perceive it, except those who had been given a true knowledge (of this kind of thing). This is what is meant by God's saying: "Nay, they are in utter confusion with regard to the new creation." And there never occurs even a moment in which they cease to see what they have seen (at the preceding moment).[29]

Now if the truth of the matter is as I have just described, the moment of the disappearance of the throne from its original place coincided with the moment of its appearance in the presence of Solomon as a result of the "new creation" occurring with every Breath. Nobody, however, notices this discrepancy (between two moments of the "new creation").

Nay, the ordinary man is not aware of it (i.e., the "new creation") even with regard to himself. Man does not know that he ceases to exist and then comes to existence again with every single breath.[30]

As we see, Ibn 'Arabî here writes that man ceases to exist at every moment and then (*thumma*) comes to existence again. But he immediately adds the remark that the particle *thumma*, meaning "then" or "after that," should not be taken as implying a lapse of time.

You must not think that by the word *thumma* I mean a temporal interval. This is not correct. The Arabs use this word in certain particular contexts to express the priority in causal relationship.[31] . . . In the process of "the new creation with each Breath," too, the time of the non-existence (i.e., annihilation) of a thing coincides with the time of the existence (i.e., re-creation) of a thing similar to it (i.e., the thing that has just been annihilated). This view

29. This annihilation/ re-creation is done so quickly that man does not notice any discontinuum between the two units of time in his sense perception and imagines that everything continues to be as it has been.

30. *Fus.*, pp.195-196/ 155.

31. "A *thumma* B" in certain contexts means that A, as the cause of B, logically precedes the latter. It does not imply that A necessarily precedes B in terms of time; A and B may very well occur simultaneously.

resembles the Ash'arite thesis of the perpetual renewal of the accidents (*tajdîd al-a'râz*).

In fact, the problem of the transportation of the throne of Bilqîs is of the most recondite problems understandable only to those who know what I have explained above about the story. In brief, the merit of Âsaf consisted only in the fact that (thanks to him) the "re-creation" in question was actualized in the presence of Solomon. . . .

When Bilqîs (thereafter came to visit Solomon and) saw her own throne there, she said: "It is as though (*ka'anna-hu*) it were (my throne)" (XXVII, 42). (She said "as though") because she knew the existence of a long distance (between the two places) and because she was convinced of the absolute impossibility of the throne's having been locally transported in such a (short) period of time. Her answer was quite correct in view of the above-mentioned idea of the "renewal of creation" in similar forms. And in reality it was (i.e., it was the same throne of hers in terms of its permanent archetype, but not as a concrete individual thing). And all this is true, just as you remain what you were in the past moments through the process of the perpetual re-creation.[32]

Quite incidentally, Ibn 'Arabî mentions in the passage just quoted the atomistic thesis of the Ash'arite theologians and points out the existence of a certain resemblance between his and their atomism. But what is more important and more interesting for our purpose is rather the difference between them which Ibn 'Arabî does not state explicitly in this passage, but which he explains in considerable detail in another part of the *Fusûs*.

The most salient feature of Ash'arite atomism is the thesis of the perpetual renewal (*tajdîd*) of accidents. According to this theory, of all the accidents of the things there is not even one that continues to exist for two units of time. Every accident comes into being at this moment and is annihilated at the very next moment to be replaced by another accident which is "similar" to it being created anew in the same locus. This is evidently the thesis of "new creation."

Now if we examine Ibn 'Arabî's thought in relation to this Ash'arite thesis, we find a striking similarity between them. Everything is, for Ibn 'Arabî, a phenomenal form of the Absolute, having no basis for independent subsistence (*qiwâm*) in itself. All are, in short, "accidents" which appear and disappear in the one eternal-

32. *Fus.*, p.197/ 156-157.

everlasting Substance (*jawhar*). Otherwise expressed, the existence itself of the Absolute comes into appearance at every moment in milliards of new clothes. With every Breath of God, a new world is created.

From the point of view of Ibn 'Arabî, the atomism of the Ash'arites, though it is not a perfect description of the real structure of Being, does grasp at least an important part of the reality. Mentioning together with the Ash'arites a group of sophists known as *Hisbâniyyah* or *Husbâniyyah*, he begins to criticize them in the following manner:[33]

> The Ash'arites have hit upon the truth concerning some of the existents, namely, accidents, while the Hisbânites have chanced to find the truth concerning the whole of the world. The Philosophers consider these people simply ignorant. But (they are not ignorant; the truth is rather that) they both (i.e., the Ash'arites and the Hisbânites) are mistaken.

First, he criticizes the sophists of the Hisbânite school. The Hisbânites maintain that nothing remains existent for two units of time, that everything in the world, whether it be substance or accident, is changing from moment to moment. From this they conclude that there is no Reality in the objective sense. Reality or Truth exists only subjectively, for it can be nothing other than the constant flux of things as you perceive it in a fixed form at this present moment.[34]

> Though the Hisbânites are right in maintaining that the world as a whole and in its entirety is in perpetual transformation, they are mistaken in that they fail to see the real oneness of the Substance which underlies all these (changing) forms. (They thereby overlook the fact that) the Substance could not exist (in the external world) if it were not for them (i.e., these changing forms) nor would the forms be conceivable if it were not for the Substance. If the Hisbânites could see this point too (in addition to the first point), their theory would be perfect with regard to this problem.[35]

33. *Fus.*, p.153/ 125.
34. The Name *Hisbâniyyah* is derived from the root HSB (the verb *hasiba*) meaning, "to opine," "to surmise," i.e., the subjective act of estimation. The appellation implies that Reality or Truth consists in the subjective estimation of this or that individual person, and that, consequently, there is no such thing as an objectively universal Truth (cf. Affifi, Com., p. 153).
35. *Fus.*, p.153/ 125.

Thus, for Ibn 'Arabî, the merit and demerit of the Hisbânite thesis are quite clear. They have hit upon a part of the truth in that they have seen the constant change of the world. But they overlook the most important part of the matter in that they do not know the true nature of the Reality which is the very substrate in which all these changes are happening, and consider it merely a subjective construct of each individual mind.

Concerning the Ash'arites, Ibn 'Arabî says:[36]

> As for the Ash'arites, they fail to see that the world in its entirety (including even the so-called "substances") is a sum of "accidents," and that, consequently, the whole world is changing from moment to moment since no "accident" (as they themselves hold) remains for two units of time.

And al-Qâshânî:[37]

> The Ash'arites do not know the reality of the world; namely, that the world is nothing other than the whole of all these "forms" which they call "accidents." Thus they only assert the existence of substances (i.e., atoms) which are in truth nothing, having no existence (in the real sense of the word). And they are not aware of the one Entity ( *'ayn*) which manifests itself in these forms ("accidents" as they call them); nor do they know that this one Entity is the He-ness of the Absolute. This is why they assert (only) the (perpetual) change of the accidents.

According to the basic thesis of the Ash'arite ontology, the world is reduced to an infinite number of "indivisible parts," i.e., atoms. These atoms are, in themselves, unknowable. They are knowable only in terms of the "accidents" that occur to them, one accident appearing in a locus at one moment and disappearing in the next to be replaced by another.

The point Ibn 'Arabî makes against this thesis is that these "accidents" that go on being born and annihilated in infinitely variegated forms are nothing but so many self-manifestations of the Absolute. And thus behind the kaleidoscopic scene of the perpetual changes and transformations there is always a Reality which is eternally "one." And it is this one Reality itself that goes on manifesting itself perpetually in ever-new forms. The Ash'arites who overlook the existence of this one Reality that underlies all "accidents" are,

36. *Fus.*, pp.153-154/ 125-126.
37. p.154.

according to Ibn 'Arabî, driven into the self-contradictory thesis that a collection of a number of transitory "accidents" that appear and disappear and never remain for two moments constitute "things" that subsist by themselves and continue to exist for a long time.

> This (i.e., the mistake of the Ash'arites) comes out clearly in their definitions of things. In fact, when they define anything, their definition turns the thing into (a collection of) accidents. And it is clear that it is all these accidents enumerated in the definition that constitute the very "substance" and its reality which (they consider to be) self-subsistent. However, even that substance (being a totality of the accidents) must ultimately be an accident, and as such it is not self-subsistent. Thus (in their theory) accidents which do not subsist by themselves, when put together, produce something that subsists by itself.[38]

The passage is explicated by al-Qâshânî as follows. The Ash'arites, whenever they define something, define it as a whole (*majmûʿ*) of accidents. Defining "man," for example, they say: "a rational animal." The word "rational" (*nâtiq*) means "possessed of reason" (*dhû nutq*). The concept of "being possessed of" is a relation, and "relation" is evidently an accident. "Reason" (*nutq*), on the other hand, being something added to the essence of "animal," is also an accident. Thus to say that man is "a rational animal" is to say that man is "an animal with two accidents." Then the Ash'arites go on to define "animal" by saying that it is a "physical body that grows, perceives, and moves by will." The "animal" turns in this way into a whole of accidents. And the same procedure is applied to the definition of the "(physical) body" appearing in the definition of "animal." As a result, "man" ultimately turns out to be a bundle of accidents which are by definition momentary and transitory. And yet this bundle itself is considered to be something subsistent by itself, a substance.

The Ash'arites, Ibn 'Arabî continues, are not aware of the fact that the very "substance," which they consider a self-subsistent entity, is of exactly the same nature as "man," "animal," and other things; it is also a bundle of accidents.

> Thus, in their theory, something (i.e., a bundle of *accidents*) which does not remain for two units of time remains (i.e., as a *bundle of*

38. pp.154-155/ 125-126.

accidents) for two units of time, nay, for many units of time! And something which does not subsist by itself (must be said to) subsist by itself, according to the Ash'arites! However, they do not know that they are contradicting themselves. So (I say that) these are people "who are in utter confusion with regard to the new creation."[39]

Ibn 'Arabî brings out the contrast between the "wrong" view of the Ash'arites and the "true" thesis upheld by the people of "unveiling" by saying:[40]

> As to the people of "unveiling," they see God manifesting Himself with every Breath, no single self-manifestation being repeated twice. They see also by an immediate vision that every single self-manifestation gives rise to a new creation and annihilates a creation (i.e., the "creation" that has preceded), and that the disappearance of the latter at every (new) self-manifestation is "annihilation" whereas "subsistence" is caused by what is furnished (immediately) by the following self-manifestation.

Thus in Ibn 'Arabîs thought, everything in the world (and therefore the world itself) is constantly changing, but underlying this universal flux of changing things there is Something eternally unchanging. Using scholastic terminology he calls this unchanging Something the "Substance," the absolute substratum of all changes. In this particular perspective, all things—not only the "accidents" so called but the "substances" so called—are represented as "accidents" appearing and disappearing at every moment. It is interesting to observe how the theory of Divine self-manifestation becomes transformed, when translated into the language of the scholastic philosophy of "substance" and "accident."

39. Fus., p.154/ 126.
40. *ibid.*

*You are plurality transformed into Unity.*
*And Unity passing into plurality:*
*This mystery is understood when man*
*Leaves the part and merges in the Whole.*

*— Shabistari*

*Chapter 10*

# Of Metaphysics and Polynesian Navigation

## *James Barr*

To begin, I must relate that although a seaman and a navigator, I am not an expert in ethnology, or in any related field: I make no claims on such modern Western attempts at "studying" other cultures. I did not attempt to read any ethnographic or anthropological material at all until long after I left the South Pacific. Essentially, these are my own observations, and if they contain error, then such is mine own responsibility. In order to study any aspect of any culture, one must attempt to come into the culture in question with the fewest preconceived ideas, with the least cultural baggage possible. One must endeavor to learn the language spoken by one's hosts as completely and thoroughly as possible; one must become completely immersed in the culture, without prejudice, and such is the method I employed.

The vastness of Oceania must be experienced in order to comprehend the greatness of the Polynesian achievement. Oceania is comprised of small islands and coral outcroppings, isolated by thousands of sea-miles of blue water.[1] On these isolated islands, the various groups of Polynesians were able to build quite remarkable cultures, based upon a sacred world-view.[2] In fact, the cultural differences between the various islands are slight enough that the Polynesians can be said to hold a more or less unified world-view, with only minor variations. In order to explain such a unity, one must

---

1. "Blue water" is a seaman's term (British in origin) for water over one hundred fathoms in depth. (One fathom is six feet.)
2. "Sacred world-view" is used here as employed by H.H. the Dalai Lama, to explain the way the phenomena of the world are viewed by traditional cultures. I use the term here because I choose to include the Polynesian cultural group as an Asiatic traditional culture. For material on the Asian origin of the Polynesian cultural group, see Peter Bellwood, *Man's Conquest of the Pacific: The Prehistory of Southeast Asia and Oceania* (Oxford: Oxford University Press, 1979), ch's. X-XIII.

needs look to the method of transportation used to cross the watery abyss. One must seek out the navigators and their craft.

On several occasions in the early 1980s, I chose to study with four men who held the craft of open sea navigation. These venerable gentlemen were Tranhei Théki (Maori), J.W. Kei (Tahiti), Jacques Koah (Bora Bora), and Matthew Burke Moi (Rorotonga and Western Samoa).[3] My studies, excepting those with Théki, all took the form of discourse while at sea, for I served as a deckhand and cook aboard their vessels.[4] Before my service, I had no idea that the art of navigation (in the traditional sense) was still alive in Oceania. Still less did I know the nature of the traditional Polynesian world, and its similarity to other systems with which I was familiar.[5]

I had boarded the schooner Vé in early 1980, intent upon visiting the Marquesas archipelago before returning to Vanatu and to work, and it did not take me long to notice that Captain Moi used no sextant, nor did he seem to own charts.[6] In fact, Captain Moi seemed to do little at all to determine our direction or position. I resolved to ask about this, and was informed that the swell, the color of the sea, the clouds, and the positions of the stars were his guides. I begged further information, and was informed that in order to learn I must know Samoan.

After I achieved proficiency in Samoan, I was able to hold various conversations with Captain Moi about his art. The captain was not particularly articulate about some of the art's finer aspects, but he did explain that there were three levels to it. Because there was

3. In order to learn anything whatever of the navigational art from these gentlemen, I was forced to learn their languages, even though Théki spoke English, and Kei, Koah and Moi spoke French. Of the four, only Moi was under age sixty.

4. Each of these men, with the exception of Théki, was in the shipping trade, using a sailing vessel to move cargo from one island to another. Their vessels were all about five hundred tons each, and were rigged as schooners or ketches. I was asked to work the rigging and to prepare meals as a crewman aboard these vessels. Théki is a traditional canoe builder and magician who resides in the various homes of his many relatives on the northern island of what is now termed New Zealand.

5. I have not attempted to write a treatise to this effect; however, I find Polynesian concepts regarding the sea similar to Celtic and Shinto understandings. I base this observation upon my own experience only.

6. "Work" was aboard a vessel of Black Cat Lines of Vanatu. I was not aboard my own vessel, "Scathacha," because she was in dry dock in Port Moresby, Papua New Guinea.

no specific set of terms used to define the process, I have chosen to use these: "literal," "moral," and "anagogical."[7]

The first level—the literal—entailed watching the clouds, the sea birds, the waves, and the color of the sea. To accomplish this one must clear the mind of all excess thought and focus one's full attention upon phenomena as they arise. I was made to understand that years of practice were involved in this process. One must be taught to "look," to "see" the subtle aspects of change, and to apply these to the task of direction finding.

Captain Moi could say very little as to the exact nature of the second level (moral) except that it involved the evocation of the sea deity. Tuaraati, the Ocean Lord, is addressed in a series of recited prayers, and a coconut is broken open, the juice of which is allowed to fall into the sea as a libation, while Tuaraati is asked to guide the mind of the navigator over his realm.[8] Captain Moi indicated that this was done directly, but he was unwilling to demonstrate. Of the third level I will speak in a moment.

In order to accomplish the first level of navigation, the navigator had to spend a great deal of time at sea, alone in a small canoe. During this period the practitioner was to recite various prayers and offer these to Tuaraati. Gradually the mind was said to be "filled with the sea," as the body is filled with blood.[9] On land, the navigator was taught the traditional chants which convey the information on natural phenomena needed to navigate. One's teacher was expected to impart these chants by memory and one was expected to commit them to memory verbatim. The corpus of these chants

7. Essentially these correspond to the Vajrayana Buddhist concepts of body, speech and mind, as well as to the "three worlds" of Hermetism. I use the term "anagogical" to mean the absolute level of reality, i.e., Brahma or Dharmakaya. In essence, this is the level wherein words become meaningless—empty—being beyond concepts. The term "moral" I use to indicate the level below the absolute, the subtle realm which is not solid, or rigid, yet draws one higher. And the term "literal" I use to indicate the physical world of solid manifestation—the gross level of manifestation.

8. The pouring of libations is essential in all forms of traditional theurgy. In the Polynesian system, libations correspond to the words of the priest (or navigator).

9. Literally, the term used was "heart," but as "heart" is used to indicate "consciousness," I have inserted the term "mind." I hope the reader will pardon me for my Buddhist interpretation, but I have found no other teaching to use which could render justice to the art of navigation.

was rather extensive, and years of study were required to learn the entire cycle.[10]

The natural phenomena one was taught to observe in order to navigate included the behavior of cetaceans, birds, and fish, wave actions, cloud formations, the taste of the water, and the positions of the stars. Small cetaceans are always attracted to the activities of humans at sea, and by watching them play about the vessel, the navigator is able to determine direction of passage and distance from land. The dolphins are said to abandon a vessel at the approach of heavy weather, and in the presence of reefs. In the open sea, the long-snouted spinner dolphin (stenella longirostris), the Pacific spotted dolphins, (stenella frontalis), and the common dolphin (delphinus delphis), are the cetaceans observed for purposes of navigation. Closer to archipelagos, the bottlenose dolphin (tursiops truncatus) is most often observed. In essence, the navigator "reads" the dolphins' speed and breaching patterns.

The navigator "reads" other creatures' patterns as well. Flying fish and squid indicate extreme depth (blue water), while Portuguese Man-o-war indicate great distance from land. Surface-feeding great white or hammerhead sharks indicate reefs nearby. Flocks of gulls indicate the presence of land nearby, though possibly out of sight, and by observing gulls' flight patterns, the navigator could determine both distance and direction of the land mass. Likewise, the Pacific albatross is carefully observed by the navigator, for the albatross is often sighted as much as forty miles from an archipelago, and its flight patterns are "read" in order to determine its course from land.

Additionally, the skilled navigator is able to recognize more than twenty distinct types of waves. Each of these has a separate and distinct name and function, and provides the navigator with information about direction, distance from land masses, and speed. Waves are directly associated with the winds, which are many in number and function as well. I was not told much by my mentors about these winds, as each is viewed as a very powerful

10. Navigators took over twenty years of study before they were able to master the art. I do not know whether this practice continues or not. I believe it does, but only on a very limited basis. Western ideas have put an end to much of Polynesian culture, and in the major island groups one is hard pressed to find anyone with even a smattering of traditional lore. The Christians have done their work well.

daemon,[11] knowledge of whom should not be imparted to the neophyte. These wind daemons are thought to be associated with the Lord of Waters as his companions.

Several varieties of cloud formation were used by my mentors to determine the position of archipelagos. The majority of these consisted of thunderheads, which form in the higher elevations of islands. Thunderheads formed over land look different to the trained observer than those formed over water. In general these clouds are seen as manifestations sent by the Lord of Waters to guide the navigator toward harbor. This is relatively similar to the Western mariner's ideas about St. Elmo's fire in storm conditions: both are seen as signs of Divine protection.

As to water's taste, I can say little, for though I watched Captain Moi taste water repeatedly, I have no idea how it is done. I tried it, but could taste only brine. Tasting the sea is an art.

As to the stars: the brightest stars in the southern hemisphere are Sirius in the constellation Canis Major, Canopis in the constellation Carina, Rigil Kentaurus in the constellation Centaurus, Rigel in Orion, and Fomalhaut in Piscis Austrinus. All of these are watched closely by navigators: Lamda, Mu, and Nu Scorpii are known to Polynesians as the "fishhook of Maui," Maui being a cultural hero, son of Tangaroa. Another important aid to navigation is the Southern Cross.

After teaching these aspects of the first, or literal level, Captain Moi was able to direct me to the navigator Jacques Koah of Bora Bora who was said to be a master of the system taught in that group of islands. Captain Koah was retired from a life at sea on board a small coastal freighter, and because he was fluent in French, we conversed in that language until I was able to pick up the local dialect.[12] From him I learned something of the second and third levels of navigation, for mastery of the "literal" and "moral" aspects depended upon one's understanding of the third level, the "anagogical."

---

11. Not to be confused with the demon (evil spirit) of the Judeo-Christian tradition. See the author's explanation of the daemon below which may be compared with the "tutelary spirit" (daemonian) of Socrates (see Plato's *Apology*, 31d; and *Republic*, 496c). *Ed.*

12. There are rather considerable differences between the various Polynesian languages, and I had to spend much time attempting to comprehend the structure and vocabulary of Bora Boran.

In order to enter this level, in order to have one's mind "filled with the sea," one must learn to "see with the heart," and to "breathe with the feet."[13] In essence, one must fill one's lungs to capacity and concentrate all one's attention upon the act of breathing. This must be done while in a vessel far enough from land that one can feel the rising and falling of the swells. One attunes one's breath to the swells, so that as the vessel is lifted, one inhales deeply, "all the way to the feet," and as the vessel descends, one must exhale slowly with the swell. By this practice one's mind "becomes the sea," and one is able to commune directly with the element, so that any change is noticed at once. One must "commune with the body of the Lord of Waves," so as to know His mind as one's own.[14]

One must call the Lord of the Sea (Tuaraati) and listen to His instruction via His body, and then "know His mind." "Knowing" Tuaraati, one then is able to know the "Supreme One" Tangaroa; "He is the One who sails your canoe."[15] One "knows" the sea, one "moves with it," and through Tangaroa via Tuaraati, one sails one's canoe to the destination.

But this is not all that one would have to know about the art of navigation, for Captain Koah mentioned the stars as well. He did not know how to commune with them, but he was able to indicate their nature. Essentially, the stars are living entities which can be approached if one's mind is "filled with the sea," as discussed above.[16] They must be approached via the Lord of Waves (Tuaraati) and known through Him. These beings are able to provide both direction (literal), and advice (moral), but they must be known or approached via the medium of the Lord of Waves, and hence Tangaroa (anagogical).

These star daemons are considered as separate entities, each with his own attributes and manifestations. The Fetia Virua Raa (sacred spirit stars) are associated with the stars Sirius, Lambda, Mu,

13. Here I have attempted to relay exactly what I heard from Captain Koah.

14. Literally: "To make his heart one's own." In essence, one's consciousness is made to "merge" with the element in every possible way.

15. Tangaroa is the supreme creator, rather like Brahma of the Hindu teaching. Tangaroa created the world with the aid of his female partner Huna (rather like Shiva and his Shakti). I can make nothing other than "gnosis" of Captain Koah's statements about Tangaroa. One's mind must be filled with the essence of Divinity, and so one sails in harmony with the currents of the world.

16. I can only interpret this as a kind of daemon which acts in harmony with the sea deity.

and Nu Scorpii (the "fishhook of Maui"), Fomalhaut, and Venus (known as Fetiapopoi Hiti). These Fetia Virua Raa can be evoked at sea in time of need, though the actual theurgical rite I do not know. On the whole, they are very *tapu*, very *Raa* (sacred), but are not *Mau Atu* (gods), rather being angelic in nature. In Samoan these beings are *Agaga fetu* (star spirits).

No doubt to be a full practitioner of this navigational art, one must be spiritually transformed and purified. Captain Koah said that the navigator was a very *tapu* person who must only eat a diet specified by tradition, and must follow a very strict code.[17]

In order to verify his understanding, Captain Koah consulted with Captain Kei of Tahiti, the skipper of the Moa, a trading ketch. Neither of these gentlemen would attempt to explain the actual method of practice, but both were obviously adept at it. Eventually they passed me into the hands of Théki , a Maori practitioner who spent time on Tahiti, and in the Bora Bora area.

Théki was able to describe to me the process of breathing in order to allow ones mind to enter into harmony with the sea, though he would impart little else. The spiritual nature of this art has not totally escaped me, but again I have no words with which I can describe it. Gradually I gained a modicum of his trust by discussing my conversion to Buddhism, a religion of which he had heard, and knew to be non-Western. Théki said that his people, and all the other Polynesian peoples had been harried by Christian missionaries and by anthropologists, and what little remained of their traditions could not be transferred to a person not of their culture. He would teach only the bare fundamentals, and not a word more.

I was taken out in a small yacht tender, and asked to sit quietly and watch the sea. After two weeks of this practice, I was taken out of sight of land in a canoe. On this occasion I was asked to watch the swell, to feel the vessel rise and to breathe with it as it rose and fell. After a time, the effect was rather like the practice of zazen.[18] Other than this, I have no words that can describe my experience.

17. Unfortunately, none of the details of either diet or code were imparted to me.
18. I do not wish this statement to be taken literally. Zazen—Zen Buddhist meditation—is the closest experiential situation I have had with which the experience at sea could be compared. rDzog Chen—a meditation praxis in Tibetan Buddhism—is utterly different.

The spiritual nature of this art has not totally escaped me, but again I have no words with which I can describe it. I have learnt to some degree how to apply the art of navigation, yet I am not skilled enough to stop using the sextant. Still, I believe that if followed correctly, the traditional art of navigation could indeed be a means toward understanding many truths. Unfortunately, I cannot hope to complete a course of training, and so must base my conclusions upon my very poor understanding alone. No doubt in some ancient time the Pacific peoples were either influenced by, or a part of the great Primordial tradition, and this being the case, we can only wonder at what was destroyed by Western encroachment and conquest. Indeed, I shall never know, nor shall any European fully know the extent of what might have been in that watery civilization of the past.

### Eskimo: The Great Sea

*The great sea*
*Has sent me adrift,*
*It moves me as the weed in a great river,*
*Earth and the great weather*
*Move me,*
*Have carried me away*
*And move my inward parts with joy.*

*Chapter 11*

# The Underlying Order:
# Nature and the Imagination

## *Kathleen Raine*

It is heartening to see that at last the long unquestioned assumptions of naive materialism that have dominated the modern Western world are beginning to seem less certain, less self-evident than they were even a few years ago. When I was a student—more than fifty years ago—I was torn between two possible choices. I intended to be a poet—that was certain—and it seemed therefore obvious to those who advised me that I should read English literature at university. But to me this was by no means obvious—why need to be taught how to read the literature of one's own language when books were available in libraries? I felt I had no need to seek the opinions of others on my fellow-writers, and I have had no reason to regret my decision to read instead natural sciences. For that was the other alternative. Always, from infancy—and in this I was perhaps no different from every child born into this marvelous world—nature had been my passion, and I thought I could best learn to contemplate and know its inexhaustible order and meaning by becoming a botanist or a marine biologist. But my love of nature was really a poet's love for meaning and beauty, rather than for fact or for manipulations and applications of scientific knowledge for practical ends. I found great delight in my studies of nature at that time, in contemplating that order and beauty that is to be found throughout the whole structure of the world, whether as it appears to the eye, or in those minute worlds revealed by microscope or beyond the visible altogether. But my love of these things was a poet's love first and last. When a year or two ago one of my grand-daughters showed me one of her examination papers in

---

* Editor's Note: This paper was originally written for the 1985 Conference of the Center for Spiritual Studies, whose theme was The Underlying Unity.

botany and asked me which questions I could answer, I had to say that once I could have answered question 4 but that at no time any of the others! For science, knowledge is ever changing; what is "knowledge" when we are young is no longer so when we are old.

But poetry and the other arts relate to the everlasting. One might say that all art is contemporaneous, the cave-paintings of Lascaux with those of Ajanta and Ellora; Greek classical sculpture with that of Chartres; the music of Monteverdi is not superseded by that of Mozart or of Wagner; Murasaki is as close to us as Marcel, the people of Shakespeare, with Homer's Hector and Achilles, with Rama and Arjuna, and all these are ourselves.

Orthodoxy, in our world, means scientific orthodoxy, and although the conclusions of science in some particular area may be open to question, the premises of the materialist ideology are not. To question these is to invite exclusion from any discussion whatsoever. As I understand it, science as we know it presumes a universe which consists of something called "matter," which, whatever else may be said about it, is measurable, quantifiable, and constitutes an ordered and autonomous system, coherent and unified in all its parts and as a whole, the space-time continuum of the universe. Newton—and psychologically do we not still live in the Newtonian era?—conceived the material universe to be a mechanism functioning autonomously by the so-called "laws of nature" which are the Ten Commandments, so to speak, of science. Within this great self-coherent order, value judgments are superfluous. It is "unscientific" to attribute to "nature" any purposes, or qualities; any of those invisible and immeasurable human qualities such as joy and sorrow and love, or meaning of whatever kind. The human mind, according to Locke (the philosopher of the Newtonian system) thus becomes "passive before a mechanized nature." These words are Yeats's, who was a disciple of Blake, the sole lonely prophet to call in question, at the end of the eighteenth century, this whole structure of thought.

Thus the materialist hypothesis—for it is no more—attributes order and reality to the outer world, leaving mind itself, consciousness itself, as the mere mirror or receptacle of impressions. All knowledge comes from without, the mind of an infant is a blank page on which these impressions can be written. Even now the *reductio ad absurdum* of this theory—behaviorism—keeps its hold on transatlantic thought. At this point human beings are themselves conceived as mechanisms activated by so-called reflexes—mindless parts of a mindless material order, with consciousness itself degraded to a mere attribute of matter. Paradoxically—and no wonder—transatlantic mythology shows a marked tendency to treat machines as if these possessed human qualities, computers as if they possessed "knowledge," even as the brain is treated as a short-lived computer. Such assumptions, consciously or unconsciously held, continue in a large measure to determine the kind and quality of the world we live in—the products of the machines, and all the advertising that goes with the age of the multinationals, all the direct or indirect propaganda for material values. Yet we are in reality living in a world whose assumptions and values rest on the no-longer tenable hypothesis that "nature" operates in independence of the perceiving mind, and is itself the source and the object of all knowledge. The great regions of consciousness itself are deemed unreal because immeasurable. The mind is popularly identified with the brain; knowledge is stored away in right or left lobes as it is in a computer; you can tell that people are meditating or dreaming by affixing electrical apparatus to their heads, but what does that tell us of *what* is thought, or of the dream itself, or of the *experience* of meditation? Nothing at all. The human kingdom—the kingdom of consciousness—is excluded by definitions which see the real as identical with the measurable. It is not our conclusions but our premises that are false. We might even reverse them and say that reality is what we experience, and that all experience is immeasurable.

According to another view—and we must remember that this is the view the Eastern world, in various forms, has held over millennia—"nature" is a system of appearances whose ground is consciousness itself. Science measures the phenomena which we perceive, and which Indian philosophical systems call *maya. Maya* has sometimes been termed illusion, but it is, more exactly, appearances. Blake used the word "visions": this world, he wrote, "is one continued vision of fancy or imagination." But if the materialist premises are reversed, then "reality" is not material fact but meaning itself. And it follows that in those civilizations grounded on this premise—our own included, up to the Renaissance—the arts, as expressions of the value-systems of a culture, have been held in high regard as expressions of knowledge of the highest order. Is not our human kingdom in its very nature a universe of meanings and values? For these are inherent in life itself, as such, the Vedantic *sat-chit-ananda*, being-consciousness-bliss: being *is* consciousness, and the third term *ananda* (bliss) is the ultimate value of being and consciousness. We are made for beatitude, as the theologians would say; Freud, indeed, said something not dissimilar when he spoke of the fundamental nature of "the pleasure principle" as the goal all seek. Plotinus wrote of "felicity" as the goal and natural term of all life, and attributed it not only to man and animals but to plants also. Beatitude—felicity—is not an accident of being and consciousness: it is our very nature to seek, and to attain, joy; and it is for the arts to hold before us images of our eternal nature, through which we may awaken to, and grow towards, that reality which is our humanity itself.

This view of reality Blake defended in its darkest hour, at the end of the rationalist eighteenth century and the beginning of the materialist nineteenth. Few heeded him or understood him when he said, "all that I see is vision" and "to me this world is one continued vision of imagination." That is the sort of thing unpractical poets and painters do say! But Blake was in earnest and spoke as a metaphysician sure of his ground when he wrote of the living sun:

> "What," it will be Questioned, "When the Sun rises, do you not see A round disk of fire somewhat like a Guinea?" O no, no, I see an Innumerable company of the Heavenly host crying "Holy, Holy, Holy Is the Lord God Almighty." I question not my Corporeal or Vegetative Eye any more than I would Question a Window concerning A Sight. I look thro' it and not with it.[1]

Plato had used the same words about looking "through not with" the eye. And what else, after all, could that innumerable multitude of beings proclaim, being themselves not objects in a lifeless mechanism, but an epiphany of life which not only has, but is, being, consciousness and bliss? The real, therefore, is ultimately—and this again has been understood by all traditions—not an object but a Person. A "Person" in this sense not by a human act of personification of something in its innate reality neither living nor conscious; but rather human "persons" are a manifestation in multitude of the single Person of Being itself, from which consciousness and meaning are inseparable, these being innate qualities of life itself,

---

1. Geoffrey Langdon Keynes, ed., "A Vision of the Last Judgment" from *The Complete Writings of William Blake* (London, Oxford University Press, 1966), p.617.

as such. Not "life" as a property of matter, but life as experienced. "Everything that lives is holy" summarizes Blake's total vision of reality—not holy because we choose to think it so, but intrinsically so. The "holy" is, again, a reality that cannot be defined but can be experienced as the ultimate knowledge of consciousness. It cannot be measured, but neither can it be denied, if by knowledge we mean what is experienced. Within the scope of human experience there are degrees of knowledge and value, self-authenticating, of which those who have reached the farthest regions tell us, the vision of the holy, and the beatitude of that vision is the highest term. And therefore Blake's stars and grains of sand can say no other than "Holy, Holy, Holy."

> To see a World in a Grain of Sand
> And a Heaven in a Wild Flower,
> Hold Infinity in the palm of your hand
> And Eternity in an hour.[2]

That is not poetic fancy: it is profoundest knowledge.

How deeply we are all immersed in the world of duality is clear in the bewilderment we must all share through our Western conditioning in the matter of "inner" and "outer." Blake was very clear in his understanding that the externalization of nature is a tragic consequence of what he called the "wrenching apart" of the apparently external world from the unity of the wholeness of being. This has created an unhealed wound in the soul of modern Western man, leaving nature soulless and lifeless, and the inner world abstracted from the natural universe, its proper home. In the *unus mundus* the very terms "inner" and "outer" are not applicable at all. Both soul and nature have suffered; nature by being banished, in Blake's words, "outside existence" in "a soul-shuddering vacuum," natural space. At the same time the soul can no longer inhabit nature, and the "afterlife" is situated—again in Blake's words—"in an allegoric abode where existence has never come." But, for the universal spiritual teaching, mind is not in space, but space in mind. "Nothing," as it is said in the *Hermetica*, "is more capacious than the incorporeal."

It is hard to reverse the more or less unconscious assumptions of a culture, and to turn our heads, like the prisoners in Plato's Cave

2. *Ibid*, p.431, "Auguries of Innocence."

who had taken the shadows of things for realities and were at first dazzled and bewildered by the light. But such a reversal—and more and more leading scientists are themselves coming to think so—the times demand, not of a learned few but of the world as a whole. Science itself has come full circle to this confrontation with the observing mind as an element in the phenomena observed. Many can see clearly, and many more obscurely feel, that some essential thing is lacking in our ways of life and thought. We have reached this confrontation; and I believe a change of the premises of our civilization is about to take place, that naive realism is already an obsolete hypothesis and—again the words are Yeats's—"wisdom and poetry return." Nothing in history is static and we are moved by invisible powers, call these what we will.

What is only now dawning on the Western mind was already plain to William Blake, when he wrote:

> . . . in your own bosom you bear your heaven
> And Earth and all you behold.
> Tho' it appears Without it is Within,
> In your Imagination, of which this World of Mortality is but a
> Shadow.[3]

A shadow, an image in a mirror; "for now we see in a glass, darkly, but there face to face."

"Matter" is in any case—and this the scientists themselves have taught us—such a mysterious and insubstantial thing, if it exists, as such, at all. That stone Dr Johnson kicked seemed to him real and solid enough when he said with such naive assurance (referring to Berkeley, who held the same view as Blake and the Neoplatonists and the *Hermetica*), "thus I refute him." All those spinning fields of force the scientists tell us of seem far from Dr Johnson's stone, and much nearer to "matter" as Plotinus understood it, as a shadowy *non-ens* which, the more we pursue, the more it recedes into its "labyrinths" of mystery. No-one knows what matter is in its ultimate nature. Stones were quite solid for Berkeley also, and tulips quite real, but for different reasons: because he saw them. And we too have to realize, in Yeats's words (referring to Berkeley) that:

> This preposterous, pragmatical pig of a world, its farrow that so
> solid seem

---

3. *Ibid*, p.709, "Jerusalem," plate 71, lines 46-9.

Would vanish on the instant, did the mind but change its theme.[4]

—the mind that is, in the words of Laurens van der Post's bushmen, "a dream dreaming us."

You may ask if it really matters whether we believe nature to be a mechanism outside mind and consciousness, or hold the opposite view, that it is an ever-changing panorama passing through our minds, a *maya*. Do we not all see the same world, whatever we may think about it? I suggest that though the sense-impressions may be the same, the experiences are different. The difference is between the factual observation and a living encounter. To the materialist the natural world is other, it is mindless, lifeless, meaningless. With the advent of materialism, consciousness itself changes, as Blake understood when he wrote, "They behold/ What is within now seen without," and this externalized nature becomes "far remote, in a little and dark land," where all is diminished and emptied of meaning and value. But once the ground is removed from the observed object to the observing mind, that "wrenching apart" of outer and inner of which Blake spoke is healed. The universe is then not alien to us; in Martin Buber's words, it is no longer an "I-it" but an "I-thou" relationship. The universe is one with us not merely in the sense in which the matter of our bodies is continuous with the entire material system, but in quite another sense nature lives with our lives, it "comes alive," it has meaning, qualities, and a kinship with us. Nothing in nature is alien to our moods and thoughts, our aspirations and sorrows, our delights and laughter; all find in nature their language. We can love our world, we experience everything as a kind of unending dialogue, and not with sentient beings only but with sun and mountains and trees and stones. They tell us those things which constitute our wisdom in a way far deeper than the mere measurement of scientific experiment. We are one with nature not merely as insignificant parts in a vast mechanism, or as detached observers of its phenomena: nature itself becomes a region of our humanity. It becomes, in other words, human. It is our world, created for us, with us, by us, and it lives with our life.

Of course consciousness cannot be transformed by a mere change of opinion; rather it involves a change of our whole recep-

4. W.B. Yeats, "Blood and the Moon" from *Collected Poems* (New York, Macmillan, 1956), p.268.

tivity, an opening of the heart, the senses and the imagination. Consciousness is in the Vedantic writings described as synonymous with being, and being with bliss: *sat-chit-ananda.* Bliss is a word Blake also used, and he too associated it with the principle of life itself:

> And trees and birds and beasts and men behold their eternal joy.
> Arise, you little glancing wings, and sing your infant joy!
> Arise, and drink your bliss, for every thing that lives is holy.[5]

Plotinus writes of "felicity" as proper to all living beings, animals and plants no less than humanity, when these attain the fullness of their development, as a plant expands in the sun. Consciousness and nature are not two separate orders, but one and indivisible; to know this, to experience this, is to heal the divided consciousness, in modern jargon the "schizophrenia" of modern secular thought, which since the Renaissance has grown ever deeper. It is to restore a lost wholeness, the *unus mundus,* that unity of inner and outer, nature and the soul, sought by the alchemists. It is the secret that can transform crude matter into the gold of the "philosopher's stone," into something of infinite value.

Is it not, besides, an experience very familiar to us, for in childhood did we not know instinctively the values and meanings of all we saw? Can we not all remember a time when not only did we talk to animals and birds and plants and stones and stars and sun and moon, but they to us? C.S. Lewis in his Narnia children's books writes of "talking animals," who communicate meaning, not perhaps in words, but none the less clearly and unmistakably. One of the disastrous consequences, as Blake saw it, of the materialist philosophy is that we could no longer communicate with the things of nature:

> . . . a Rock, a Cloud, a Mountain
> Were now not Vocal as in Climes of Happy Eternity
> Where the lamb replies to the infant voice, and the lion to the
> man of years
> Giving them sweet instructions; where the Cloud, the River and
> the Field
> Talk with the husbandman and shepherd.[6]

---

5. Geoffrey Langdon Keynes, ed., *op.cit.,* p.195, "Visions of the Daughters of Albion," plate 8.
6. *Ibid,* p.315, "Vala VI," lines 134-7.

The natural world "wanders away" into the "far remote," and the animals "build a habitation separate from man." "The stars flee remote . . . and all the mountains and hills shrink up like a withering gourd." These are not changes in the object but in the consciousness of the perceiver.

Blake addresses one of the four sections of his last great prophetic book, *Jerusalem*, "To the Jews" and appeals to the Jewish esoteric tradition of the primordial man, Adam Kadmon, when he writes:

> You have a tradition that man anciently contain'd in his mighty limbs all things in Heaven and Earth: this you received from the Druids. "But now the Starry Heavens are fled from the mighty limbs of Albion."[7]

—the Giant Albion, who is the English national being: we are Albion.

To those unaccustomed to the symbolic language in which alone it is possible to speak of invisible realities this may seem remote from anything that can concern us today. In fact this is by no means so, and the esoteric teaching that "'Man anciently contain'd in his mighty limbs all things in Heaven and Earth" is perhaps only now becoming comprehensible in terms other than mythological. Blake, here as throughout his writings, is taking issue with the materialist philosophy that separates all things in heaven and earth from the "body" of man.

Let us examine what he is in reality saying. The human "body" as Blake uses the term is much more than the physical frame, to which indeed Blake always refers as "the garment not the man." In this respect he is following Swedenborg, his earliest master, who is himself drawing on that primordial tradition to which Blake refers. Plato wrote that "the true man" is intellect; Blake changed the term to "imagination," which he called "the true man." Under either term the meaning is that man is not merely his physical but his mental and spiritual being. According to Swedenborg this human "body" is neither large nor small, not being in space at all; it is a spiritual and mental body which is not contained in the material universe. Mind is not in space, but space in mind, which contains the entire universe that we see, hear, touch and know. This "body" Swe-

---

7. *Ibid*, p.649, "Jerusalem II," plate 27.

denborg called the "Divine Humanity," a phrase most of us associate rather with Blake, who borrowed it, and identified the term (as did Swedenborg) with the Eternal Christ, Blake's "Jesus, the Imagination." "This world of Imagination is the world of Eternity," Blake writes, "All Things are comprehended in their Eternal Forms in the divine body of the Savior, the True Vine of Eternity, the Human Imagination."[8] "I am the true vine," Jesus says, "I am the vine and ye are the branches"; and so the mystics have ever understood his words. All humanity is incorporated within this great spiritual organism; not a mechanism but being, living and conscious, a "person," whom Swedenborg described as "the Grand Man of the Heavens," the collective spiritual being of all humanity.

Some of you may here recall Plato's parable of the first human beings, who were spherical. And it seems that this was more than a joke by Aristophanes at the banquet; for is not the universe of the scientists said to be spherical because of the curvature of the path of light? And is not each of us, in this sense, the center of a spherical universe which "contains all things in heaven and earth?" And as all see the same sun, so from our myriad centers we each contain not a part of the universe but the whole. It is this tradition—the primordial tradition of that first religion of all humanity that Blake attributes, rightly or wrongly, to "the Druids," that Blake in his address "To the Jews" recalls. In symbolic terms the Jewish Adam Kadmon, humanity as first created "in the image of God," is the same as Blake's and Swedenborg's "Divine Humanity," and the Christian's mystical body of Christ present in and to every created human individual. Man in reality still contains in his mighty limbs all things in heaven and earth but through the "wrenching apart" of inner and outer worlds, the "mortal worm," the "worm of sixty winters" has lost his spiritual body and his universe is all outside him. It is through the materialist philosophy that modern man has come to this pass, summed up in Blake's line:

> But now the starry heavens have fled from the mighty limbs of Albion.[9]

Albion is the English nation, and it is in England that Bacon, Newton and Locke (whom Blake holds responsible for the

---

8. *Ibid*, pp.605-6, "Vision of the Last Judgment."
9. *Ibid*, p.649, "Jerusalem II," plate 27.

"wrenching apart") elaborated the materialist system which has since overspread the whole world. (There was of course also Descartes, but Blake was an Englishman.) The "starry heavens" are Newton's especial domain; and by, as Blake understood the matter, separating the stars from the mountains, the mountains from man, and postulating a space-time universe outside mind itself, man becomes only "a little groveling root outside of himself," and the physical body, which is in reality only a "form and organ" of boundless life, seems all. How differently the world appears when the rift between man and his universe is healed, Blake has sought to express in the poem *Milton*, whose theme is the world of imagination. Answering Newton, for whom space is an external system, Blake writes of the same universe seen as within the human imagination. "The Sky is an Immortal Tent," he wrote:

> And every Space that a Man views around his dwelling-place
> Standing on his own roof or in his garden on a mount
> Of twenty-five cubits in height, such space is his Universe:
> And on its verge the sun rises and sets, the Clouds bow
> To meet the flat Earth and the Sea in such an order'd Space:
> The Starry heavens reach on further, but here bend and set
> On all sides, and the two Poles turn on their valves of gold:
> And if he move his dwelling-place, his heavens also move
> Where'er he goes, and all his neighborhood bewail his loss.
> Such are the Spaces called Earth and such its dimension.[10]

Spaces are, according to Blake, "visionary," and time and space come into being by the creative power of the imagination, measured out "to mortal man every morning." For him it is all so very simple, not at all because he took issue with Newton on the "facts" or arguments of his system (which within its own terms is not to be faulted) but because his premises were quite other.

Teilhard de Chardin has made an attempt to situate the theory of evolution within a spiritual rather than a materialist context; the divine humanity (to use Blake's term) is implicit in the alpha, to emerge as the omega of creation by the One who says "I am alpha and omega, the first and the last." Naive materialism must deem man an accident in a blind mechanism. Somehow the less can produce the greater by the laws of chance. Was it Bertrand Russell who calculated the chances of a thousand monkeys at a thousand type-

10. *Ibid*, p.516, "Milton," plate 29, lines 4-13.

writers producing the plays of Shakespeare? Absurd as the notion is, it is a calculation that has to be made by those who deny spiritual cause. It seems self-evident that a mechanism cannot produce spirit; but spirit can embody itself. The greater can produce the less, but the less cannot produce the greater, nor can the laws of chance write the plays of Shakespeare, who could write, on this very subject,

> What a piece of work is man! How noble in reason! How infinite in faculty! In form, in moving, how express and admirable! In action how like an angel! In apprehension, how like a god! the beauty of the world! the paragon of animals! And yet, to me, what is this quintessence of dust!

Can dust of itself produce such a quintessence? The materialist would have it so; and Blake, with his genius for going to the heart of things, saw no third alternative: "Man is either the ark of God or a phantom of the earth and of the water." If the naive materialist supposes that "nature" can produce man, that man is a product of nature, sacred tradition sees, on the contrary, "nature" as the domain of man.

Blake insisted continually on the "human" character of the natural world, in its whole and in its parts; for "nature" is the human imagination when understood not as a mechanism but as a "vision," a reflection of the one living and indivisible universe.

> ... Each grain of sand,
> Every stone on the Land,
> Each rock and each hill,
> Each fountain and rill,
> Each herb and each tree,
> Mountain, hill, earth and sea,
> Cloud, Meteor and Star
> Are Men Seen Afar.[11]

"All is Human, Mighty, Divine," he wrote; not in an excess of emotion but with the certitude of a profound understanding.

Swedenborg—who as we have seen was in the eighteenth century the principal defender of this mode of thought—elaborated his famous theory of "correspondences." If every creature is seen as the "correspondence" of its inner nature—for such is Swedenborg's teaching—we find in the outer world continually and everywhere, in beasts and birds down to the minutest insects, the expression of

---

11. *Ibid*, p.805, "Letter to Thomas Butts," 2 Oct. 1800.

"spirits of different orders and capacities" whose outer forms bear the imprint of their living natures. Swedenborg was by profession a scientist (he was Assessor of Minerals to the Swedish Government) and his pages on the rich variety of living creatures, understood as "correspondences" of states of being, certainly inspired Blake, who in his battle against materialism does not fail to make use of this view of nature as an expression of the living Imagination. He too presents the creatures not as objects but as forms of life:

> Does the whale worship at thy footsteps as the hungry dog;
> Or does he scent the mountain prey because his nostrils wide
> Draw in the ocean? does his eye discern the flying cloud
> As the raven's eye? or does he measure the expanse like the vulture?
> Does the still spider view the cliffs where eagles hide their young;
> Or does the fly rejoice because the harvest is brought in?
> Does not the eagle scorn the earth and despise the treasures beneath?
> But the mole knoweth what is there, and the worm shall tell it thee.
> Does not the worm erect a pillar in the moldering church yard
> And a palace of eternity in the jaws of the hungry grave?[12]

Everything in nature has its inner no less than its outer being. The "mortal worm" is "translucent all within" and of "the little winged fly smaller than a grain of sand," Blake writes:

> It has a heart like thee, a brain open to heaven and hell,
> With inside wondrous and expansive; its gates are not clos'd:
> I hope thine are not: hence it clothes itself in rich array:
> Hence thou art cloth'd with human beauty, O thou mortal man.[13]

Yet another version of the figure of the Universal Man who contains in himself all things—Blake's Divine Humanity, the Imagination, is the One distributed in the Many, like the Egyptian God Osiris, scattered throughout the universe, whose "body" is reassembled by the devotion of his wife Isis:

> So man looks out in tree and herb and fish and bird and beast
> Collecting up the scatter'd portions of his immortal body
> into the Elemental forms of every thing that grows. . . .
> In pain he sighs, in pain he labors in his universe,
> Screaming in birds over the deep, and howling in the wolf

12. *Ibid*, p.193, "Vision of the Daughters of Albion," plate 5, lines 33-41.
13. *Ibid*, p.502, "Milton," plate 20, lines 28-31.

Over the slain, and moaning in the cattle, and in the winds . . .
his voice
is heard throughout the Universe: wherever a grass grows
Or a leaf buds, The Eternal Man is seen, is heard, is felt,
And all his sorrows, till he reassumes his ancient bliss.[14]

Blake is following the Swedenborgian doctrine of "correspondences" which is, of course, a continuation of the earlier Alchemical
and Astrological doctrine of "signatures." Everything in nature,
according to this pre-materialist view, bears in its outer form the
"signature" of its qualities. Plants, animals, minerals are classified
according to their qualities by an elaborate system of "signatures"
from planets and the houses of the Zodiac, themselves deemed to
be under the guidance of heavenly influences. Albeit modern
thought has discarded the literal interpretation of these influences
as coming from "the stars" or planets in a physical sense, nevertheless this older cosmology can be understood as a projection of the
Imagination into the natural universe, a model of the *unus mundus*
which affirms the intrinsic qualities and order of the visible world.
Applied to human nature astrological correspondences similarly
describe and affirm the unity of inner and outer, man the microcosm within the macrocosm of the universe. Or, as Blake and Swedenborg would have it, the outer universe is within man. Dismissed
as an inexact and rudimentary science, are we not now obliged to
re-examine alchemy, astrology and the rest—as C.G. Jung has
done—as pertaining rather to our inner universe, and to the indi-
visibility of inner and outer? As the alchemists, and before them the
Neoplatonists understood, "nature" is a mirror, a looking-glass in
which we see reflected everything that is, and everything we are. We
are once more in a living universe, a universe moreover whose life
is not alien to us but indistinguishable, inseparable, part and parcel
of what we ourselves are. This, it seems to me, is the point at which
we, at this time, are; where human knowledge has brought us. I suggest that we are not in a phase of further development of materialist
science in directions already foreseeable, but at the moment of a
reversal of premises, a change of direction. Not, indeed, that anything of the scientific observation of the natural phenomena will be
denied or invalidated; science in the modern sense is one of the
ways of observing the world, nor is it necessary in order to study

14. *Ibid*, p.355-6, "Vala VIII," lines 561-83.

what Owen Barfield many years ago named the "appearances" to accept the materialist standpoint. The greater knowledge does not invalidate the partial, but can include it. It is the claim of the natural sciences to be that all-inclusive knowledge that is no longer tenable.

Would such a change—will such a change—or dare I say, *is* such a change—a venture into a new and unknown experience, or is it not rather something already familiar, which in our heart of hearts we already know? There have been societies, indeed civilizations, where the unity and wholeness of being which our own has gradually lost, has been understood by the wise and the simple alike. Blake supposes it to be man's primordial condition to contain in his mighty limbs all things in heaven and earth. Have we not all read Laurens van der Post's poignant accounts of the doomed African Bushmen whose physical survival was precarious indeed, but who felt themselves, so he tells us, to be perfectly at one with their world, because nothing in that world was alien to them, nothing without meaning? I quote from his latest book *Testament to the Bushmen*:

> The essence of this being, I believe, was his sense of belonging: belonging to nature, the universe, life and his own humanity. He had committed himself utterly to nature as a fish to the sea. He had no sense whatsoever of property, owned no animals and cultivated no land. Life and nature owned all and he accepted without question that, provided he was obedient to the urge of the world within him, the world without, which was not separate in his spirit, would provide. How right he was is proved by the fact that nature was kinder to him by far than civilization ever was. This feeling of belonging set him apart from us on the far side of the deepest divide in the human spirit.

And Laurens van der Post goes on to write:

> We were rich and powerful where he was poor and vulnerable: he was rich where we were poor, and his spirit led to strange water for which we secretly longed. But, above all, he came to our estranged and divided vision, confident in his belonging and clothed as brightly as Joseph's coat of dream colors in his own unique experience of life.

Above all the Bushman experienced always "the feeling of being known." And the author confesses that he himself experienced an overwhelming sense of nostalgia:

for this shining sense of belonging, of being known and possessing a cosmic identity of one's own, recognized by all from insect to sun, moon and stars which kept him company, so that he felt he had the power to influence them as they influenced and helped him.

Earth was not only the Bushmen's home, source of material nourishment and shelter, but also of their spiritual food. The earth is full of meaning; tells them those marvelous stories of Mantis and the Lynx and the Morning Star, of lizard and beetle and wild freesia, living in their rich and manifold lives some one or other aspect of the world's one and indivisible being. As Blake says, earth would "talk" with the husbandman and the shepherd. All is a subtle, profound, mirthful and delightful continuous epiphany of the great mystery in which we live and move and have our being.

With this imaginative apprehension goes always a sense of the sacred; for the sacred is an experience of a certain kind, precluded by the materialist mentality whose world is a lifeless world. But for primitive peoples of all times and places—the Australian aborigines no less than the indigenous North American peoples—Blake's words are true, that "everything that lives is holy." Sacred rocks, sacred trees, sacred animals and totem birds and holy mountains. But where are the holy places of the modern technological world? But do we need holy places, all those sacred springs and wells and rivers and trees and anthills and caverns and mountains where the gods live? I would reply that, since we have the capacity to experience awe and wonder and love, these are within the range of human experience without whose use we are diminished, as by blindness or deafness. Modern secular man finds no burning bush, no Presence which commands "Take thye shoes from off thye feet for the place whereon thou standest is holy ground." But in losing the capacity for awe, for wonder, for the sense of the numinous, the sacred, what we lose is not the object but that part of ourselves which can find in trees or churinga-stone or the dread cavern of the pythoness the correspondence of an aspect of our humanity of which these are the objective correlative, the correspondence, the mirror, the "signature." The Presence that spoke to Moses from the Burning Bush speaks on in every age: "I am that I am." A mystery insoluble!

For the secular mind, in common modern parlance, a "mystery" is a problem to be solved, a puzzle in the manner of a Sherlock Holmes story in which something that seems frightening, inexplicable, or mysterious proves after all to be simple, explicable and trivial. Such is the reductionist spirit of our culture that has invented Sherlock Holmes as the embodiment of the prevalent reductionist mentality. That shallow rationalism can exorcise the Hound of the Baskervilles or the Speckled Band for us. Yet they live on in the depths. The terror that they evoke is more real than the exorcisms that banish them. But to a child a pebble can speak, or a withered leaf, or the eye of a bird, or a tree or a running stream, the cosmic word "I am that I am." For these are Presences, not objects merely, as to the "detached" mind of the investigator. Have we not all memories of this world of presences, fearsome and beautiful—infinitely strange and infinitely familiar?

We will never, certainly—nor should we wish to do so—return to the innocent world of the Stone Age. We can never un-know what the scientific investigation of nature has presented to us. It has described in the minutest detail and the grandest scope that image in the "vegetable glass of nature." But until we have experienced the unity of all things not as a natural fact but as a living presence we shall never, in the early mystic Traherne's words, know the world "aright."

What this learned and cultured divine has written re-echoes down the ages from the Stone Age to ourselves:

> You never enjoy the world aright, till the sea itself floweth in your veins, till you are clothed with the heavens, and crowned with the stars: and perceive yourself to be the sole heir of the whole world, and more . . . because men are in it who are every one of them sole heirs as well as you . . . Till your spirit fills the whole world, and the stars are your jewels.[15]

In our secular world it is customary to look at scientists for truth, to the arts for entertainment: I suggest that this attitude is deeply mistaken. Perhaps it should be reversed, for it is the part of the poet to present to us that total view and experience of reality which includes all aspects of our humanity in the context of every age. Or that situates every age, rather, in the context of the everlasting. Such poets have, even so, written in this century—I think of Valéry and Claudel, of Rilke and of Yeats, indeed of T.S. Eliot and of Edwin Muir and Vernon Watkins, of Robert Frost—and there are others less complete or less illustrious. I know no poetry that goes beyond

15. Thomas Traherne, *Centuries of Meditation* (London, 1950).

that of Rilke in stating—suggesting rather—who we are, what our place is in the universe. Rainer Maria Rilke, near the end of his life, in a brief period of continuous and prophetic inspiration, completed his two greatest poetic works, the *Duino Elegies* and the *Sonnets to Orpheus*. Rejecting institutionalized religion he was the more free to experience those "angels," intelligences of the universe, "beyond the stars." What are we, he asks, beside these great transhuman orders? And he replies:

> Praise this world to the Angel, not the untellable; you can't impress him with the splendor you've felt; in the cosmos where he more feelingly feels you're only a novice. So show him some simple thing, refashioned by age after age till it lives in our hands and eyes as a part of ourselves. Tell him *things* . . . [16]

To the things of this earth it is mankind who gives their reality. It is these only we can tell the Angel:

> . . . Above all, the hardness of life,
> The long experience of love, in fact purely untellable things. But
> later, under the stars, what use? the more deeply untellable stars?
> For the wanderer does not bring from mountain to valley a
> handful of earth, for all untellable earth, but only a word he has
> won, pure, the yellow and blue gentian. Are we, perhaps, *here* just
> for saying: House, Bridge, Fountain, Gate, Jug, Fruit-tree,
> Window—possibly: Pillar, Tower . . . [17]

It is we who give meaning to these things by our words, by performing Adam's appointed task of "naming" the creation. Thus we bestow on the creatures not a merely natural, but a human, an imaginative and *in*visible reality. And Rilke continues his thought that we are here "just for saying" the names:

> . . . but for *saying*, remember,
> oh, for such saying as never the things themselves
> hoped so intensely to be. Is not the purpose
> of this sly earth, in urging a pair of lovers,
> just to make everything leap in ecstasy in them?[18]

The world finds in us an intenser, a totally new mode of being; as if we are here to perform an alchemical transmutation of crude base

---

16. J.B. Leithman and Stephen Spender, trans., *Duino Elegies* (New York, W.W. Norton & Co., 1939), IX.
17. *Ibid*, IX, 1, pp.25-35.
18. *Ibid*, pp.35-9.

"nature" into the gold of Imagination. And to the Angel we can show "how happy a thing can be, how guileless and ours"; even in its transience:

> . . . These things that live on departure understand when you praise them: fleeting, they look for rescue through something in us, the most fleeting of all. Want us to change them entirely, within our invisible hearts into—oh, endlessly—into ourselves. Whosoever we are.[19]

Whosoever we are. That is a mystery which we cannot in our very nature hope to resolve. It has been the *hybris* of science to hope to know everything. The poet, more humble, seeks to discern who and what we are within a totality greater than ourselves, a finally unknowable order. We are nevertheless the custodians and creators of that order of values and realities that are properly human, that human kingdom of the Imagination "ever expanding in the bosom of God." That "divine body," the human Imagination, is the underlying order which bounds, embraces and contains the human universe.

Within the tradition of spiritual knowledge which I have indicated the underlying order is not some system of natural laws but being itself, at once the "person" and the "place" of the universe. Boehme called it the "imagination" of God, and Blake, following him, "Jesus the Imagination." To the Jews it is Adam Kadmon, to Swedenborg the Grand Man of the Heavens, the Self of the Upanishads. The unity of this Being—of Being itself—is not that of a mechanism but of a consciousness, "in whom we live, and move, and have our being." Within this whole we are, in our present state, aware only of the limited field of our own lives. We are aware of other lives, and great fields beyond us, other times and places and being and modes of being surrounding us like unexplored forests or unclimbed mountains or unsailed seas. A sort of fragrance, or music, is sometimes borne to us on an invisible wind from those far-off fields of knowledge and experience, and we wish we could experience more of that whole of which each of us is at once an infinitesimal part and an infinite center.

At the British Museum I walked from one exhibit to another at the recent exhibition of Buddhist scriptures, devotedly and

19. *Ibid*, pp.64-8.

minutely transcribed in languages unknown to most of those who
visited that exhibition, on tablets of wood or pages of palm-leaves,
by forgotten monks whose days were spent in meditating the truths
of a great civilization that rose like a tide over the Eastern world, to
ebb again, and whose records end in a museum as in an honored
grave. And before, the unwritten knowledge and unrecorded
visions of civilizations still more remote. And again beyond the vast
regions of the once known and the knowable, that given an infinite
number of lifetimes—perhaps that very infinite number of which
there are, or have been or will be, human lives—there may be other
beings attuned not to the spectrum of our human senses but to
other, ampler magnitudes. And in every hedgerow are there not
minute lives of birds and bees and insects, whose worlds are to us
impenetrable? And yet in us something seems to discern an underlying order, a unity of being, "the One" of which Plato wrote, the All,
the God Itself. Or, as the subtler, deeper wisdom of India in one of
the Vedic hymns takes us to the extreme limit of the known and the
knowable:

> But, after all, who knows, and who can say
>> whence it all came, and how creation happened?
> The gods themselves are later than creation,
>> so who knows truly whence it has arisen?
> Whence all creation had its origin,
>> he, whether he fashioned it or whether he did not,
> he, who surveys it all from highest heaven,
>> he knows—or maybe even he does not know.[20]

20. A.L. Basham, *The Wonder That Was India* (New York, Grove Press Inc., 1954),
p.248.

*Flower in the Crannied Wall*

*Flower in the crannied wall,*
*I pluck you out of the crannies,*
*I hold you here, root and all, in my hand,*
*Little flower—but if I could understand*
*What you are, root and all, and all in all,*
*I should know what God and man is.*

— *Alfred Lord Tennyson*

*Chapter 12*

# Hierophanic Nature

*Arthur Versluis*

It has become something of a commonplace to blame Christianity for the modern divorce between man and nature. Some go back to Genesis, where man is given dominion over the creatures of the earth, and find there a source for our technologism, for our Cartesian belief in nature as merely a grand machine, and for our relentless despoliation of the natural world. Others see the origin of the modern anti-nature worldview in Protestantism, with its anti-iconic, often Puritanical stance. But in reality, the origin of modernity lies not in the Judeo-Christian tradition so much as in the jettisoning of that tradition in favor of scientistic ratiocentrism. The truth is, Christianity has always contained within it an esoteric understanding of nature as hierophany, and it is upon this understanding that we will focus.

However, I ought to begin with a few comments on recent tendencies within Western Christianity. Numerous recent writers have brought against Protestantism the charge that it entailed a diminution of the Western Christian tradition, a kind of denaturing, which in turn allowed the wholly desanctified modern worldview to appear. Protestantism, seen from this perspective, was historically necessary in order that eventually a wholly profane modernity could take root in the West. But this conception of Protestantism, while it has some merit, wholly ignores the emergence of the German and French theosophers, men like Jacob Böhme, Johann Gichtel, and Friedrich Oetinger, and Protestant-influenced Catholics like Louis Claude de St. Martin, and Franz von Baader, to name only the most outstanding.

The theosophical movement of the seventeenth, eighteenth, and nineteenth centuries—which had nothing whatever to do with the Madame Blavatsky's late nineteenth century Theosophical Society—was an authentically spiritual counterbalance to precisely the barrenness of Protestantism. If Protestantism entailed the abandoning of Roman Catholic ceremonialism and iconography, with its rich pageantry and imagery, in favor of bare pews and a plain wooden cross, it also was responsible for the astonishingly rich inward imagery one found not only in the Rosicrucian movement of the seventeenth century, but also in the works of Jacob Böhme, the Lutheran visionary, as well as in the theosophical movement of which he was prime mover.

Not all the theosophers were Protestant, of course—Franz von Baader remained Roman Catholic to the end of his life, and was never censured even though he had fiercely opposed the institution of the papacy and of the Vatican for much of his life and through most of his writings. But exactly this opposition to the papacy characterized Protestantism, and makes of Baader the exception that, in the end, proves the rule: the richness of theosophical writings complemented the Protestant movement's attempt to return to the origins of Christianity.

Now central to the theosophical movement was precisely the opposite tendency to that which René Guénon recognized in Protestantism: if Protestantism represented the beginnings of the modern, profane view of nature, the theosophical movement represented a renewed awareness of nature as theophany, as, finally, divine revelation. Whether it was Jacob Böhme in *De Signatura Rerum*, Louis Claude de St. Martin in his *Tableau Naturel,* or Franz von Baader with his *Philosophie der Liebe* (Philosophy of Religious Eros) theosophy entailed a deep understanding of nature as embodying for us the divine language, the *Logos* speaking to us from forest and brook.

It is well known that in shamanism all over the world there is said to be a secret language of nature. The shaman is able to understand the speech of birds and animals and even of stones—and he is able to speak to them. This archaic unity between humanity and nature reflects a primordial state that, in Christian terms, cannot be other than paradisal. Indeed, it was exactly this unity referred to when Adam gave the creatures of the earth names while in the garden of Eden; those names were none other than the "secret language of nature" that marks the paradisal state in which the *logos* can be recognized in all created things.

Christian Hermeticism, or theosophy as displayed in the writings of Paracelsus, Böhme, Saint-Martin, Baader and Oetinger, also understands that there is a "secret language" of nature—but for them it is an emblematic language rooted in alchemical imagery and, even more, in the science of correspondences. This theosophical tradition derives its basis from a concept expressed in the *Tabula Smaragdina* (the Emerald Tablet): what is below reflects what is above. In other words, there is a correspondence between spiritual truth and what we see in the natural world. One sees this in the many parables of the New Testament, which use natural images to reveal the most transcendent of spiritual truths about the human condition.

Hence Valentin Weigel wrote, "O my creator and God, through thy light I know how wonderful I am created: Out of the world am I created, and I am in the world, and the world is in me. I am also created out of you, and remain in you, and you in me . . . I am your child and son . . . and all that is in the greater world is also spiritually in me; thus am I and it one."[1] This is a mystical unity between humanity, nature, and God that the traditional formulation "man is a microcosm" does not completely express. Here we see a theosophic understanding of humanity, the world, and God that one cannot reduce to formulations, but that certainly reflects the alchemical science of transmutation and imagery, as well as the German theosophy of, for example, Eckhart.

The theosophers drew their conception of an emblematic language in nature at least in part from alchemy, which is above all a science of correspondences between the cosmos and man. For example, we might take the alchemical recognition of three essential principles in the natural world: mercury, salt, and sulfur. As we know, each of these principles has fundamental characteristics, mercury being fluidic, salt crystalline, and sulfur fiery. These same principles are operative in the natural world, in the human body, and in the human psyche. What is more, each of them presents an image of certain *qualities* inherent in all nature.

Precisely here the science of alchemy diverges from the technological science of modernity—for whereas modern science is almost exclusively concerned with quantitative analysis, traditional sciences like alchemy are concerned with qualities. We might add that such a concern with qualities entails a natural limit on technology—some alchemists knew the explosiveness of gunpowder, for instance, but

1. In *Nosce te ipsum*, p. 244; see F.-W. Wentzlaff-Eggebert, *Deutsche Mystik Zwischen Mittelalter und Neuzeit,* (Berlin: de Gruyter, 1969), pp. 177-178.

were not concerned with it—whereas modern science is fundamentally concerned with quantitative technological effects, and so there is no limit to its technological applications, which indeed seem to spin out of control, as if like the fabled golem they had taken on a life of their own.

Although alchemy has often been reviled as a materialistic search for gold, and as the "primitive" predecessor of modern chemistry, in fact alchemy is above all the science of correspondences and signatures, and ultimately a secret language in images that reveals the spiritual truths hidden in nature herself. The alchemist is concerned with the subtle qualities that inform both nature and man; and any changes or transmutations that we work in nature occur without because they correspond to changes within. The alchemical tradition that most influenced the theosophers like Böhme and Baader was based in the medical and cosmological thought of Paracelsus, the remarkable medieval spagyric physician.

The German and French theosophical tradition, then, derived from the confluence of two streams—the alchemical stream represented most completely in Paracelsus, and the gnostic German stream perhaps best represented by the figure of Meister Eckhart. From the alchemical current comes the use of images, figures, and principles in such writers as Martinez de Pasqually, teacher of Saint-Martin; and from the gnostic current of Eckhart comes the supracosmological understanding that informs virtually the whole of the theosophical perspective. Briefly, we may say that the alchemical perspective offers an understanding of how the spiritual informs nature; and the gnostic perspective offers an understanding of that which not only informs, but transcends nature.

One can see the confluence of these two streams in the *natur-theologie* of Friedrich Christoph Oetinger, who wrote:

> It is the most pestilent of ideas that nature can be envisioned as outside the presence of God. There is in all men an uncontradicted awareness or feeling of the invisible powers that animate nature. There is also in us a secret "yes" or "amen" to the presence of wisdom within and without us. This secret awareness causes us to recognize the beauties of nature as copies of the primordial Right.[2]

2. Oetinger, "Die güldene Zeit," *Theosoph. Schriften*, 2. Abth., Bd. 6, §52.

The "secret 'amen'" to the presence of wisdom reflects the gnosis of Eckhart or Tauler; and the awareness of the invisible powers animating nature reflects the cosmological gnosis of the alchemists.

But not all people are willing to recognize this awareness of the invisible powers that inform nature—indeed, precisely during Oetinger's lifetime (1702-1782) arose a materialistic science, which held nature to be, not the emblematic representation of divine wisdom, but a kind of machine or clock that perhaps God wound up. To this divorce of humanity, God, and nature, the theosophical movement of which Oetinger was a part directly opposes a unified understanding of man as microcosm and of nature as analogical macrocosm, both informed by and reflecting divine power.[3]

In a very real sense, one may speak of the esoteric theosophy of Böhme, Oetinger, Saint-Martin and Baader as having appeared as a direct counterbalance to growing materialist scientism and atheism in Europe at that time. Each of these writers presented a complete and unified spiritual understanding of the cosmos and of hierophanic nature that was utterly antithetical to the kind of reductionist dualism and mechanistic view of nature Descartes and others put forth. For the theosophers, nature is like scripture, a divine revelation through parables and emblems, through figures and images. All things are the manifestations of the *Logos* and their signatures can be read.

The historical appearance of the theosophers and their understanding of nature—both in their dual inheritance from the German gnostics and from the alchemists, and in their counterbalance both to Protestant anti-iconolatry and to materialist science—is nothing less than providential. Unfortunately, however, their importance has not been adequately recognized. Certainly in an era in which the failures of materialist scientistic premises have become obvious, and the societal collapse of modernity—which has no concept of how a culture can be theocentric—is upon us, it is important

---

3. "In diametric opposition to materialistic atheism is idealistic Theism, ... which is based in the unity and objectivity of the unending spiritual Ur substance." So wrote Franz Josef Molitor, in his *Philosophie der Geschichte*, II.42. Likewise, Franz von Baader well remarked—in an extension of the Aristotelian idea that man is created to know—that "Just as it is man's need to know (in both the sense of knowledge and of becoming familiar with), so too it is man's need to know God." So too, Molitor adds that just as it is a human necessity to will, so too it is a human necessity to will toward God and to live in God. II.55 §87.

that we at least consider what possible alternatives to our present worldview might help us out of our impasse.

Theosophy is relevant to our current situation. Environmentalists or ecologists today present arguments about the "biosphere," and about the earth as a single living organism, but such arguments still present nature based on materialist premises; they entail no concept that nature might be understood in light of a unified religious understanding. Some criticize Christianity as having been responsible for the birth of the modern world and its destruction of nature, but in fact it was the progressive erosion or disintegration of a religious center in the Judeo-Christian world that gave birth to modernity. The absence of Christianity—in any complete sense—is responsible for the divorce between humanity, nature, and God that many now feel, and its reestablishment alone can restore the *hieros gamos*, or sacred marriage between man, nature, and God in the West.

Such a reestablishment of what can only be called a normal culture in the West may come about through a yet unforeseen spiritual illumination coming from three main sources: the gnostic mysticism represented in Roman Catholicism by Tauler and Ruysbroeck and Franz von Baader, in Protestantism by Böhme and Oetinger, and in Eastern Orthodoxy by virtually the entire tradition itself. Only these three sources are capable of representing from within Christendom itself a complete understanding of the proper relations between human beings and nature. This proper relationship has certain fundamental characteristics, the most essential of which is its religious center.

For the right relationship between humanity and nature can only take place in a spiritual context. Saint-Martin expresses the proper human function as that best exemplified in Christ, who he calls the Repairer, and who restores to man and nature the spiritual equilibrium lost in the Fall. Christ, who is the pillar between heaven and earth, is the means by which man is able to "bind and loose" on earth and in heaven. That is, Christ is the means by which the terrible catastrophes and evil let loose by the primordial angelic Fall are reversed. This function of "repairing" directly manifests the proper human relation to nature—for man in his primordial state is Christ-like, manifesting heaven on earth.

According to Saint-Martin, who is only following Böhme in this—for it is a view expressed by Baader and others in the theosophical tradition as well—nature itself reflects the fall of the angels and of humanity.[4] In other words, there was on the horizon of time a catastrophe of which we can only glimpse the outward manifestations or signs, but which produced the evil we can see manifested not only in the destructive aspects of nature, but even more in the evil acts of destructive people. That modern man is a fallen creature is a doctrine not happily admitted in the modern university, dedicated as it is to the premises of materialist science; but even the modern biologists and chemists are busy cataloguing the catastrophic effects on nature that modern humanity is having.

This theosophical recognition of evil is not a mere "dualism," however—rather, it is a cosmological understanding of how powerful are the effects of sin, sin conceived not just as individual miscreance, but as cosmological disequilibrium. In Islamic tradition, in particular in Ismaili gnosis, theosophers recognize that ours is but one of a long series of temporal cycles, cycles which are the result of Adam's fall, itself a cosmic "event" that ultimately produced our contemporary entrapment in history.[5] The Fall is a fall into time, both our gift and our punishment, shared with all living creatures.

Since the Fall, nature is like a widow longing to be in a state of marriage, or unity. Baader wrote:

> Thus cursed, nature could no longer bring forth heavenly fruit (paradisal); and her impotence followed upon that of man. Throughout the beauties of nature, man perceives, now more, now less, the melancholy plaint through the widow's veil for what she must bear for the guilt of man.[6]

It may not be possible for man to restore his paradisal state *in toto*, now, at the end of a temporal cycle; but it is certainly possible on an individual level for man to return to an harmonious relation to nature. Such a relation is glimpsed in the way saints like St. Francis live, around whom one sees prefigurations of the lion lying down with the lamb.

4. See Saint-Martin, *Tableau Naturel*, I.100: "The wisdom and bounty of the Divine Being are manifested by the birth of man into terrestrial life. He is thus placed in a position to soothe by his labor a part of the evil which the first crime caused on earth."
5. See Henry Corbin, *Cyclical Time and Ismaili Gnosis*, for an extended discussion of the Fall as cosmic disequilibrium.
6. Baader, "Urbild der Menscheit," in *Schriften*, (Frankfurt: Insel, 1966), p. 70.

This spiritual restoration can only appear out of freedom from time and its constraints. Our current terrestrial condition reflects our fall from an earlier, angelic state; but it also represents our opportunity to re-ascend to that state through spiritual practice. Spiritual practice entails the transcendence of temporal limitations, from which derives the restoration of paradise. Böhme writes:

> Every particular thing, be it herb, grass, tree, beast, bird, fish, worm, or whatsoever it be . . . has proceeded from the separator of all beings, from the Word . . . For this visible world with all its host and being is nothing but an objective representation of the spiritual world, which spiritual world is hidden in this material, elemental world, like the tincture in metals and herbs.[7]

In every being there are two aspects, according to Böhme: the spiritual, or eternal, and the natural or outward.[8] The spiritual aspect manifests as the light of glory, and is above time; the natural aspect is its fiery reflection in the physical, temporal realm.

From these observations we can see how throughout nature, through its beauties, we can see the reflection of the paradisal state that is still there—not in historical time, nor in our physical world, which is itself a fall from a higher state, but glimpsed through nature as if seen reflected in water. In this we can see too exactly how religious man, *homo religiosus*, is the uniter of heaven and earth. For we alone are capable of "seeing through" nature; we alone are capable of being the pillar that reaches from the timeless to the temporal, from the transcendent to the physical, from the celestial to the tangible. This doctrine of course emphasizes to us once again just how profound is the human task on this earth, and how few of us even begin to approach our proper way of living.

This proper way of living does not necessarily mean that we live in the virgin wilderness and do nothing to disturb it, even though the virgin wilderness reminds us with great force of our obligations to the transcendent, both of how small and of how significant we are. Rather, to live properly and to fulfill our human vocation to be *homo religiosus*, our obligation is first of all to realize upon earth how we form a connection between heaven and earth, and how nature

---

7. Böhme, *Theoscopia, or Divine Intuition*, III.§34, §35. For a contemporary selection from Böhme's profound works, see *The Wisdom of Jacob Böhme*, A. Versluis, editor, (St. Paul: New Grail, 2003).

8. Böhme, *Mysterium Pansophicum* V.§1 ff.

reflects its divine origin just as we do. When people are organized aright—when the earthly kingdom reflects the heavenly kingdom, when earthly gardens reflect the gardens and orchards of paradise—then nature too is justified and restored.

This is why in the alchemical texts, one often sees in the culminating illustrations—the king and the queen crowned and together in a paradisal landscape. The alchemical mysteries indeed lead to a paradisal state, in which the mysteries of nature yield their secrets to the one who has made himself worthy of them, and who has come to understand the "secret language," the emblematic language of the soul's truths. This harmonious state, in which humanity and nature are both restored, is possible today for the individual, but is also possible on a broader scale for an entire state or countryside— a kind of late reflection of the golden age.

Clearly the theosophical and alchemical teachings offer us a coherent cosmological science as yet quite unfamiliar. There is an alternative and completely integral, unified understanding of hierophanic nature accessible not far off in the exotic Himalayas, but right at home, so to say, in the European Christian theosophic tradition. To understand the spiritual truths ensconced in nature, it is not necessary to go far afield in one's search, but even if one does, in the end one may return to the traditions to which one was born, where unexpected treasures may be found.

As John Pordage wrote in his *A Treatise of Eternal Nature*:

> The Divine Nature and glory of the Deity is hid in Nature, as a Jewel in a Cabinet, or as a treasure hid in a field. Indeed, in pure Nature this Jewel is easily found, for there it lies open ... but in impure Nature it lie's deep hid and buried, and cannot be discovered, but with great pains and difficulty.[9]

By "pure nature," Pordage means what he and Böhme termed "eternal nature," meaning unfallen transcendent existence in the divine; but even in impure, temporal nature, the glory of the deity is visible. It is no doubt the case that the glory hid in nature is less visible to us today than it was to someone for whom there still was a nature untouched by the hand of man, unsullied by venomous rain and the drifting poisons of urban, mercantile humanity. But it is

---

9. Pordage, *A Treatise of Eternal Nature*, (London: 1681), p. 161. For a contemporary version of Pordage's classic work, see *The Wisdom of John Pordage*, A. Versluis, editor, (St. Paul: New Grail, 2003).

always possible to see beyond the apparent to the visionary reality that, far from being fantasy, possesses an authenticity of being which far exceeds the mutable world before us.

It was not so long ago, nor was it in a world so different from our present one, that the poet George William Russell (AE) could feel the inward calling of the breath of celestial nature even while in some urban office surrounded by bustle and paperwork. Indeed, it was not so long ago that he was called out into the open lands of England where he saw the earth transfigured before him, saw celestial beings of surpassing splendor, and felt a delight inexplicable and overwhelming. It is possible, too, for such hierophanies to take place in America, or Australia, or Europe, or anywhere on earth—there are many sacred places that still bear within them the power to transmute, and to be transmuted. To this truth, theosophic Christianity stands both as reminder and as path.

*A fish cannot drown in water,*
*A bird does not fall in air.*
*In the fire of creation,*
*Gold doesn't vanish:*
*The fire brightens.*
*Each creature God made*
*Must live in its own true nature;*
*How could I resist my nature,*
*That lives for oneness with God.*

*— Mechthild of Magdeburg*

## Chapter 13

# The Symbolism of Water

## *Titus Burckhardt*

The modern economy, in spite of all the research findings at its disposal, has for a long time almost completely left out of account one of the most important bases of our life as well as of its own existence, namely the living purity of water. This fact bears witness to a unilateralness of development which, quite apart from the question of water, is also harmful to many other things, not the least of which is the psyche or soul. When the balance of Nature is not disturbed, the earth's waters themselves continually re-establish their purity, whereas, when this balance is lost, death and pollution are the result. It is thus not merely a coincidence that the "life" of the waters is a symbol for the "life" of the human soul.

When one considers whether there is anything that could possibly alert non-scientifically minded people to the menace of water pollution, one quickly realizes that the natural sense of beauty that enables us spontaneously to distinguish a diseased tree from a healthy one, should also be able to sound a warning here. That it has not done so—or hardly done so—comes from the fact that modern man completely separates not only "the beautiful" from "the useful," but also "the beautiful" from "the real." This way of thinking is like a split in one's consciousness, and it is difficult to say whether it is cause or effect of a state of affairs which, on the one hand, drives man systematically to destroy, on an ever-widening front, the natural balance of things and, on the other, impels him periodically to flee the artificial world which in this way he creates. Never before have there been such enormous concentrations of buildings of stone, concrete and iron, and never before did city-dwellers, in such enormous numbers, periodically leave their homes in order to re-discover Nature at the seaside or in the mountains—that very Nature which they themselves have so inexorably banished. It would not be true to say that, in so doing, people are merely seeking to preserve their health. Many, if not all, are at the same time seeking a relaxation of soul that is accorded only by surroundings whose still unspoilt and harmonious state has ensured the preservation of such beauty as gives peace to the soul and frees the mind from the pressure of calculating thoughts. However, the same people who, when on holiday, consciously or unconsciously seek this beauty, quickly reject it as "romanticism" whenever it stands in the way of their utilitarian interests. In this, the good or bad intention of the individual scarcely plays a role; everyone is under the pressure of economic forces, and it is usually unconscious self-defense if one hides from oneself the destructive consequences of certain developments. In the longer view, however, such an attitude is disastrous.

Beauty always represents an inward and inexhaustible equilibrium of forces; and this overwhelms our soul, since it can neither be calculated nor mechanically produced. A sense of beauty can therefore permit us the direct experience of relationships before we can perceive them, in a differentiated manner, with our discursive reason; in this, incidentally, there is a defense for our own physical and psychic well-being, something that we cannot neglect with impunity.

To this it may be objected that men have always distinguished between the useful and the beautiful; a pleasure-grove was always a luxury, while a wood was usually viewed in a utilitarian manner. It might even be said that it took modern education to create the desire to protect a given piece of nature on purely aesthetic grounds.

However, in earlier times there were also sacred groves, which no axe might fell. They catered neither for use in the usual sense of this word nor for luxury. Beauty and reality—two qualities which the modern world spontaneously separates—were (and, for men who have a pre-modern view regarding the sacred, still are) united. Even today there are sacred woods in Japan and India, just as there were in pre-Christian Europe; we mention them here only as one example of sacred nature, for there are also sacred mountains, as well as—and this touches us more closely—sacred springs, rivers, and lakes. Even within Christendom, which generally avoids the veneration of the various phenomena of Nature, there were and are springs and lakes—for example, the well at Chartres and the spring at Lourdes—which, because of their connection with miraculous events, have come to be regarded as sacred. What is important here is not that some particular mountain or spring is regarded as sacred, and therefore inviolable; but that one particular phenomenon is invariably an example of a whole range of related things, of a complete order of Nature, which for a larger or smaller community of men is of vital importance, and expresses a higher or supernatural reality: thus, for the ancient Germans, the forest was the indispensable basis of their very life, and at the same time something of a temple, a place that harbored the Divine Presence. All forest had this quality and, in this sense, was inviolable. Since, however, the forests also had to be used, there were special sacred woods whose function was to recall the principial and spiritually significant inviolability of the forest as such. The case of the sacred cow among the Hindus is similar: in reality, for the Hindus, everything living is sacred, in other words, inviolable and symbolical, for, according to their doctrine, all consciousness participates in the Divine Spirit. Since, however, it is impossible everywhere and always to avoid the killing of living creatures, the law of inviolability was in practice limited to a few symbolic species, amongst which the cow, as the incarnation of the maternal mercy of the cosmos, assumes a special position. By renouncing the slaughtering of cows, the Hindu in principle venerates all life and at the same time protects one of the most important bases of his way of life, which for thousands of years has depended on cultivation and the raising of cattle. Likewise the sacred springs, of which there were many in Medieval Christendom, drew attention to the sacredness of water as such; they were a reminder that water is a symbol of grace, something that can readily be seen in the symbolism of baptism. The sacred is that which is the object of veneration and awe; it is the reflection of something eternal, and therefore indestructible; and the inviolability which it enjoys stems directly therefrom.

Depending on which faith a people adheres to, and depending on their hereditary mentality, there are other natural or artificial things that they may regard as sacred. The four elements—air, fire, water, and earth—which are the most elementary modes of manifestation of all matter to offer themselves to our senses, are almost everywhere—with the exception of the modern, rationalistic world—endowed with the quality of sacredness; from this point of view, earth is illimitable, air is ungraspable, fire in its very nature is undefilable; only water is open to violation, and therefore commended to special protection.

To recapitulate: for pre-modern cultures, there are realities which transcend the level of mere utilitarianism and have precedence over them. These realities are in themselves of a purely spiritual or divine nature. They are however reflected in certain sensory appearances, which may consequently become the object of veneration and awe. These are then, either completely or in part (as representative symbols), withheld from the violent interference of men. Such an attitude is naturally very different from that of aesthetic sensitivity, which may also cause us, all considerations of usefulness apart, to admire and protect a natural phenomenon. But the sense of beauty is somehow contained within the veneration of the sacred; for the truly beautiful is that which lies hidden in the inexhaustible richness of harmoniously united possibilities. The same holds true for the sacred, and indeed for all phenomena and elements pertaining to the very bases of life, so that awe of the sacred also more or less directly contributes—not always in a predictable way—to the maintenance of life itself.

A few remarks should be made here regarding the elements: these have naturally nothing to do with what are called elements in modern chemistry but, as we have already said, represent the most elementary modes of manifestation in which the "stuff on which the world is made" communicates itself to our five senses: the solid, the liquid, the aerial, and the fiery modes of manifestation. There are indeed other liquids besides water, but none has for us the same aspect of purity, and none plays such an important role in the preservation of life. Likewise there are other gaseous substances besides air, but none of them can be breathed.

Cosmically, then, the four elements are the simplest manifestational modes of matter. From an inward point of view, on the other hand, they are also the simplest images of our soul, which as such is ungraspable, but whose fundamental characteristics can be likened to the four elements. This is what St. Francis of Assisi has in mind when he praises God for the four elements, one after the other, in his famous *Canticle of the Sun*. In regard to water, he says: "Praised be Thou, O Lord, for sister water, who is very useful, humble, precious, and chaste (*Laudato si, o Signore, per sor acqua, la quale è molto utile ed umile e preziosa e casta*)." That may sound like pure poetic allegory, but in fact it signifies very much more: humility and chastity well describe the quality of water which, in a river, takes on all forms, without thereby losing its purity. Herein also lies an image of the soul, which possesses the capacity to take in all impressions and to follow all forms while remaining true to its own undivided essence. "The soul of man resembles water," said Goethe, thereby reiterating an image that occurs in the Scriptures of both Near and Far East. The soul resembles water, just as the Spirit resembles wind or air.

It would lead us too far to mention all the myths and customs in which water appears as an image or reflection of the soul. An awareness that the soul recognizes itself when it beholds water—finding animation in its play, refreshment in its rest, and purity in its clarity—is perhaps nowhere more widespread than amongst the Japanese. The whole of Japanese life, to the extent that it is still formed by tradition, is penetrated by a sense of purity and pliant simplicity that finds its prefiguration in water. The Japanese make pilgrimages to the famous waterfalls of their country and will gaze for hours at the unruffled surface of a temple pond. Significant is the story of the Chinese sage Hsuyu—a recurring theme of Japanese painters—who received a message that the Emperor wished to hand over his kingdom to him; he fled to the mountains and washed his ears in a waterfall. The painter Harunobu represented him allegorically in the form of a young and noble maiden who, in the solitude of the mountains, washes her ear in the vertical fall of water.

For the Hindus, the water of life finds embodiment in the Ganges which, from its source in the Himalayas, the mountains of the Gods, irrigates the largest and most populous plains of India. Its water is held to be pure from beginning to end, and in fact it is preserved from all pollution by the fine sand which it drags along with it. Whoever, with repentant mind, bathes in the Ganges, is freed from all his sins: inner purification here finds its symbolic support in the outward purification that comes from the water of the sacred river. It is as if the purifying water came from Heaven, for its origin in the eternal ice of the roof of the world is like a symbol of the heavenly origin of divine grace which, as "living water," springs from timeless and immutable Peace. Here, as in the similar rites of other religions and peoples, the correspondence of water and soul helps the latter to purify itself or, more exactly, to find anew its own—originally pure—essence. In this process, the symbol prepares the way for grace.

Water symbolizes the soul. From another point of view—but analogously—water symbolizes the *materia prima* of the whole universe. For, just as water contains within itself, as pure possibilities, all the forms which, in flowing and sparkling, it may assume, so *materia prima* contains all the forms of the world in a state of indistinction.

In the Biblical story of creation it is said that, in the beginning, before the creation of the earth, the Spirit of God moved upon the face of the waters; and the holy books of the Hindus tell us that all the inhabitants of the earth emerged from the primordial sea. In these myths, water is not meant in the ordinary sense of the word; and yet the picture they create in our imagination is in its own way correct, and as apt as possibly can be, for nothing conveys better the undifferentiated and passive unity of *materia prima.*

The myth of the creation of all things from the primordial sea finds an echo in the Koranic words: "We have created every living thing from water." The Biblical allegory of the Spirit of God moving upon the waters has its counterpart in the Hindu symbol of the divine swan Hamsa which, swimming on the primordial sea, hatches the golden egg of the world; and each of these allegorical representations is finally echoed in the Koran, where it is said that, at the beginning, the Throne of God was upon the water.

The opened lotus flower, the seat of Indian divinities, is also a "throne of God" floating upon the water of *materia prima,* or upon the water of principial possibilities. This symbol, which was transmitted from Hindu to Buddhist mythology and art, brings us back from water as the image of the primordial substance of the world to water as the image of the soul. The lotus-stream of the Buddha or Boddhisattva rises up from the waters of the soul, just as the spirit, illumined by knowledge, frees itself from passive existence. Here water represents something which has to be overcome, but in which nevertheless there is good, because in it is rooted the flower whose calyx contains the "precious jewel" of *Bodhi,* the Divine Spirit. The Buddha, the "Jewel in the Lotus," is himself this Spirit.

That must suffice as a survey of the meanings which water can have as a symbol, though many other examples of this kind could be mentioned. But it is not merely a question of demonstrating that in all cultures that can be called pre-rationalist—and the term is not used pejoratively—water has more than a purely physical or biological meaning; the spiritual realities, of which it is the symbol, are never attached to it arbitrarily, but are directly and logically derived from its essence. The contemplative beholding of Nature which, through essential and constant appearances, perceives the timeless prototypes or causes of these appearances, is not something that is merely sentimental, nor is it bound to time and place, and this despite the fact of the modern world, from which this kind of contemplation seems to have been banished. We say "seems," for such a contemplation of things is too deeply rooted in the human heart to be able to disappear completely. It even continues unconsciously, and it would not be difficult to show how the mysterious attraction of water as something sacred, as a symbolic and manifested expression of a psychic or cosmic reality, lives on in art, especially in painting and poetry. Who, when confronted with a pure mountain lake or with a spring gushing forth from the rock, has never felt at least something of the awe and veneration that are inseparable from anything sacred? The people of earlier times knew better than we that one does not disturb the balance of nature with impunity. Our superior scientific knowledge is totally insufficient to protect us from all the effects of a disturbed nature; and even if we could insure ourselves against every negative reaction on the part of the physical environment, we would still have no guarantee that the psychic or subtle world would not take its revenge on us. A glance at Asia and Africa, where the spiritual equilibrium of ancient cultures has been disturbed on all sides, and their very existence called into question, is sufficient to let us sense that it may still come to a destruction of "living waters," in comparison with which the pollution of our physical waters will seem harmless.

In conclusion, and by way of indicating that even in modern Europe there are still sacred waters, mention should be made of Lough Derg in Donegal, the most northerly county in Ireland. In this lough is an island on which are a number of Christian shrines dating from the Middle Ages and also a cave, which represents the entry to the underworld. It is called "St. Patrick's Purgatory," for it is said that it was here that St. Patrick, the Apostle of Ireland, made hell and the Mount of Purgatory appear to the heathen in a vision. Since the early Middle Ages, the island has been a place of pilgrimage, with which very strict rules are associated. The pilgrims, who are brought to the island by boat, must walk on it fasting and bare-footed, and carry out certain spiritual exercises during a stay of three days. These consist principally in kneeling on the rocks and praying before a number of crosses that have been erected in honor of the most important of the Irish saints. Each time a pilgrim completes his devotion before these "stations," set out like the beads of a rosary, he makes his way to a large rock that rises out of the water at a little distance from the shore of the island, and, after a few prayers, recites aloud the creed, looking out over the water of the lake. People who have performed this pilgrimage declare that these moments of solitude, in contemplation of the unruffled lake, surrounded by uninhabited hills, release in their hearts something that is indescribable.

*The water is clear all the way down.*
*Nothing ever polished it. That is the way it is.*

*— Keizan*

## Chapter 14

# Divine Beatitude: Supreme Archetype of Aesthetic Experience

## *Reza Shah-Kazemi*

Most of the studies which deal with sacred art only focus on its objective aspect, that is, on its formal manifestations; our intention here is to focus rather on the spiritual dimensions of one of the subjective aspects closely connected with sacred art, that is, the aesthetic experience of the perceiving subject, the beholder of art. By aesthetic experience we mean the existential ramification of the perception of beauty; the experience of expansiveness, marvel, serenity and in its higher reaches, the feelings of bliss that can be generated in the contemplation of beautiful forms; and we take sacred art in its widest meaning, to encompass not only the formal productions of *homo religiosus*, but also the handiwork of the Creator: that is, virgin nature, with all the beauties found therein.

Just as terrestrial beauty both reflects and participates in the Divine archetype of Beauty, so the experience of beauty, the aesthetic sensation, must derive from an archetype situated on a transcendent plane. But whereas in the case of formal beauty, participation in the archetype is rigorously objective and unconditional, in the case of aesthetic experience, participation in the archetype is critically dependent on the subjective capacity of the individual to make of his experience a spiritual foretaste of heavenly felicity and thereby a "remembrance of God." Beautiful vision on earth should foreshadow the Beatific Vision in Heaven, it should heighten one's resolution to conform to the requirements of this celestial reward; it should, in other words, lead one to God. The experience of beauty, far from being a question of merely aesthetic sensibility, is essentially an invitation to union: union with the Divine Principle, which both projects Beauty and attracts by means of Beauty. One speaks of being entranced, enthralled, enraptured by beauty: these terms clearly indicate the spiritual potential inherent in aesthetic experience, for the individual is not fully himself in the face of a beauty that overwhelms him; indeed, a certain mode of extinction can even be said to have taken place.

Whether or not this spiritual potential will be realized depends on whether the perceiving subject is interiorized or exteriorized by his experience; that is, whether the perception of beautiful form leads one to the formless source of beauty within the heart, to the "kingdom of God that is within you," to God "who is closer to man than his jugular vein;" or whether, on the contrary, the experience of beauty gives rise to a fixation on the transient forms as such and thus to a cult of aestheticism, an art for the sake of art. In this case, the experience of beauty becomes a substitute for God, rather than a pathway to Him; it generates a *ghaflah*, a forgetfulness of God, rather than a *dhikr*, a remembrance of God; it gives rise to an unstable, false and fleeting plenitude which inflates the ego, rather than to a contemplation of the transcendent essences of beauty in the face of which the hardness of the ego is dissolved, and the limitations and pretensions of the ego are transcended. In the words of Frithjof Schuon:[1]

> ... the born contemplative cannot see or hear beauty without perceiving in it something of God. The Divine that is contained in it allows him the more easily to detach himself from the appearances of things. As for the passional man, he sees in beauty the world, seduction, the ego, so that it takes him away from the "one thing needful."

Now all men have an existential need for beauty, for on the one hand man is "made in the image of God" (*khalaqa Allahu 'l-Adam 'ala suratihi*); and on the other, "God is Beautiful and He loves Beauty" (*inna Allaha jamilun yuhibbu 'l jamal*). The substance of man's innermost being is woven of Beauty, and like God, he loves Beauty. Consequently, love of beauty imposes itself upon man as an ontological imperative; it is far from being just a sentimental attraction.

"Beauty is in the eye of the beholder." This English saying accords perfectly with a key Platonic principle: the eye must itself be of a luminous nature for it to be able to register light; the truth must be immanent in the intellect for the intellect to be able to recognize

---

1. *Spiritual Pespectives and Human Facts* (London, Faber and Faber, n.d.), p.272.

truth. It is because beauty is of the essence of man's spirit that he is able to perceive and love beautiful forms; but it must be added that this capacity to intuit the essence in forms depends not only upon one's contemplativity, but also on the degree to which the individual's inherent beauty of soul is actualized: in other words, whether virtue and piety adorn the soul.

According to Plato again: "Beauty is the splendor of the True." Now what this implies, among other things, is that one cannot come to know the Truth without also coming to know and love Beauty, which is found in all its infinite glory only in the Truth. This same fundamental principle is implied in the *hadith qudsi*:

> I was a hidden treasure and I loved to be known, so I created the world.

The fact that God loved to be known implies that man, in proportion to his coming to know God, will ineluctably come to love Him. The Truth, his coming to know God, will ineluctably come to love Him. The Truth, then, reveals the essence of Beauty, but beauty does not necessarily reveal the truth: it can both enlighten and delude, hence the drama of man's perennial quest for a beauty that is imperishable.

If this beauty is not sought in its Divine source, by means of contemplation, in the necessary framework of prayer and virtue, then it will be sought in its manifested forms; and these forms will become divinized, that is, adored, if not worshipped, as idols. To paraphrase Frithjof Schuon: Beauty attached to God is sacrament, cut off from God it becomes an idol.[2] One might add: the aesthetic sensation attached to God is *dhikr*, cut off from God it is *ghaflah*. The beautiful object will then be detached from the Divine source that imparts to it all its meaning, all its liberating power; it will be adored for its own sake, or more specifically, for the sake of the concupiscent gratification of the senses, a gratification which is the vulgar parody of that blissful contemplation of the archetypes that is the authentic fruit of aesthetic experience.

There is then a fundamental ambiguity inherent in aesthetic experience; in order to serve its proper spiritual purpose the experience of beauty must consciously be related to God. And it must be stressed that the ultimate function of this experience is to provide a

---

2. *Esoterism as Principle and as Way* (Pates Manor, Perennial Books, 1981), p.182.

foretaste of that beatitude which is one with the absolute Reality, a foretaste which is as an invitation to participate in the Divine Presence with all one's being, and not just with one's surface sensibility.

Given the fact that the Divine Reality is at once transcendent and immanent vis a vis all formal beauty, it is incumbent on man to take account of both of these dimensions; one must see all beautiful things in God, and God in all beautiful things. Failure to see all beautiful things in God violates the aspect of transcendence: for it is blind to the fact that all beautiful things are prefigured in the Divine Principle which infinitely transcends the world; and failure to see the Divine Beauty in all beautiful things violates the aspect of immanence, by being blind to the fact that objects are beautiful only by virtue of the Divine Beauty that is rendered present through and by them.

The rest of this paper will attempt to highlight the metaphysical relationship between aesthetic experience and Divine Beatitude, pointing out these two dimensions of transcendence and immanence. We shall begin by positing three fundamental degrees of Being: the terrestrial, the celestial and the Divine. Notwithstanding the distinctions that can be made within the celestial realms and the Divine Nature, this tripartite distinction is adequate for the purposes of our central thesis here: that aesthetic experience is a reflection of celestial felicity and that this felicity in turn is derived from its archetype, the Beatitude proper to the Absolute. This assertion can be derived from three main sources: intellectual self-evidence; scriptural exegesis; and the fruits of spiritual realization.

Turning first to self-evidence: given the fact that man is made in the image of God, all the essential truths are inscribed in his innermost spirit; it is then altogether "normal" that the innate knowledge of the beatific nature of the Absolute should shine forth as a self-evident reality for primordial man, or man still attuned to his primordial nature, the *fitrah*. And this spiritual intuition of ultimate Reality as the Sovereign Good, steeped in its own Beatitude, will comprise an understanding that this beatitude is the supreme archetype of all blessings and modes of happiness on the celestial and terrestrial planes. For the contemplative, every beautiful object on earth proves the Divine archetype of Beauty, and every aesthetic experience testifies to the Divine archetype of Beatitude. Beauty and Beatitude are indistinguishable in the Essence; it is only on the basis of the initial bi-polarization of the One Reality into Subject and Object that one can distinguish the archetype of objective beauty and the archetype of subjective beatitude. As Dr Lings says in his book *Symbol and Archetype*, it is God's consciousness of His own Infinite Perfection that constitutes the archetype of all marveling at perfection[3].

This intellectual certitude of the Divine source of all beatitude, of the blissful nature of ultimate Reality, can also be actualized upon contact with Revelation: that is, as a result of reflection upon and contemplation of scripture. The descriptions of God's nature as intrinsic beatitude, goodness, mercy and compassion—encapsulated in the *basmalah*[4]—can awaken the dormant knowledge of these realities within the heart of man. The descriptions of Paradise can serve as a means of Platonic remembrance: for Paradise is not only the final resting-place of man, it was also his original home. For this reason, Plato asserts that music on earth can act as a reminder of the heavenly harmonies which man heard prior to this earthly exile. And, according to the Gospel, "no man hath ascended up to Heaven but he that came down from Heaven."[5]

Of the numerous Qur'anic verses describing the felicity of Paradise, we should like to draw attention to one in particular, from the *Surah al-Baqarah*:[6]

> Whenever the dwellers of Paradise are given to eat of the fruits of the Garden they say: this is what we were given to eat before. And they were given the like thereof.

This verse establishes in a most direct manner the relationship between the earthly experience and the celestial archetype of every good. "Fruit" may be taken here to denote the varieties of beatific experience, so the dwellers of Paradise are asserting here that there is a continuity of essence between the delights offered them in Paradise and all positive, noble and beautiful experiences on earth; every mode of happiness on earth is thus a foretaste of a heavenly fruit.

As between the earthly symbol and the celestial archetype, however, there is both continuity and discontinuity, deriving respectively

---

3. *Symbol and Archetype* (Cambridge, Quinta Essentia, 1991), p.57.
4. The Muslim formula of consecration: "In the name of God, the Infinitely Good, the All Merciful" (*Bismi'Llahi ar-Rahman ar-Rahim*), *Ed.*
5. St. John 3:13
6. Qur'an 2:25

from immanence and transcendence: there is continuity in respect of essential content and discontinuity in respect of existential degree. The dwellers in Paradise express the aspect of continuity in saying, "this is what we were given before"; whereas the statement immediately following qualifies this affirmation of identity by saying "they were given the like thereof." In other words, from the point of view of immanence, the earthly experience of beauty participates in its celestial archetype through essential identity, while from the point of view of transcendence, the lower existential degree of this world renders all earthly experience incommensurable with the infinite plenitude of celestial realities. Hence on the one hand, the celestial Garden is described in images that are immediately intelligible in terms of our earthly experience, and on the other hand we are told in a *hadith*[7] that God has prepared for the righteous a Paradise that no eye has seen, no human heart can conceive.

One of the most vivid symbolic illustrations of this two-fold nature of all cosmic realities is to be found in the image of the spider's web. Frithjof Schuon elucidates the meaning of this natural symbol in the following terms:[8]

> . . . the spider's web, formed of warp and weft threads or of radii and concentric circles, represents the Universe under the two-fold relationship of essential identity and existential separation . . . from the point of view of the radii a given thing is the Principle represented in this scheme by the central point; from the point of view of the concentric circles, a given thing only represents that Principle.

This same image can be derived from the Muslim community at prayer: the Ka'bah is then the center of a structure delineated by the innumerable radii and concentric circles constituted by the worshipping believers.

Returning now to the exegesis of scripture, the Qur'an mentions numerous degrees of Paradise, which may be taken as the differentiated radiation of the Beatitude or *Ridwan* mentioned in a *hadith* as being that which is "better" than Paradise, and which is also called "greater" than Paradise in the Qur'an.[9] Being greater and better than paradisal bliss this *Ridwan* can only be the archetypal source of this, and all possible blissful experience. It refers to

---

7. A saying of the Prophet of Islam, *Ed.*
8. *In the Tracks of Buddhism* (London, George Allen & Unwin, 1968), p.27

the beatific contentment proper to the Absolute, alone; for only the Absolute is identical with all that is loveable. We shall return to this point below.

In the *Surah al-Rahman* mention is made of two pairs of Gardens; following Kashani's esoteric commentary, the lower pair consists of the Gardens of the Soul and the Heart, the upper pair being those of the Spirit and the Essence. Consideration of this latter pair will lead to the third part of our discussion, that of spiritual realization. For Kashani writes, in regard to the two fruits symbolizing the abodes, the date and the pomegranate:

> And the "date palm"—that which containeth food and enjoyment, the contemplation of the celestial lights and the manifestations of the Divine Beauty and Majesty in the abode of the spirit, for in its garden the kernel of the individuality still remaineth . . . and the "pomegranate"—that which containeth enjoyment and medicinal balm in the abode of totality, in the Garden of the Essence. It is the contemplation of the Essence through pure extinction in which there is no individuality to be fed.[10]

This extinction in the Essence is not only a posthumous possibility: the highest saints also taste it in the most sublime moments of contemplation, even in this life. The paradoxical combination of extinction and contemplation is summed up in the title of one of Ibn Arabi's works: *Kitab al-Fana' fi'1-Mushahadah* (The Book of Extinction in Contemplation). This extinction of individuality through contemplative absorption in the blissful nature of the Essence is indeed a point on which saints from the most diverse religious traditions converge. To the extent that metaphysical realization is total, the mystics affirm, through their concrete experience, an ineffable Reality that not only transcends all formal dogma but also infinitely surpasses the individuality as such. To take just three of the most important mystics in history, Shankara, Ibn 'Arabi and Meister Eckhart, we find the following strikingly similar characterizations of the supreme reality "tested" and realized in mystical absorption: according to Shankara the Absolute is *Sat-Chit-Ananda*, Being, Consciousness and Bliss;[11] Ibn 'Arabi writes: *wujud wijdan al-*

9. Qur'an 9:72
10. Dr. Lings' unpublished translation.
11. *Atma-Bodha* (Self-Knowledge) (Madras, Sri Ramakrishna Math., 1975), p.217.

*Haqq fi' l wajd*—Being is the consciousness of the Real in ecstasy;[12] and Eckhart writes that the content of the highest realization is "immeasurable power, infinite wisdom and infinite sweetness."[13]

The Bliss, Beatitude or Ecstasy that all three affirm is not an aspect of the Real; rather it is absolutely identical with Reality and with Consciousness. The three elements are distinguishable only on the plane of relativity; they are absolutely undifferentiable in the Essence. To say absolute Reality is to say absolute Beatitude and absolute Consciousness.

It is through the immanence of the Divine in the depths of the soul that the mystics are able to realize the beatitude proper to the Absolute. But the aspect of transcendence is in no wise compromised, for there is no common measure between even the most blissful state attainable by the individual, on the one hand, and the realization of the Absolute, on the other. All experience that remains conditioned by the "kernel of individuality" is *ipso facto* relative; it is for this reason that, in their quest for the pure Absolute, the three mystics cited above methodically reject all blissful experiences that can in any way be qualified as individual. Just as the Absolute is, according to Shankara, *prapancha-upashama*—"without any trace of the development of manifestation"—so there can be no trace of the individual condition in the realization of the Absolute. Shankara comments as follows on the transcendent bliss:

> It is peace . . . liberation. It is indescribable . . . for it is totally different from all objects . . . it is unborn because it is not produced like anything resulting from empirical perceptions.[14]

In other words, the non-transcendent degree of bliss is something like an "object"; it resembles that which results from empirical perception, and therefore, it is conditioned by the relationship between a subjective agent and an object distinct from the subject. This object, even if it is internal to the subject, is nonetheless constitutive of a particular experience of the relative subject. It is only through the transcendence of this ontological dualism, as ground

12. *The Sufi Path of Knowledge*, W. C. Chittick (Albany, State University of New York Press, 1989), p. 212.
13. *Meister Eckhart—Sermons and Treatises*, Tr. M.O'C. Walshe (Dorset, Element Books, 1979), Vol. 1, pp. 60-61.
14. *The Mandukhyopanisad with Gaudapada's Karika and Sankara's Commentary* (Mysore, Sri Ramakrishna Ashrama, 1974), 3:47.

of all subjective experience, that one can speak of the realization of that bliss which is proper to the Absolute, a bliss that is absolutely indistinguishable from the Absolute.

Thus, it is not a state of bliss that defines realization; rather, it is the transcendence of all duality, the conscious realization of the supreme identity, which necessarily entails transcendent bliss. Just as it was stated above that the Truth invariably reveals the essence of beauty, but beauty does not necessarily reveal the truth, so now it can be seen that realization invariably entails bliss, while bliss does not necessarily imply realization. To conclude: whether it be grasped as intellectually self-evident, understood as the result of scriptural exegesis or "tasted" to whatever degree in spiritual realization, this Divine Beatitude is the archetype of all beatific experience in Heaven, which in turn is the archetype of blissful contemplation of beauty on earth, including even the primary aesthetic experience.

For the spiritual man, the experience of formal beauty outside himself enhances and enriches the formless beauty within himself, that is, virtue in an integral sense. Only on the basis of a degree of inward beauty of soul can the experience of outward beauty be spiritually turned to account. For the profane man, on the other hand, the aesthetic experience is at best a temporary relief from the suffocating egotism that is the inescapable result of a life lacking a meaningful relationship with God, and at worst, the aesthetic experience strangles even further the egotistic soul by giving it an illusory plenitude, a sensuous justification of a life without God, an existential proof of "wisdom according to the flesh." Instead of being a foretaste of a beatific Hereafter, the experience of beauty becomes the prop of an irreligious here-below, an expropriation of the immanent beauty of God by the self-seeking and self-satisfied soul.

Nonetheless: "the more he blasphemes, the more he praises God." This elliptical saying of Eckhart can be applied in the present context, for no matter how much the profane man idolizes beauty, his idolatry is only possible by virtue of the immanence of the Divine in all beauty; his idolatry thus unconsciously and indirectly "praises" the Divine Beauty.

Conscious and direct "praise" on the other hand, is performed by the spiritual man who transforms his experience of beauty into a "remembrance of God"; in the measure that this remembrance is operative, the possibility of attachment to the passing forms of beauty recedes, because, in the words of Frithjof Schuon:

> . . . all the treasures of art and those of nature too are found again, in perfection and infinitely, in the Divine Bliss; a man who is fully conscious of this truth cannot fail to be detached from sensory crystallization as such.[15]

Thus, from one's experience of beauty on earth, one can derive an existential foretaste of the higher ontological degrees of bliss, for even the most elementary aesthetic experience participates to some extent in its supreme archetype, Divine Beatitude. But this foretaste deriving from the Immanence of the Divine is spiritually valuable only if it be accompanied by an awareness of the Divine Transcendence and by the accomplishment of the moral and spiritual imperatives that flow from man's total dependence upon God: only then will the foretaste be consummated in a Hereafter which is, as the Qur'an tells us, "better and more lasting."[16]

15. *Understanding Islam* (London, George Allen & Unwin, 1963), p.135.
16. Qur'an 87:17.

The rivers all in Paradise
Flow with the word Allah, Allah
And every longing nightingale
He sings and sings Allah, Allah.

— Yunus Emre

## Chapter 15

# The Yin and the Yang in Nature

## *J.C. Cooper*

Nowhere is the balance of the *yin* and the *yang* in Nature shown better than in the development of the typical Chinese garden, which was essentially Taoist in origin. The Han Emperors had earlier created vast artificial landscapes and parks with mountains, ravines, forests, rivers, lakes and open spaces to provide a habitat for hordes of game for hunting; but during the time of the Six Dynasties and the Tang, when Taoism prevailed, there developed the quiet intimacy of the Taoist garden, intended to reflect heaven on earth. It became a symbol of Paradise where all life was protected and sheltered. The park had been given over to the grandiose, the artificial, extravagant and luxurious, to the hunter and aggressor; the Taoist garden was a place of naturalness and simplicity, a haven for Sage, scholar and nature lover as well as animal, bird and plant life.

Both landscape painting and garden-making owed their development to the Taoist philosophers who derived their inspiration from Nature as the Mother of All Things, the womb of life, eternal renewal, with all her rhythms and moods. What was said of the painting of a landscape applied equally to the creation of a garden; "Chinese painters intuitively felt these same forces to be the visible, material manifestations of a higher all-embracing Reality; the Word made—not flesh—but Living Nature."[1] Or: "The Sages cherish the Tao within them, while they respond to the objective world . . . As to landscapes, they both have material existence and reach to the realms of the Spirit . . . the virtuous follow the Tao by spiritual insight and the wise take the same approach. Landscapes capture the Tao by their forms and the virtuous take pleasure in them. Is this not almost the same thing? . . . The Divine Spirit is infinite, yet it dwells in forms and inspires likeness and thus truth enters into

1. Michael Sullivan, *The Birth of Landscape Painting in China* (R.K.P., 1962).

227

forms and signs."[2] But while landscapes portray the vastness and grandeur of Nature, the garden reveals the intimate aspect.

All forms of art are the outward and visible expression of *Ch'i*, the Cosmic breath or Energy, with which all creation must be in accord, whether it be painting, poetry, music or the creation of a garden. Indeed, all these arts are developed side by side, for the Chinese scholar was expected to be capable of interpreting the same inspiration in all three arts together and the place of both their inspiration and expression was most usually the garden, this term being applied also to the rural retreat of a Sage or hermit, where, in some remote and beautiful scenery, a hut had been built and round it trees planted. In a well-designed garden it should be difficult to distinguish between the work of man and Nature. One should "borrow scenery from Nature" and the ideal place was "among trees in the mountains." Wherever it was, the garden was a place of quiet, meditation and communion with Nature, whether in wild scenery beside a waterfall, or a trickling stream, or in a bamboo grove, or courtyard of a city dwelling.

The garden is "the natural home of man" and house and garden were situated according to *feng-shui* (wind and water) influences in harmony with the currents of *Ch'i*; these were held in balance in both house and garden, as in Nature, by the *yin-yang* force. The *yin* lunar and *yang* solar powers were represented by the *yin* valleys and waters and the *yang* mountains and sky with all their endless *yang* and *yin* qualities such as sunshine and shadow, height and depth, heat and cold.

However small the space utilized, the garden was never laid out as a flat expanse from which all could be viewed at once. This removal of any definite boundary made for succession, expansion, rhythm and the sense of unlimited time and space. The garden, like Nature, is ever-changing, a place of light and shade with a life-breath (*Ch'i yün*) which is in harmony with the rhythms of the seasons and their contrasts in weather. Irregularity of line also suggests movement and life. "Everything that is ruled and symmetrical is alien to free Nature."[3] Or, as it has been said: "The awareness of change, the interaction symbolized by the *yin-yang* theory, has caused Chinese gardeners to seek irregular and unexpected fea-

2. From the *Hua shan-shui hsu*. Preface to painting by Tsung Ping.
3. From the *Yüan Yeh*, a Ming treatise on gardening.

tures which appeal more to the imagination than to the reasoning faculty of the beholder. There were certain rules and principles for gardening, but these did not lead to any conformity. The basic elements were the same as for landscape painting, *shan shui* or 'mountain and water.'"[4] This "mountain and water" might be either imposing scenery or simply a pond and rocks. The smallest space could be converted into an effect of depth, infinite extension and mysterious distance; groves, rockeries, bushes, winding paths, all helped to lure on beyond the immediate scene. As Rowley says of Western and Chinese art: "We restrict space to a single vista as though seen through an open door, they suggest the unlimited space of Nature as though they had stepped through that open door."[5]

The entire garden must be considered in association and relationship with all things in Nature. Chang Ch'ao says: "Planting flowers serves to invite butterflies, piling up rocks serves to invite the clouds, planting pine trees serves to invite the wind . . . planting banana trees serves to invite the rain and planting willow trees serves to invite the cicada." These are all traditionally symbolic associations.

In the past in China, though man was the mediator between Heaven and Earth, he was not the measure of the universe; his place was simply to maintain the balance and harmony between the *yin* and the *yang*. It was Nature which was the Whole, the controlling cosmic power. The garden helped man in his work of maintaining harmony; it also had an ethical significance and influence. According to Ch'ien Lung it had "a refreshing effect upon the mind and regulated the feelings," preventing man from becoming "engrossed in sensual pleasures and losing strength of will." Its pleasures were simple, natural and spiritual. A Suchou poet wrote of the garden: "One should enter it in a peaceful and receptive mood; one should use one's observation to note the plan and pattern of the garden, for the different parts have not been arbitrarily assembled, but carefully weighed against each other like the pairs of inscribed tablets placed in the pavilions,[6] and when one has thor-

---

4. Yang Yap and A. Cotterell, *The Early Civilization of China.*
5. *Principles of Chinese Painting* (Princeton, 1947).
6. Pairs of tablets were inscribed with parallel quotations which corresponded in tonal value and content.

oughly comprehended the tangible forms of objects one should endeavor to attain an inner communication with the soul of the garden and try to understand the mysterious forces governing the landscape and making it cohere."

The garden was for all seasons with their changing moods and colors, flowers and trees; so the pavilion and open gallery were necessary for enjoyment in the heat of summer or the cold of winter and became an integral part of the scenery. Even in winter one sat in the pavilion to admire the beauties of the snow and watch the budding of the almond and plum blossom. A portable brazier of glowing charcoal kept one warm and a large brazier was used to melt the snow to make the tea. The garden was particularly evocative by moonlight, and the new and full moons, times of spiritual power, had their own festivals—especially the festival of the mid-autumn moon. Other festivals were also celebrated in the pavilion or garden; the vernal equinox, observed on the twelfth day of the second month of the Chinese year, was known as the Birthday of the Flowers.

Pavilions and galleries obviously had to blend with their surroundings. The *Yüan Yeh* says: "Buildings should be placed so as to harmonize with the natural formation of the ground." When pavilions were connected by galleries, these followed the rise and fall and curves of the land or winding of the waters which were often crossed by bridges, bringing in all the symbolism of the crossing of the waters, of transition, of communication between one realm or plane and another, as well as of man as mediator, occupying the central position between the great powers. Added beauty and symbolism was introduced in the "moon bridge," a lovely half-circle which when reflected in the clear water below formed the perfect circle of the full moon.

Roofs were curved and painted and the lattice work of the balustrades was lacquered and painted in harmonizing and symbolic colors. Harmony and proportion had to be maintained, but symmetry was alien to Nature. Thus the garden contained no such thing as clipped lawns or hedges or stiff geometrically designed flower beds, or flowers marshaled in rows or patterns. Any "landscaping" had to absorb buildings and, like planted trees, make them look as if they had grown there. "One erects a pavilion where the view opens and plants flowers that smile in the face of the spring breeze."[7] It was

7. The *Yüan Yeh*.

a place for both relaxation and active enjoyment, for solitary meditation and study or for convivial gatherings of friends to meet and drink tea or wine or take *al fresco* meals. There they composed poetry and music, painted, practiced calligraphy or discussed philosophy. One amusement was to compose a poem in the time that it took a floating wine cup and saucer to drift from one end to the other on a meandering water-course set in the floor of the pavilion. A poet failing to complete his poem in the time had to catch and empty the cup. These water-courses could also be constructed in symbolic forms such as the swastika, or the cross-form of the Chinese character for the number ten, or in the shape of a lotus or open flower. Sometimes the water tumbled over small waterfalls or rocks.

Pavilions were given names such as the Pavilion of the Hanging Rainbow, the Fragrance of the Lotus, the Secret Clouds, or the Eight Harmonious Tones, Invitation or Contemplation of the Moon, Welcoming Spring, Pleasant Coolness, and so on. In some gardens there were Halls of the Moon. These were constructed in the shape of a hemisphere, the vaulted ceiling painted to represent the nocturnal sky with innumerable small windows of colored glass depicting the moon and stars. The total effect was one of subdued light like a summer's night. Sometimes the floor was planted with flowers, but more usually it contained running water, the moon and water being closely allied: "The moon washes its soul in the clear waters"; but although moon and waters are both *yin*, water is also symbolically related to the sun since it catches and reflects back the sun's light, the *yang*. These halls could be large enough for holding banquets or of a smallness suitable for intimate sitting about in conversation or listening to poetry and music. Here, in the garden, where heaven and earth meet, music and poetry became the natural form for the expression of harmony.

While the pavilion was built in and for the garden and was open to it, this breaking down of the distinction between in and out of doors applied also to the dwelling house which was not only sited for *feng-shui* but for fitting as naturally as possible into the scenery and giving access so immediately to the garden that there seemed no dividing line. Doors either did not exist or were left open. (Socially, closed doors were not considered courteous since they implied exclusion, while the open door symbolized the welcome extended by the essentially out-going Chinese temperament with its spontaneous and natural relationships developed over the ages in the highly socialized life of a large family or clan.) Doors were often only a means of enhancing a view into the garden or the scenery beyond, such as was the moon door, a beautifully placed circle framing some special outlook Not only was every aspect used to its full natural advantage but "if one can take advantage of a neighbor's view one should not cut off the communication, for such a 'borrowed prospect' is very acceptable."[8]

The house opened on to the garden and the garden came into the house; rooms opened on to the courtyards where flowering shrubs and trees grew and ferns and flowers fringed a central pool, usually with golden carp swimming in it, for the garden was a place for animal and bird life also. Indeed, animals and plants were not considered the only "living" things; everything shares in the cosmic power and mountains and rivers also "live." Nor was it at all unusual for the house to go out into the garden, for the lover of Nature would move a bed out of doors, beside some special tree, shrub or flower which was coming into bloom, so that no stage of its development and beauty would be lost; or one would sit up all night to enjoy the effect of the moonlight. "The moonlight lies like glittering water over the countryside. The wind sighs in the trees and gently touches the lute and the book that lie on the couch. The dark rippled mirror of the water swallows the half-moon. When day dawns one is awakened by the fresh breeze; it reaches the bed and all the dust of the world is blown out of one's mind."[9]

The garden was not, however, merely aesthetic but creative and a reminder of, and contact with, the creative forces of the earth and the great cycle of the seasons, birth, maturity, decay, death and rebirth.

The merging of the native Taoism with imported Buddhism in Ch'an, or Zen, carried on the tradition of the intimate relationship between man and Nature. Ch'an Buddhism and gardens were two facets of Chinese inspiration which were adopted and carried on by the Japanese, but in later decadent times the original symbolism of the garden as a reflection of Paradise was lost and gardens became mere pleasure grounds, except where attached to monasteries, in which much of the symbolism was taken over and where the associations with meditation remained. In these gardens of the effete

8. The *Yüan Yeh.*
9. The *Yüan Yeh.*

times artificial extravagances crept in; windows were made in shapes which bore no relation to symbols, such as teapots, animals, vases and fans, although some of these forms had, in fact, a symbolic content. But these aberrations were stigmatized by the *Yüan Yeh* as "stupid and vulgar" and "intelligent people should be careful in such matters."

The garden was a reflection of the macrocosm and embodied all the *yin-yang* dualisms projected in manifestation. Mountains, valleys, rivers, lakes, were all represented. As Cheng Pan ch'iao said: "The enjoyment of life should come from a view regarding the universe as a garden . . . so that all beings live according to their nature and great indeed is such happiness."

The importance of water in the Chinese garden was not only due to *yin-yang* symbolism but to the wide significance of water itself as, next to the Dragon, the greatest Taoist symbol. It is strength in weakness, fluidity, adaptability, coolness of judgment, gentle persuasion and passionlessness. While mountains and rocks are the bones of the body and the earth its flesh, rivers and streams are the arteries and blood, life giver and fertilizer. Flowing water and still water symbolized movement and repose, the complementary opposites, and water-worn stones symbolized the interaction of the soft and the hard. Still water also takes on all the symbolism of the mirror.

Water could be introduced by forming lakes and rivers in the earth excavated for making mountains, though mountains were most frequently represented by rocks, hollow and weather-worn, fretted out by the restless sea or the elements or formed from the strange shapes of petrified trees. These rocks were carefully selected for their color, texture, grain and shape; some were upright and towering, others, larger at the top than at the base, gave the effect of disappearing into the clouds; others, lying down, took fantastic animal shapes, some gave out a note when struck, others were mute. Sometimes the rocks formed grottoes, but whatever the shape they always appeared as natural to the setting and were as near to the forms of wild mountain crags as possible, giving the impression of Nature, untamed and capricious. (In this "naturalness" it must be remarked that the mountains of China in the Yangtse gorges, the far West and the southern provinces have been worked by Nature herself into fantastic and sometimes grotesque shapes.) "Try to make your mountains resemble real mountains. Follow Nature's plan" but "do not forget they have to be built by human hands."[10]

Symbolically, the mountain is, of course, the world axis, but in the Chinese garden it also represented the *yang* power in Nature with the waters as the *yin*. The "mountain" is traditionally placed in the middle of a lake or pond, the rock being the stable and eternal, the water the flowing and temporal. This mountain-and-water (*shan shui*) symbolism also obtains in landscape painting. The rock and the shadow it casts are also *yang* and *yin*. Rocks are "silent, unmovable and detached from life, like refined scholars." Their ruggedness also suggests the challenging and dangerous element in the mountains and life.

In larger gardens the mountains were sufficiently high for the formation of small valleys and dales, with winding streams opening out into lakes on which boat journeys could be taken and where water could be spanned by bridges. Sometimes a series of islands or rocks were so connected. Tunnels in the rocks gave the same effect and carried the same symbolism as bridges in passing from one world to another. But "even a little mountain may give rise to many effects . . . a small stone may evoke many feelings."[11] Shen Fu says: "In the designing of a rockery or the training of flowering trees one should try to show the small in the large and the large in the small and provide for the real in the unreal and the unreal in the real. One reveals and conceals alternately, making it sometimes apparent and sometimes hidden."

Both the *yang* mountain and the *yin* tree are axial and so represent stability and balance between the two Great Powers; they also offer a line of communication for man between the celestial *yang* forces coming down to earth and to earthly *yin* forces reaching up to heaven, with man again as central and responsible for the maintenance of balance and harmony in responding equally to both powers.

Trees were an essential feature of both the domestic and hermitage garden, particularly the latter where they were often the only addition made by man to the natural scenery; their variety was almost as important as the trees themselves. While all trees are beautiful and symbolize the feminine power, some were especially noted

10. The *Yüan Yeh.*
11. The *Yüan Yeh.*

for their *yin-yang* qualities. Though *yin* as a tree, the pine and cedar express *yang* masculine dignity and rigidity in contrast to the feminine gracefulness, pliability and charm of the willow, both these trees were considered necessary for the maintenance of the *yin-yang* harmony. Flowering trees such as the almond, cherry, plum and peach were esteemed—one should say loved—for their beauty and their symbolism. The almond, as the first flower of the year, is in many traditions the Awakener, watchfulness. Flowering in winter it is also courage in adversity. The cherry depicts delicacy of feeling and purity on the *yin* side and nobility on the *yang*. The plum, a symbol of winter and beauty, also signified strength, longevity and the hermit; it is one of the favorite subjects for artists. The plum, pine and bamboo were called "the three friends of winter." The almond and plum are both symbolic of new life coming in spring, but the plum should have a gnarled trunk and branches, called "sleeping dragons," as the *yang* aspect, to offset the delicate blossoms of the *yin*; they also represent the old and the new together. Just as lovers of the garden would move their beds out under trees, so we read of artists who wandered all night in the moonlight to catch every phase of the beauty of "the dry limbs clad in jade-white blooms."

The peach holds a special position as the tree of the Taoist genii or Immortals; it is the Tree of Life at the center of Paradise. It is also the Tree of Immortality and one bite of the fruit growing on the tree confers immediate immortality. Peach stones were apotropaic and were beautifully and symbolically carved and kept, or worn, as amulets and talismans. The tree is a symbol of spring, youth, marriage, wealth and longevity.

Pre-eminent among flowers were the lotus, peony and chrysanthemum. The peony is the only purely *yang* flower. Flowers, with their cup shape, naturally depict the *yin* receptive aspect in nature, but the peony is a royal flower, flaunting the red, fiery, masculine color; it is also nobility, glory, riches. The chrysanthemum, on the other hand, is a flower of quiet retirement, the beloved flower of the cultured scholar, the retired official, who was, of course, also a scholar, and of the philosopher and poet. It was so much cultivated in retirement that it became a symbol of that life and of leisure. It signifies longevity, as being that which survives the cold, and as autumnal it is harvest and wealth, but it is primarily ease, leisure, joviality and enjoyment. Yüan Chung-lang said that the retired and the scholar were fortunate in having "the enjoyment of the hills and water, flowers and bamboo" largely to themselves since "luckily they lie outside the scope of the strugglers for fame and power who are so busy with their engrossing pursuits that they have no time for enjoyment."

But the lotus, a universal symbol in the East (its symbolism is taken on by the lily and sometimes the rose in the West), is "the flower that was in the Beginning, the glorious lily of the Great Waters . . . that wherein existence comes to be and passes away." It is both *yin* and *yang* and contains within itself the balance of the Two Powers; it is solar, as blooming in the sun, and lunar, as rising from the dark of the waters of pre-cosmic chaos. As the combination of air and water, this symbolizes spirit and matter. Its roots, bedded in the darkness of the mud, depict indissolubility; its stem, the umbilical cord of life, attaches man to his origins and is also a world axis; rising through the opaque waters of the manifest world, the leaves and flowers reach and unfold in the air and sunlight, typifying potentiality in the bud and spiritual expansion and realization in the flower; its seeds, moving on the waters, are creation. The lotus is associated with the wheel both as the solar matrix and the sun-wheel of cycles of existence. Iamblicus calls it perfection since its leaves, flowers and fruit form the circle. As lunar-solar, *yin-yang*, the lotus is also the androgyne, the self-existent. It has an inexhaustible symbolism in Hinduism, Taoism and Buddhism alike. Again it appears as both solar and lunar associated with sun gods such as Surya and lunar goddesses such as Lakshimi; solar with Amitaba and lunar with Kwan-yin and androgynous in Kwannon. The lotus is the Golden Flower of Taoism, the crystallization and experience of light, the Tao. While on the spiritual level it represents the whole of birth, growth, development and potentiality, on the mundane plane it depicts the scholar-gentleman who comes in contact with the mud and dirty water of the world but is uncontaminated by it. Apart from its almost endless symbolism, the lotus is a flower of great beauty and highly evocative; as Osvald Sirén says, a sheet of lotus blossom "emanates a peculiar magic, an atmosphere that intoxicates like fragrant incense and lulls like the rhythm of a rising and falling mantra."[12]

12. *Gardens of China.*

Ancient China understood many things which are only now reaching the West and being hailed as new discoveries. She anticipated by centuries the "discovery" that flowers and plants have feelings. Yüan Chung-lang knew that they have their likes and dislikes and compatibilities among other vegetation and that they respond to care and appreciation in more than a material way. The flowers in a Chinese garden were genuinely loved, not in any "precious" aestheticism, but rather in an intimate relationship between living individuals. He said that "flowers have their moods of happiness and sorrow and their time of sleep . . . when they seem drunk, or quiet and tired and when the day is misty, that is the sorrowful mood of flowers . . . when they bask in the sunlight and their delicate bodies are protected from the wind, that is the happy mood of flowers. . . . When the ancient people knew a flower was about to bud they would move their beds and pillows and sleep under it watching how the flower passed from infancy to maturity and finally dropped off and died . . . As for all forms of noisy behavior and common vulgar prattle, they are an insult to the spirits of flowers. One should rather sit dumb like a fool than offend them."[13] Among things which flowers dislike are: too many guests; ugly women putting flowers in their hair; dogs fighting; writing poems by consulting a rhyming dictionary; books kept in bad condition; spurious paintings and common monks talking Zen! On the other hand they do like a visiting monk who understands tea!

Picked flowers and vases of flowers should never be regarded as normal, only as a temporary expedient employed by those living in cities and unnatural places deprived of hills and lakes or any garden.

For the town-dweller or for one kept indoors of necessity, the miniature garden was created. Though it was also seen in pavilions, it was most usually on the tables of scholars. It, too, symbolized Paradise, the Isles of the Blessed or the Abode of the Immortals reflected in miniature perfection with the whole range of the *yin-yang* symbolism. Exceptionally beautiful stones and shells were used and there were miniature grottoes, trees, bamboos and grasses growing among the mountains, valleys and waters. The making of these gardens was an art in itself; just as Wang Wei maintained that

13. The treatise *P'ing Shih* by Yüan Chung-lang.

the artist can bring Nature into the space of a small painting, so the creator of a garden, large or small or miniature, can concentrate the cosmos within its bounds.

Enclosing the whole garden in the city, or where the extent of the ground was limited, was the wall which was used not only as a boundary but as a setting for trees, shrubs and flowers; it could also provide an aperture which opened on to some special view. In the city, where space was restricted, walls were often a garden in themselves, sometimes built with considerable width, giving a roof-garden effect, or with trees and shrubs planted on top and ferns in the crevices below. Enclosing walls also helped to make the city garden a place where one could find "stillness in turmoil." Apart from the symbolism of the enclosed garden as Paradise, the walls brought in the *yin-yang* significance of the interplay of light and shade.

Unfortunately China now joins the industrial nations of the world in exploiting Nature. Hideous concrete blocks of flats, offices and factories insulate man from any contact with the yellow earth and even in the country, in the "communes," ugly blocks of dwelling houses and buildings scar the landscape and violate all traditional rules. Sadly, Seyyed Hossein Nasr's words can be applied: "There is nearly total disequilibrium between modern man and Nature as attested in nearly every expression of modern civilization which seeks to offer a challenge to nature rather than co-operate with it . . . the harmony between man and nature has been destroyed."[14] The *yin-yang* balance and harmony has been betrayed.

14. *Man and Nature* (London, 1968).

My Cottage at Deep South Mountain

In my middle years I love the Tao
and by Deep South Mountain I make my home.
When happy I go alone into the mountains.
Only I understand this joy.
I walk until the water end, and sit
waiting for the hour when clouds rise.
If I happen to meet an old woodcutter,
I chat with him, laughing and lost to time.

— Wang Wei

## Chapter 16

# Creation, the Image of God

## *Leo Schaya*

Lift up your eyes on high and see who hath created these?

*Isaiah 40:26*

## I

The principal aim of tradition in regard to the forms and laws of the cosmos is to connect all things with their first and divine cause and thus show man their true meaning, the sense of his own existence being likewise revealed to him thereby. Now, in the sight of the "One without a second," the whole of existence has no being of its own: it is the expression of the one reality, that is to say the totality of its aspects, manifestable and manifested, in the midst of its very infinity. Things are no more than symbolic "veils" of their divine essence or, in a more immediate sense, of its ontological aspects; these aspects are the eternal archetypes of all that is created.

If one understands creation in this way, it is revealed as a multitude of more or less perfect images of God or of his qualities, as a hierarchy of more or less pure truths leading towards the only truth; for if God is the first origin and highest prototype of creation, he is also its final end as Proverbs (16:4) testifies: "YHVH[1] has made everything for his own purpose."

The only reality cannot do otherwise than work for itself and in itself. But in its pure selfness, it does not act or wish for any; in it nothing whatsoever is determined, there is no distinction between subject and object, cause and effect, a god and a creation. In this non-duality, God rests in himself, nameless, and without any know-

---

1. The tetragrammaton YHVH represents the sacrosanct name of God in the Jewish tradition. For more than two thousand years the Jews have been forbidden to pronounce this name, and its vocalization is no longer known.

able aspect; it is only on this side of the supreme and superintelligible essence that his knowledge "makes its appearance," which is to say his intelligent and intelligible being, including his causal and efficient will. His being, his knowledge, his will and his action are indivisible aspects of his ontological unity; this unity is not affected by any of his attributes nor by any of his manifestations: the One is what he is, knows himself, through himself, and works in himself for himself without becoming other than himself.

His work is the manifestation of all the aspects of his being in the midst of his being itself. In *Sefirothic* language it is said that *kether*, the supreme principle, sees itself through *hokhmah*, the "wisdom" or first irradiation, in the mirror of *binah*, the "intelligence" or infinite receptivity. In this supreme mirror God contemplates his seven lordly aspects: *hesed*, his "grace"; *din*, his "judgement"; *tifereth*, his "beauty"; *netsah*, his "victory"; *hod*, his "glory"; *yesod*, the cosmic "foundation" or his eternal act; and *malkhuth*, his "kingdom," or immanence. The irradiations of his aspects come together in the last *Sefirah*, *malkhuth*, as in a lower mirror, and there form the multiple picture of what in reality is only one; this image of the infinite and indivisible aspects of the One is the Creation.

All created things emanate from God's being and from his knowledge; they are essentially his ontological and intelligible possibilities, the "sparks" of his light, the "ideas" that spring from his "wisdom" or "thought" like so many spiritual and existential "rays."

> When God designed to create the universe, his thought compassed all worlds at once, and by means of this thought were they all created, as it says, "In wisdom hast thou made them all" (Psalms 104:24). By this thought (*mahshabah*)—which is his wisdom (*hokhmah*)—were this world and the world above created. . . . All were created in one moment (the eternal moment of divine action). And he made this (terrestrial) world corresponding to the world above (the celestial and spiritual worlds which are themselves "pictures" of the infinite world of the *Sefiroth* or supreme archetypes), and everything which is above has its counterpart here below . . . and yet all constitute a unity (because of the causal sequence of all things and their essential identity with the only reality) (*Zohar, Shemoth* 20 a).

The knowledge of God is the *alpha* and *omega* of the work of creation. The world is born from the knowledge that God has of himself; and by the knowledge that the world has of God, it is reabsorbed into him. God made everything for this knowledge that unites to him; all other knowledge is only an ephemeral reflection of it. When the world sees God—through man—it sees its supreme archetype, its own uncreated fullness, and is effaced in its essence, in the infinite. This cognitive and deifying act is the ultimate fulfillment of the creative work; it is for that—for himself—that God created the world.

The knowledge of God does not depend on any science, but all human knowledge depends on it and derives from it. Receptivity alone, face to face with God, is enough, in principle, to obtain the influx of his light in which the spirit can see him. A science, even a revealed science such as cosmology, is only a possible, not an obligatory way of searching for knowledge of God; it is a way which makes it possible to receive the truth through his symbolic "veils," that is through the worlds, on whatever scale. To see the eternal cause in cosmic effects raises a man above the illusions of the phenomenal world and brings him closer to reality. Baal-Shem[2] said:

> At times, man has to learn that there are an indefinite number of firmaments and spheres beyond, and that he himself is located in an insignificant spot on this small earth. But the entire universe is as nothing in the face of God, the Infinite, who brought about the "contraction" and made "room" in himself so that the worlds could be created in it. But although man may understand this with his mind, he is not able to ascend toward the higher worlds; and this is what is meant by: "The Lord appeared to me from afar"—he contemplates God from afar. But if he serves God with all his strength, he actualizes a great power in himself and rises in spirit, and suddenly pierces all the firmaments, and ascends beyond the angels, beyond the celestial "wheels," beyond the Serafim and the "thrones"; and that is the perfect "service."

# II

When Baal-Shem says that "God, the infinite, brings about a 'contraction' and makes 'room' in himself where the worlds can be cre-

---

2. Israel ben Eliezer, called Baal-Shem (Master of the Divine Name), 1700-60, was the greatest Jewish saint of the last centuries. He founded Polish and Ukrainian Hasidism; this term comes from the word *hasid*, the "devout" in regard to God. His movement developed towards the middle of the eighteenth century in Poland and spread into all the Slav countries; in the last century it included nearly four million adepts.

ated," he is alluding to the Kabbalistic doctrine of *tsimtsum*. The term *tsimtsum* can be translated by "contraction," "restriction," "retreat," or "concentration"; it had been used in Jewish esotericism chiefly since Isaac Luria (1534-72) to describe the divine mystery on which creation depends. "The Holy One, blessed be he, withdrew his powerful light from one part of himself, and left a void to serve as 'a place' for cosmic expansion"; it concerns "that part of the divine essence in which the light was weakened to allow the existence of souls, angels and the material worlds."

Through this symbolic language, the Kabbalah, then, tries to express the mysterious genesis of the finite in the midst of the infinite. In reality, God, the absolute One, has no "parts," but an infinity of possibilities, of which only the creatural possibilities have the illusory appearance of separate forms; in themselves, these forms are integrated, as eternal archetypes, in the all-possibility of the One. As for that "part from which the light has been withdrawn" to make room for the "place" of the cosmos, it is nothing other than the receptivity of God that actualizes itself in the midst of his unlimited fullness; this receptivity has a transcendent aspect and an immanent aspect: "above," it is identified with *binah*, the "supreme mother," which is eternally filled with the infinite and luminous emanation of the "father," *hokhmah*; "below," it is *malkhuth*, the "lower mother," or cosmic receptivity of God. The latter absorbs both the influx from the *Sefiroth* of mercy which are luminous and overflowing, and the influx from the *Sefiroth* of rigor which are "dark" or "empty"; that is why, in contrast to *binah*, which is always revealed as filled with the infinite, *malkhuth*, or divine immanence, can take on the appearance of a dark void in the midst of its radiant fullness. Indeed, *binah* is said to be "without all rigor, although rigor emanates from it"; while *malkhuth* receives the emanations of rigor together with those of grace, to produce and dominate the cosmos and hold it in equilibrium through the interpenetration of the two simultaneously opposite and complementary influxes.

Now, the rigor which emanates from *binah* is *din*, "judgment" or universal discernment, the principle of concentration, distinction and limitation; it produces *tsimtsum*, divine "contraction," in the heart of *malkhuth*, the plastic cause. Through the effect of *tsimtsum*, the divine fullness withdraws to a certain extent from the "lower mother," and awakens creative receptivity in her; the latter, when actualized, takes on the aspect of the void or "place of the world," ready to receive cosmic manifestation. Then, all created possibilities spring up from the existential seed which is left behind by divine fullness on its withdrawal—as a luminous "residue" (*reshimu*) in the midst of immanent emptiness. Thus, thanks to the divine "contraction" and to the void it brings about in the *shekhinah*, the expansion of the world takes place; and everything living in the immanence of God is a small world created in the image of the macrocosm: it is a void to which life is given by a luminous "residue" of the only reality, by a central and divine "spark" that projects onto it the reflection of some eternal archetype.

The Kabbalah expresses the same cosmogonical process in other symbolic terms as the *pargod* or cosmic "curtain." The *Idra Rabba Kadisha* (the "great and holy assembly," included in the *Zohar*) says of the "Ancient of Ancients" that "he draws a curtain down before him" through which his kingdom begins to take shape. This image and that of the *tsimtsum* not only point to the same truth but from one point of view also complement each other. Thus it can be said that God appears to "withdraw" himself into himself to the extent that he draws down a "curtain" before him. The "curtain" hangs before him like a darkness; and this darkness in reality is nothing other than his cosmic receptivity, which allows his reality to appear through it as a light. But his infinite light appears through the dark veil only in a "weakened," fragmented and limited way, which is the mode of existence of the finite.

God is hidden in everything he creates, somewhat in the way that light is contained in the innumerable reflections that produce a mirage. To go further in this symbolism, it could be said that the desert where the mirage is produced represents the "void" or the "place" of the world made by *tsimtsum*, and the imperceptible screen on which appear the vanishing forms that lead the pilgrim astray represents the *pargod*, which is the "curtain" or "mirror" of the *shekhinah*. In fact, in the face of the "One without a second," creation—the apparition of a "second"—as well as the creative causes themselves, come to appear as existential illusions. That is why the Kabbalah brings in a third idea, in addition to those of *tsimtsum* and *pargod*, to define the nature of creation, namely, *habel*, "vanity," derived from Ecclesiastes (1:2): "Vanity of vanities (*habel habalim*), all is vanity!" The *Zohar* (*Shemoth* 10 b) teaches on this subject:

King Solomon, in his book (Ecclesiastes), treated of seven "vanities" (*habalim*, lit. "breaths") upon which the world stands, namely the seven (*Sefirothic*) pillars (of universal construction) which sustain the world in (causal) correspondence with (their first created effects) the seven firmaments, which are called respectively *Vilon, Rakiya, Shehakim, Zebul, Ma'on, Makhon, Araboth*. It was concerning them that Solomon said: "Vanity of vanities . . . all is vanity" (*ibid,* 1:1). As there are seven firmaments, with others (existential planes such as the seven earths and seven hells) cleaving to them and issuing from them, so there are seven *habalim* and others emanating from these (and filling all creation), and Solomon in his wisdom referred to them all (as well as to their causes and archetypes, the seven *Sefiroth* of construction).

The Kabbalah does not say that the seven cosmological *Sefiroth* are illusions in themselves, for they represent the creative aspects of one and the same reality; nevertheless, in so far as they project the mirage of an existential multitude in the midst of its undifferentiated unity, they manifest as so many principles of illusion or causal "vanities." But if they are considered outside of their relation with creation, they are integrated into absolute unity. In so far as the One is looking at himself alone, he does not go out of his supreme trinity, *kether-hokhmah-binah*; but when he wishes to contemplate the creative possibilities in himself, he opens his "seven eyes" or "Sefiroth of construction," projecting all the cosmic "vanities" through their look. "Vanity," according to Ecclesiastes, is to be found "under the sun"—a symbol of the *Sefirah tifereth*, which synthesizes the six active *Sefiroth* of "construction"—and is made upon the earth; now the "earth" is one of the synonyms of *malkhuth*, the receptive and substantial *Sefirah* of cosmic "construction": there alone, in the divine immanence, the mirage of creation is produced, maintained and effaced. "That is why the beginning of Genesis," says the *Tikkune Zohar*:

> is concerned only with the *elohim* (principle of immanence) designating the *shekhinah* (and not with the transcendental principle, YHVH). Everything created, from the *hayoth* and the *serafim* (higher angels) down to the smallest worm on the earth, lives in *elohim* and through *elohim* . . . The creation is the work of the *shekhinah* who takes care of it as a mother cares for her children.

The entire creation is an illusory projection of the transcendental aspects of God into the "mirror" of his immanence. The *Zohar* notes, in fact, that the verb *baro*, "to create," implies the idea of "creating an illusion." But although the creation is by nature illusory, it contains something of reality; for every reflection of reality, even remote, broken up and transient, necessarily possesses something of its cause. Even if the creation is taken as being pure illusion, that real something which constitutes its essence still cannot be excluded. Illusion itself is not a mere nothingness, for there cannot be any such thing. By its very existence it would no longer be nothing; illusion is a "mixture" of the real and the ephemeral or—in Kabbalistic terminology—of "light" and "darkness."

Creation is made from the "dark void" that God established in the midst of his luminous fullness and which he then filled with his existential reflections. This "dark void" is the "mirror" or plane of cosmic reflection, inherent in the receptivity of the *shekhinah*. Indeed, receptivity is both emptiness and darkness; but while the nature of the void is transparency or translucence, that of darkness is opacity or contraction. Thus, when the creative influx of the *Sefiroth* fills the receptivity of the "lower mother," its emptiness or translucence transmits the divine radiation in all the directions of the cosmos, while its darkness contracts, condenses and becomes substance-enveloping light. In its first and celestial condensation, substance is still subtle and resplendent with the radiation that only lightly veils it; but it becomes opaque and gross in its corporeal and terrestrial solidification, which hides the light from above, as thick clouds mask the sun.

The "vanity" of things consists in this darkness which fleetingly takes on the appearance of substance; however, substance becomes a mirror of truth when the forms it assumes are recognized as the symbolic expressions of the eternal archetypes, which are none other than the divine aspects.

# III

The ten fundamental aspects of God, or *Sefiroth*, are manifested at first on the macrocosmic level in the form of ten heavens. The three supreme *Sefiroth*, *kether-hokhmah-binah*, are revealed in the three "heavens of heavens," the triple immanent principle: that is, *shekhinah-metatron-avir*. *Shekhinah* is the immanence of *kether*, the presence of divine reality in the midst of the cosmos. *Metatron*, the manifestation of *hokhmah* and the active aspect of the *shekhinah*, is the principial form from which all created forms emanate; *avir*, the ether, is a manifestation of binah:[3] it is the passive aspect of *shekhinah*, its cosmic receptivity, which gives birth to every created substance, whether subtle or corporeal. The triple immanent principle, *shekhinah-metatron-avir*, in its undifferentiated unity, constitutes the spiritual and prototypical "world of creation": *olam haberiyah*.

The seven *Sefiroth* of universal construction, *hesed-din-tifereth-netsah-hod-yesod-malkhath*, which emanate from the supreme tri-unity, are the causes and archetypes of the seven created heavens; the latter issue from the three "heavens of heavens," as the constituent degrees of the "world of formation," *olam hayetsirah*. In this world all creatures undergo their first and subtle formation; it is situated beyond space and time, in the indefinite expansion and duration of the supra-terrestrial cosmos. *Olam hayetsirah* is imperceptible to the senses and serves as a dwelling place for souls—before or after they pass through the earth—for angels and for spirits.

Between the seven subtle heavens and the "seven earths" which issue from them, are situated as further manifestations of the *Sefiroth* of construction, the seven degrees of the "lower Eden" or earthly Paradise, inhabited by angels and blessed souls; in this intermediary world there exist also darkened inversions of the heavens, namely the seven hells or abodes of the demons and of the damned.

The corporeal universe comprising the "seven earths," is called the "world of fact," *olam ha' asiyah*; it is conditioned by time, space, the material elements and, from the microcosmic point of view, by sensory perception. The seven earths represent so many different states of our universe; they are described as "seven countries," hierarchically "super-posed and all populated"; one of them, the "higher earth," is our own, which the six others resemble without attaining its perfection; in the same way their inhabitants possess only an incomplete or unbalanced kind of human form. On the other hand, the seven *Sefiroth* of construction—which are also called the "seven days of (principial) creation"—are manifested in time in the following septenaries: the seven days of the week; the seven years forming a "sabbatical" cycle; the seven times seven years between one "Jubilee" and another; the seven thousand years rep-

---

3. Sometimes *avir* is identified, by metaphysical transposition, with the supreme principle, *kether*; it is the substantial indistinction of the ether which, in this case, serves as a "symbol" of the indeterminateness of the absolute essence.

resenting a great cycle of existence; and the "seven times seven thousand years" ending at the fiftieth millennium, on the "great Jubilee," when the world is reintegrated into the divine principle.[4] Finally, the seven *Sefiroth* of construction determine the six directions of space and their spiritual center, called the "Holy of Holies."

Man is the most perfect image of universal reality in the whole of creation; he is the "incarnated" recapitulation of all the cosmic degrees and of their divine archetypes. Indeed, through his spiritual faculties, psychic virtues and corporeal forms, he represents the most evident symbol of the ten *Sefiroth*, and his integral personality embraces all the worlds: his pure and uncreated being is identified with the *Sefirothic* "world of emanation" (*olam ha' atsiluth*); his spirit, with the prototypical "world of creation" (*olam haberiyah*); his soul with the subtle "world of formation" (*olam hayetsirah*); and his body, with the sensory "world of fact" (*olam ha' asiyah*). The law of man, the ecalogue, is a manifestation of the ten *Sefiroth*, as is the "sacred community" of Israel, which is complete only when ten Jewish men come together.

The human being is the principal "point of intersection" of the *Sefirothic* rays in the midst of the cosmos; through him, the divine riches are revealed in all their spiritual radiance and by the explicit symbolism of thought, word, forms and corporeal gestures. Of all beings, man alone—in his perfect state—is the one being whom God causes to participate fully in his infinite knowledge; and through man's intermediary God brings everything back to himself.

## IV

If creation is the image of God, cosmogony operates—just like a reflected projection—by the law of inversion or, more precisely, by inverse analogy. This law derives from the principle of divine "con-

4. When the Kabbalah says that the total duration of the world is fifty thousand years, this figure should be taken as a symbolic expression of the law which constitutes its eternal foundation. This law resides in the mystery of the seven *Sefiroth* of construction, each one of which recapitulates, in its way, the whole. Thus one is faced with a unity of "seven times seven" or forty-nine *Sefirothic* degrees, which are manifested through as many cyclical phases, its total duration being that of the indefinite existence of the cosmos; these forty-nine degrees issue from *binah* and return to it. *Binah*, as their "end," is the "fiftieth" degree, or the supreme and prototypical "Jubilee."

traction," *tsimtsum;* by the effect of this "contraction," the infinite, *en sof,* appears as *nekuda,* the causal "point" or supreme "center" of the finite, and the limits of the finite are extended and take on the appearance of unlimited existence. The "contraction" or first inversion is reflected in the midst of existence itself, with the actualization of a multitude of "central points," each surrounded by an expanse, which serves both as "veil" and "mirror" for its contents. All these "centers" are connected among themselves and with the "supreme Center," by the "middle pillar" or universal axis, which is none other than the creative, regulating and redemptive "ray" of the divine principle. The "spheres of activity," which surround their respective centers, are all the worlds, great and small, together making up the cosmic expanse; whether they appear as worlds properly so called, as beings or as things, each of these spheres constitutes, therefore, the "envelope" or "shell" of such and such a "kernel" or existential point of departure, hierarchically included in the "middle pillar." Finally, as was explained in the last chapter, every "point" representing the center, the immediate principle or prototype of such a world, itself functions as the "field of action" of a higher center, and so on up to the supreme center, which is its own "sphere of activity" embracing all the others.

Thus we are confronted by an indefinite series of existential states, formed by as many "inversions" or exteriorizations of their respective points of departure. We have just seen that all these "points" are co-ordinated, in accordance with the law of causality, in the universal axis, which is the "descent" of the "supreme point" across the center or "heart" of everything; thus, each thing, in spite of its dependence on what is hierarchically above it, contains in its innermost depth the "center of centers," the real presence of God. Every created thing is in its own way a synthesis of the whole of creation, whether in a conscious, developed or seminal mode and it includes in its essence the principle itself. The principle or universal and divine center is not comparable, therefore, to a point or geometric axis, localized in any one place:[5] it is the omnipresent medium.

---

5. It should be made clear that if the divine immanent center is not "localized" in any one place—because it penetrates all—it nevertheless reveals itself by preference in a sanctified place or being; the latter thereby represents the living expression of the universal center.

Terrestrial man, "last born" of the creation, is the "lower point" where cosmogony stops in its creative inversions and returns toward the "supreme point." When this "inversion of inversions" starts to work in man, it is said that he is seized by *teshubah*, "conversion," "repentance," or the "return" to God; indeed, when man "performs *teshubah*," with all his heart, all his soul, and all his might, he ends by being absorbed into his pure and divine "self" and by integrating—within himself—the whole of existence in the cause. This is given to man by the mystery of his inner and universal person which embraces everything from the terrestrial "world of fact" to the very principle of the "world of emanation"; that is why the voluntary "return" of man to God involves the "return" of all the worlds. "Great is *teshubah*, for it heals the world. Great is *teshubah*, for it reaches the throne of glory. Great is *teshubah*, for it brings about redemption" (*Talmud, Yoma* 86 a).

By his absorption in God, man actualizes universal deliverance in himself and thereby "hastens" cosmic redemption. The latter occurs when the entire multitude of subtle and corporeal manifestations has been exhausted in the midst of the two created worlds. At that moment the "grand Jubilee" takes place, the total and final deliverance;[6] it is the ultimate phase of *tsimtsum*, the "inversion of inversions," which is not only the "contraction" of the corporeal universe, but of the entire cosmic expanse: the "withdrawal" of the whole creation into its uncreated center and principle. Then, every immanent spiritual fight regains its transcendent brightness, and every terrestrial and celestial substance is reabsorbed in the "higher ether" (*avira ilaah*), which is eternally integrated into the infinite essence. Such is the return of the cosmic "image" to divine reality.

6. The definitive reintegration of the cosmos into the principle, which is to be accomplished at the end of "seven times seven millennia" or great cycles of existence, is prefigured by transitory restorations of the paradisal state, which take place every "seventh millennium" or "great Sabbath" of creation. One of these "moments of rest" or transient absorptions of the created into the divine immanence was the cycle of the *Fiat Lux*, the other, that of the adamic Eden; according to tradition, we are now at the dawn of a new cosmic Sabbath, the "Reign of the Messiah."

*Where I wander—You!*
*Where I ponder—You!*
*Only You everywhere, You, always, You.*
*You, You, You.*
*When I am gladdened—You!*
*And when I am saddened—You!*
*Only You, everywhere You!*
*You, You, You.*
*Sky is You!*
*Earth is You!*
*You above! You below!*
*In every trend, at every end,*
*Only You, everywhere You!*

*— Levi Yitzchak of Berditchov*

*Chapter 17*

# The World of the Icon and Creation:

## An Orthodox Perspective on Ecology and Pneumatology

*John Chryssavgis*

### I. Theology and Mystery

Any discussion of the beauty or sacredness of the world, at least from an Orthodox perspective, necessarily involves an exploration into the theology and mystery of the icon, that is to say, into the doctrine behind and the vision beyond icons. For the world of the icon not only presupposes a way of thinking and demands a way of living, but it also offers new insights into our worldview, new perceptions of the world around us, and something of the eternal in everything we see. Our generation is characterized by behavior that results from an autism with regard to the natural cosmos: a certain lack of awareness, or recognition, causes us to use, even waste, the beauty of the world. And so we are locked inside the confines of our own concerns, with no access to the outside world. We have disestablished a continuity between ourselves and the outside, with no possibility for intimate communion and mutual enhancement. The world of the icon restores this relationship by reminding us what is outside and beyond, what ultimately gives value and vitality.

The iconographer aspires to achieve the inner vision of the world, an image of the world as intended by God. The "iconic" world, however, is not an unreal world; rather, it is the real world which is called to ingress upon, and to spill over into, this world. Orthodox iconography seeks to discover and then to disclose the reality of the experience of the heavenly kingdom in this world. In fact, the icon articulates with theological conviction the faith in this kingdom and its activity in the earthly realm. Unfortunately, we have desacralized, or denaturalized, this world by disconnecting it from "heaven." The icon reverses perspective as we know it and does away with the "objective" distance between this world and the next. There is no double order in creation. There is no sharp line of demarcation between "material" and "spiritual." The icon constitutes the epiphany of God in the world and the existence of the world in the presence of God. It is neither idealism nor idolatry. Like the unborn child in the womb of its mother, the icon presents to us the visible seeds of the divinity in the world. Its art and beauty represent God's art and beauty in the creation. The icon speaks in this world, yet in the language of the age to come.

The icon is an integral part of Orthodox spirituality, a central aspect of the celebration of creation. Like the Incarnation and the Creation, the icon is meant to be the piercing of space and time, that is, matter is met by God's eternal nature. The entire church building—with its architecture, frescoes, and mosaics—accomplishes through space and matter what the liturgy does through time and praise: the anticipation of the heavenly kingdom and the participation of the divine presence. The seeming contradiction of an inaccessible God and a crucified Christ constitutes the ultimate measure of God's measureless love for the world. For it is God's freedom that makes God's limitless love so powerful that it breaks all barriers and all limitations. The God who created out of love, who was incarnated out of love, now saturates the whole world with divine energies.

The icon reveals all the tensions, conflicts, and contradictions through which one is called to transparency; every fall is inscribed on it. But there is ultimately resurrection through communion, for to encounter Christ in the icon is to encounter an image beyond suffering, solitude, and hell, an image that will never die. Therefore, the basis of the icon is christological, allowing the wholly inaccessible to be shared entirely. With the event of the Incarnation, as with the epiphany of the icon, the cycle of the nonrepresentation of the Old Testament God (cf. Exod. 20:4-5 and John 1:18) is completed.

"God became human that humanity might be deified," wrote the Christian fathers.[1] The saints are those who emanate the light of

1. See Athanasius, *On the Divine Incarnation*, 54.

deified humanity, while icons indicate the participation of humanity and the entire created world in divine life and light. As a result, faces of saints in icons are always frontal, "all eyes" (Bessarion), transparent, susceptive of divine energy.[2] I see someone also means I am seen, and therefore I am in communion.

## II. Creator and Creation

Since the doctrine of the divine Incarnation is at the heart of iconography, what is being represented is God's affirmation and assumption of the world. In color and on wood, the icon proclaims, "God was made flesh" (John 1:14). In his work entitled *On Divine Images*, John of Damascus, the eighth-century champion of icons, claims, "I do not adore creation in place of the creator, but I worship the One who became a creature."[3] And since it is through matter that "God has worked out our salvation,"[4] there is an appropriate honor due to material things. I would argue that it is this sense of the salvific power of matter that we have lost today and which we need to rediscover. As John of Damascus writes: "Because of the Incarnation, I salute all remaining matter with reverence."

In the Western High Middle Ages, the "image of God" in the human person was identified with rational nature, deemed superior to the rest of creation. Such an individualistic view of humanity has contributed greatly to the rise of our ecological problems. In the Greek fathers' view, however, the "image of God" in humanity lay in its specific value of freedom. The human person must be associated with, and not dissociated from, the created world, for it is through the human person that the created world must be transformed and offered to God. And so the world is freed from its natural limitations and becomes a bearer of life. In the words of Metropolitan John (Zizioulas) of Pergamon:

> We believe that in doing this "in Christ" we, like Christ, act as priests of creation. When we receive these elements back, after having referred them to God, we believe that because of this reference to God we can take them back and consume them no

2. Bessarion, saying 11, in *Sayings of the Desert Fathers*, trans. Benedicta Ward (London: A. R. Mowbray, 1975), 35. Reference to "all eyes" is also found in Barsanuphius, *Letters*, 120 and 241.

3. John of Damascus, *On Divine Images*, 1.4.

4. *Ibid.*, 16.

longer as death but as life. Creation acquires for us in this way a sacredness which is not inherent in its nature but "acquired" in and through Man's free exercise of his *imago Dei*, i.e., his personhood. This distinguishes our attitude from all forms of paganism, and attaches to the human being an awesome responsibility for the survival of God's creation.[5]

This view of the priestly or parapriestly character of the human person was in earlier times acknowledged by Leontius of Cyprus (seventh century):

> Through heaven and earth and sea, through wood and stone, through relics and Church buildings and the Cross, through angels and people, through all creation visible and invisible, I offer veneration and honor to the Creator and Master and Maker of all things, and to him alone. For the creation does not venerate the Maker directly and by itself, but it is through me that the heavens declare the glory of God, through me the moon worships God, through me the stars glorify him, through me the waters and showers of rain, the dew and all creation, venerate God and give him glory.[6]

Thus, an entire anthropology and cosmology are given artistic shape and utterance in the icon. This is why the two main events for Orthodox iconography are the Incarnation and the Transfiguration. The first reforms what was "originally" deformed through sin and grants to the world the possibility of sanctification. The second realizes the consequences of divinization and grants to the world a foretaste even now of the beauty and light of the last times. We are, in this world, placed at a point of intersection between the present age and the future age, uniting the two as one. In his perceptive book, *The Sacred in Life and Art*, Philip Sherrard claims that the art of the icon presents holy personages

> ready to convert the beholder from his restricted and limited point of view to the full view of their spiritual vision. For the art of the icon is ultimately so to transform the person who moves towards it that he no longer opposes the worlds of eternity and time, of spirit and matter, of the Divine and the human, but sees them united in

5. "Preserving God's Creation," *King's Theological Review* (London) vol. 13, no. 1 (1990): 5. See also the first two parts of this illuminating article in vol. 12, no. 1-2 (1989): 1-5 and 41-45. These articles have, with additional material and editorial changes, appeared in a book published in Greek, entitled *The Creation as Eucharist* (Athens: Akritas, 1992).

6. See *Apologetic Sermon* 3, "On the Holy Icons" (Migne, *PG* 93.1604ab).

one Reality, in that ageless image-bearing light in which all things live, move, and have their being.[7]

## III. The Light That Knows No Evening

The light of an icon is an uncreated, sanctifying light, a light that is not of this world and knows no evening. Perspective is abolished, history is telescoped, and proportion is altered. The icon bears witness to a "different way of life."[8] This life and light are shed from the Risen body of Christ and reveal the joy of the Resurrection.

The value of the icon is not pedagogical or aesthetic, but mystical or "sacramental.": It surpasses any opposition between this world and the next, uniting the two in an act of communion. It also transcends any opposition between figurative or nonfigurative art and appears instead as transfigurative. The icon presupposes and even proposes another means of communication, beyond the conceptual, written, or spoken word. It is the articulation of what cannot be expressed in theology.

## IV. "In the Image and Likeness of God"

The human person, too, is an icon. Created in the image of God, humanity is also a living image of the created universe. The church fathers see humanity as existing on two levels simultaneously—on the level of the spiritual and on the level of material creation. The human person is characterized by paradoxical dualities: humanity is limited yet free, animal yet personal, individual yet social, created yet creative. To attempt escaping this fundamental tension within humanity would be to undermine the Christian doctrine of humanity created "in the image and likeness of God" (Gen. 1:26) and as the image of Jesus Christ who is at once human and divine. A human being, says Gregory the Theologian (fourth century), is like "another universe,"[9] standing at the center of creation, midway between strength and frailty, greatness and lowliness. Humanity is the meeting point of all the created order. The idea of the human

---

7. Philip Sherrard, *The Sacred in Life and Art* (Ipswich, England: Golgonooza Press, 1990), 84.

8. From the Resurrection Canon chanted at Easter Matins.

9. Gregory the Theologian, *Homily*, 38.11 (Migne, *PG* 36.321-24).

person as a bridge, a point of contact and union, is developed as early as the seventh century by the lay monk Maximus Confessor.[10] As an image of the world, the human person constitutes a microcosm. Another monastic writer, Nilus of Ancyra (fifth century), makes this point very clearly:

> You are a world within a world . . . Look within yourself and there you will see the entire world.[11]

The world in its entirety forms part of the liturgy of heaven. Or, as we have already seen, the world constitutes a cosmic liturgy. God is praised by the trees and the birds, glorified by the stars and the moon (see Ps. 18:2), worshiped by the sea and the sand. There is a dimension of art, music, and beauty in the world. And the very existence of material creation constitutes a revelation of God (Eph. 4:6), awaiting its liberation through the children of God (Rom. 8:19). The world, then, becomes the clearest, albeit the most silent and inconspicuous, sermon declaring the word of God, a sign of the kingdom of heaven, the bridal chamber (Ps. 18), where God can touch the work of creation in the most intimate manner.

When Orthodox Christians enter a church, they bow down before the altar, reverence the holy icons, bow to the minister, and lower their heads at certain points of the liturgy. After receiving the Sacrament of the Eucharist, however, they depart bowing to none, for their conviction is that the life of the world and the heart of the Church are at that moment seeded and seated deeply inside their own heart. When one is initiated into the mystery of the Resurrection and transformed by the light of the Transfiguration, then one understands the purpose for which God has created all things.[12] The world is rendered as a gift—a gift received from, and returned to, God. The climax of the Orthodox Liturgy is found in the words: "Your own from your own we offer to you, in all and through all."

---

10. Maximus Confessor, *De Ambiguis*, 91. See also his *Mystagogia*, 7 (Migne, *PG* 91.672).

11. Nilus of Ancyra, *Epistles*, 2.119 (Migne, *PG* 79:252b). See also Origen, *Homily on Leviticus*, 5.2 (Migne, *PG* 12.448-50); and D. S. Wallace-Hadrill, *The Greek Patristic View of Nature* (Manchester: Manchester University Press, 1968), especially 66-79.

12. See Maximus Confessor, *Gnostic Chapters*, 1.66 (Migne, *PG* 90.1108ab). On the priestly character of humanity, see Kallistos Ware, "The Value of the Material Creation," *Sobornost* (London) vol. 6, no. 3 (1971): 154-65.

Someone who sees the whole world as an icon, experiences from this world the realities of the future and final resurrection. That person has already entered the life of resurrection and eternity. John Climacus, the abbot at St. Catherine's Monastery on Mt. Sinai, was convinced that, in the very beauty and beyond the shattered image of this world:

> such a person always perceives everything in the light of the Creator God, and has therefore acquired immortality before the ultimate resurrection.[13]

There is a sense in which this person is indicating and anticipating here and now the transfiguration of the world. The result is a prefiguration of the restored image of the world, a configuration in this world of uncreated and created elements.

## V. The Icon as Communion

When the Russian monk St. Andrei Rublev (ca. 1360-1430) painted his masterpiece, The Holy Trínity—which depicts the Old Testament narrative of the three angels who visited Abraham and Sarah (Gen. 18:1-33), sometimes also known as "the hospitality of Abraham"—he was in fact representing the open communion of the triune Godhead, a love that is showered upon the face of the earth and in the hearts of people. The Rublev icon is an image of what the Trinity is: a celebration and communication of life. This is why there is an empty or open place at the table of communion. The three persons of the Trinity are seated on three of the four sides of the rectangular table, allowing for, or rather inviting, the world to communion. Indeed, the very contours of their bodies create and reproduce in macro-image the communion chalice about which these angels are seated.[14] The potential sacredness of the world is more than a mere possibility; it is a vocation.

---

13. John Climacus, *The Ladder of Divine Ascent, Step 4*, 58 (Migne, *PG* 88.892d-893a).

14. For a detailed description of selected icons, including that by Rublev of the Trinity, see Paul Evdokimov, *The Art of the Icon: A Theology of Beauty*, trans. Fr. Steven Bigham (Redondo Beach, Calif.: Oakwood Publications, 1990). About the icon of Rublev, Pavel Florensky once exclaimed: "there is Rublev's Trinity, therefore there is God." See V. V. Bychkov, *The Aesthetic Face of Being* (Crestwood, N.Y.: St. Vladimir's Seminary Press, 1993), 42.

# VI. The Image of Christ

There is no thing, no place, no time, and no person that escapes, or is excluded from, the comprehensive love of Christ (John 1:9). For Christ is God's categorical affirmation and assumption of the whole world. And there is, as a result, no condition, no tragedy, no experience outside the embrace of Christ. To be an imitator of Christ is to be assimilated to him. One can then walk on Earth as Christ and in the authority of Christ: "For it is not I who lives but Christ lives in me" (Gal. 2:20).

The Christ dimension is also suggested in Orthodox icons of the enthroned Jesus, particularly in the truly magnificent mosaic of the late thirteenth century which still survives in the Constantinopolitan monastery of Chora (later known as the Kariye Cami). The icon of Christ over the door to the nave is entitled "The land [*Xôra*] of the living." The same notion of the resurrection of the dead or newness of life is envisaged in our personal spiritual life through the dynamic stage of for-give-ness (*sun-Xôrè-sis*), which implies a death to self and "allowing room for others," making space (*Xôra*) for the rest of the world, giving up of the self, and opening up in communion and acts of giving and givenness. Nothing and no one is excluded. Symeon the New Theologian poetically describes this cohabitation, or co-indwelling, of Christ in the world:

> You make of all Your home and dwelling-place; You become a home to all, and we dwell in You.[15]

Everything therefore assumes a Christ dimension; everything is in some way sacramental. All depends on the receptiveness and openness of our hearts. By the same token, everything is rendered unique, inasmuch as it has its particular place and meaning. Nothing is secular or profane; nothing is pagan or foreign.[16] Indeed, if God were not visibly present in the material creation,

15. Symeon the New Theologian, *Hymn*, 15.132-33. As with the concept of "*sophia*," so also the notion of "*chora*" may equally be applied to the Virgin Mary (cf. the Akathistos Hymn, Stasis 1: She "contained [*choresasa*] the One who contains [*chorei*] the universe"). On the relationship between liturgy, iconography, and creation, see the articles in *Orthodoxy and Ecology: Resource Book* (Bialystok: Syndesmos, 1996), 72-81.

16. See Leonardo Boff, *Sacraments of Life-Life of Sacraments* (Washington, D.C.: Pastoral Press, 1987), 49-51.

then we could not properly worship him as invisible. Were God not tangibly accessible in the very earthliness of this world, then he would not be the loving, albeit transcendent author of the universe. This is surely the implication of the basis of the Christian faith, namely, that "the Word assumed [or became] flesh" (John 1:16), which we all too often, in a reductionist manner, take to mean, "became human." Yet, the early Christian writers categorically stated that, "what God did not assume, God did not heal."[17] What God did not reach out and touch, did not come down and sanctify, cannot possibly be related to or loved by God. And unless Christ may be discovered "in the least of his brethren" (Matt. 25:40) and in the least particle of matter, then he is too distant to matter. There is a wonderful saying attributed to Jesus, which expresses the reality of his presence everywhere:

> Lift up the stone, and there you will find me; cleave the wood, and I am there.[18]

Matter is not merely an object for our possession and exploitation. The earth has not only economic but also moral and sacramental value. For "the earth and all its fullness" (Ps. 23:1) is a bearer of God, a place of encounter with Christ, the very center of our salvation. In the words of Leonardo Boff:

> All things are sacraments when viewed in God's perspective and light. The word, human beings, and things are signs and symbols of the transcendent.[19]

## VII. Theology in Color

The theological statement made by the icon is, therefore, threefold:

1. That the world was created good, and therefore needs to be loved;

---

17. Gregory Nazianzus, *Letter 101 to Cleidonius* (Migne, *PG* 37.181c).

18. In Joachim Jeremias, *Unknown Sayings of Jesus*, trans. Reginald H. Fuller (London: SPCK, 1957), 95.

19. Boff, *Sacraments*, 38. Pierre Teilhard de Chardin wrote in similar fashion echoing Maximus Confessor's image of the "cosmic liturgy." See Teilhard, *Mass on the World*, in *Hymn of the Universe*, trans. G. Vann (New York: Harper and Row, 1972), 16: "Once again the fire has penetrated the earth . . . the flame has lit up the whole world from within."

2. That at the Incarnation, Christ assumed a human body, thereby affirming the intrinsic value of the whole created world; and

3. That salvation embraces all of created matter, as well as human body and soul.

The entire world is an icon. The whole of creation constitutes an icon painted before all ages, an image eternally engraved by the unique iconographer of the Word of God, namely, the Holy Spirit. This image is never totally destroyed, never fully effaced. Our aim is simply to reveal this image in the heart and to reflect it in the world. Yet, the image itself, the icon, is indelible, for the world has been forever "sealed with the gift of the Holy Spirit."[20] In our age, green is perhaps most fittingly the color of the Holy Spirit, recalling as it does Greek patristic thought[21] and indicating the renewal of life itself and the revival of all things.

## VIII. Pneumatology and Ecology

This brings me to emphasize the close connection of pneumatology and ecology. Nature speaks a truth scarcely heard among theologians: the world relates in very tangible terms the spiritual connection between the uncreated and the creation.

Just as the Spirit is the "air" that the whole world breathes, so too the earth is the "ground" which we all share. Were God not present in the density of a city, or in the beauty of a forest, or in the sand of a desert, then God would not be present in heaven either. So if, indeed, there exists today a vision that is able to transcend—perhaps transform—all national and denominational tensions, it may well be that of our environment understood as sacrament of the Spirit. The breath of the Spirit brings out the sacramentality of nature and bestows on it the fragrance of resurrection.

Eastern theological thought has been concerned with the metahistorical or the spiritual dimensions of this world seen in the light of the kingdom of heaven and the liturgical nature of time. Facts and figures are considered in terms of the Holy Spirit; power is understood from the perspective of the Sacrament of the

---

20. From the Service of the Sacrament of Baptism in the Orthodox Church.
21. See Dionysius the Areopagite, *Celestial Hierarchy*, 15.7 (Migne, *PG* 3.336bc).

Eucharist; the world around is appreciated in relation to the heavens above. The understanding is that eschatology is not an apocalyptic teaching, the last chapter of the New Testament, or perhaps an unnecessary chapter of a Christian manual of doctrine. Rather, it is the teaching about the "last-ness" and "lasting-ness" of all things.

## IX. Ascetic Theology

A second characteristic of Orthodox spirituality is the ascetic tradition. The discipline of ascesis is the necessary and critical corrective for the excess of our consumption. We have learned all too well and only too painfully that the ecological crisis both presupposes and builds upon the economic injustice in the world. Ascesis is a reality of the spiritual life because it is the reassurance of our difficult and painful struggle to relate our theology to the world, our justice and our economy to the poor.

Ascesis is not primarily an achievement, but an attitude of attendance to and expectation of the Spirit. Hence, once again, the liturgical aspect of ascesis is a continual invocation (*epiclesis*) of the Paraclete. As one Orthodox theologian puts it: "we are called not just to do something, but simply to stand there." Ascesis is not another or a better way of acting; it is, in fact, a way of inaction, of stillness, of vigilance. We are called to remember that the present ecological crisis is a result precisely of our action—of considerable human effort and success to "change" or "better" the world—and not only of our greed or covetousness. The primary cause of our devastation and destruction is the relentless pursuit of what many people consider a good or desirable thing—namely, the modern, industrial-technological model of development. Yet, this "developmental" ideology has not created a sustainable world for everyone; it has encouraged exploitation and an unsustainable world.

Ascesis means allowing room for the Spirit, for an action beyond our action. It means "leaving space" (lit., "for-give-ness" or *synchoresis*). The patristic term *peri-chore-sis* has the same root etymologically as *syn-choresis*: *synchoresis* includes the aspect of reconciliation, while *perichoresis* includes the dimension of joy and celebration toward nature for the sake of future generations. When we reduce the spiritual or religious life to ourselves (to our concerns, to our needs, and to our interests), then we forget the calling of the Church to implore God—always and everywhere—for the salvation of the whole polluted cosmos, to the least of our brothers and sisters, and to the last speck of dust in the universe.

It is always alarming to see how easily the term "spirituality" is used without reference to the Spirit which is the giver of all gifts. The Greek patristic tradition does not even have an equivalent term for spirituality; preferring rather to speak about the action of the Holy Spirit in the world. It is not always clear in contemporary theological writings if the Spirit is anything more than just certain abstract nouns—love, justice, peace, or perhaps green peace—with capital letters. The Spirit, of course, "blows where it wills" (John 3:8), as Christ confided to one of his friends on a rooftop. We only know of the Spirit what we may experience on a rooftop on a hot summer's day with a cool breeze blowing: we know that we are touched, that we are refreshed, and that our clothes move a little. The Spirit is only known in contact and in communion with our environment.

The distinction between the "Spirit of God" and the "Spirit of Creation" was one that early Christian ascetics experienced in their very bodies, in their intense struggle to maintain the interdependence of body and soul. The Spirit is indeed the "giver of life" and of all forms of life. It penetrates and permeates the world and cannot be conceived apart from this world. Yet, if the Spirit and the earth are conformed, or confused, then the Church is no longer called to transform the world; then the Spirit itself ceases to be something that is promised, and becomes something that is compromised. This is why the patristic tradition underlined that the divine Spirit is at once known and unknown, both seen and unseen, revealed and veiled alike. Such is the conviction of Symeon the New Theologian and of Gregory Palamas. Such is the depth of the distinction between divine essence and divine energy. In his treatise *On Divine Names*, Dionysius the Areopagite describes the divinity as en-cosmic, as peri-cosmic, and as hyper-cosmic.[22]

---

22. Dionysius the Areopagite, *On Divine Names*, 1.6 (Migne, *PG* 3.596) and 13.1-2 (Migne, *PG* 3.977); translation mine. For the works of Dionysius, see *Pseudo Dionysius: The Complete Works*, trans. Colm Luibheid, The Classics of Western Spirituality (New York: Paulist Press, 1987).

# X. Apophatic Theology

This brings me to a third characteristic of Orthodox theology, the close connection between theology and poetry, between "ascetics" and "aesthetics." Often, our theology does not have sufficient poetry. There has undoubtedly occurred an unfortunate shift in emphasis: from God to man, from body to soul, from theological symbolism to mathematical analysis. Yet, in the tradition of the Orthodox, certainly the greatest and most acclaimed of theologians were also poets: John the Divine, Gregory of Nazianzus, and Symeon the New Theologian. There is always much more to be said than can ever be expressed. This is why the emphasis in the East is on the apophatic dimension of all theological talk and thought. I believe that this apophatic dimension is wonderfully, indeed "naturally," fostered in creation. The breadth and beauty of this earth is a reflection of the boundlessness and splendor of divine grace; and our respect toward the environment results in a parallel allowance for the surprising abyss of God. Our admiration for creation reflects our adoration of the absolute, a vocation to the beyond, an invitation to transfiguration.

*Apophasis* is an element of *askesis*; the silence of poetry is a form of surrender to the living God; it is like dying to the flesh in order to live fully in the Spirit. Silence and death go hand in hand; to be utterly silent can feel like death. Silence and ascesis issue in resurrection and new life through the Spirit.

# Conclusion

If, indeed, there is a Spirit of God, and it is the very Spirit of Creation; if this world is the Body of God, the actual flesh of the divine Word; if, in fact, the Spirit of God reveals the Image of God in creation, beyond the brokenness and shatteredness of this world; then there is a sense in which this earth is not merely a reflection,[23] but

---

23. This is a significant point of divergence between Christian theology and Platonist philosophy. The Hellenistic conception of the created world as a "mirror," or "image," of the eternal realm is a privilege as well as a problem in terms of the value and sacredness of creation. Perhaps this is also the reason for the "ambivalence" of the patristic texts themselves, which will sometimes underline the creation of this world by a loving God, while at other times undermine the intimate connection between the Creator and the creation. The result is an apparent paradox between

even a perfection of heaven. Just as we are incomplete without the rest of the animal and the material creation, so, too, the kingdom of God remains incomplete without the world around us.

a "monarchical" theology and its consequential "dualistic" anthropology and cos-mology to which Sallie McFague and others rightly react.

### Responsory for Virgins

Green life, most noble,
Rooted in the sun,
Bright and serene,
You shine in a sphere
Beyond all earthly excellence.

You are enfolded
In the embrace of
Divine ministries.

You blush like the dawn,
And like the sun's flame,
You burn.

— Hildegard of Bingen

## Chapter 18

# Becoming Part of It

## *Joseph Epes Brown*

In talking about sacred dimensions in Native American life, I must proceed not just as a descriptive ethnographer but also as an historian of religion, and with what I hope is a basic humanistic concern; that is, I believe it important to ask about the relevance of these primal values to a dominant contemporary world with life-ways which are oriented towards very different directions and with contrasting priorities. One notices very clearly today our increasing malaise and sometimes even fear, which—at least in certain segments of our society—is leading to a growing mood for re-evaluation and reassessment, a wish even to take a backward look, so to say, at "progress," that concept which for so long has been an unquestioned quasi-religious dogma in our lives. Many of those early studies of Native American peoples and cultures suffered from the kinds of prejudices that came out of this prevailing concept of progress.

An expression of this new and growing mood is found in an increasing concern to seek out our ancient origins, with a view to rediscovering and perhaps even identifying with what is our own proper heritage. I put the question in this manner because very often when I speak about the relevance and the reality of American Indian values, I am misunderstood, especially by students who like to believe that what I am trying to say is that they should go out and be and live like American Indians; this is not my point at all, because for those of us who are non-Indians it is an impossibility. One has to be brought up in these cultures and traditions, one has to live the languages, in order truly to identify with the ethos of an American Indian people. What I am trying to say is that these traditions could

* Editor's Note: Originally given as an address at the American Museum of Natural History in January 1982 as a part of a program entitled "I Become Part of It," presented by the Society for the Study of Myth and Tradition.

be taken as models which might provide us with answers to some of the dilemmas with which we are currently struggling in our own society.

In the 1960s, in our restlessness with where we found ourselves, we began to turn to the religions and methods of the Orient, with all the attractions and mystique which distance provides. By the 1970s, however, with our rapidly growing ecological concerns, there developed an increasing awareness that certain answers could be found in the spiritual traditions of the Native Americans; for here the sacred values which so many of us were seeking out were actually rooted in this land, where they have survived through some sixty to eighty thousand years. Out of this mood there has come a vast array of new literature, both genuine and spurious, relating to Native American life ways and world view; and even if the approach has often been overly romantic, there is here a change from earlier attitudes and prejudices, which is a positive sign even if it is only a beginning.

Although greatly oversimplified and generalized, let me give at least a brief sampling of what I think are some of the core Native American values and perspectives, through which we can perhaps come to relearn a little bit about ourselves and about our own proper spiritual heritage, the hope being that what has been lost can still be rediscovered. Certainly the Native American people themselves, especially the younger ones today, are trying to regain and revitalize their own traditions which may have been lost, or taken from them through a variety of pressures and prejudices. We have, I suggest, in this struggle a model for our own proper quest. What are some of its contours?

Tribal cultures, it seems to me, present a model of what a religious tradition is; and this is a basic reality which we have lost sight of. That is, what really is a true religious tradition? What does it encompass, what are its dimensions? These cultures demonstrate how all components of a culture can be interconnected; how the presence of the sacred can permeate all life ways to such a degree that what we call religion is here integrated into the totality of life and into all of life's activities. Religion here is so pervasive in life that there is probably no Native American language in which there is a term which could be translated as "religion" in the way we understand it. As Peter Nabokov tells us in his book, *Indian Running*, when you track down a seemingly isolated or minimal feature of Indian life, such as running, the whole system opens before your eyes; and this is true because of the interrelatedness of all the components of a genuine tradition. Obviously in such a system life cannot be fragmented, due to that binding and interconnecting thread of the presence of the sacred.

In terms of interconnections, a dominant theme in all Native American cultures is that of relationship, or a series of relationships, that are ways reaching further and further out; relationships within the immediate family reaching out to the extended family, to the band, outward again to the clan, to the tribal group; and relationships do not stop there but extend out to embrace and relate to the environment; to the land, to the animals, to the plants, and to the clouds, the elements, the heavens, the stars; and ultimately those relationships that people express and live, extend to embrace the entire universe.

In the Plains area, to give an example, one of the most profound rites is that of the smoking of the pipe. In this ritual smoking of the pipe, all who participate are joined in a communal ritual, and when it is finished, everybody who has shared in the smoking of the pipe recites the phrase, in Lakota in this case, "*mitakuye oyasin*"—"we are all relatives." We are all related, because in this rite we have all become one within a mystery that is greater than any of its parts. I shall talk more about the general importance of rituals and ceremonies later.

Associated with relationship there should be mentioned the theme of reciprocity which permeates so many aspects of North American cultures. Put very simply, reciprocity here refers again to that process wherein if you receive or take away you must also give back. This is a living statement of the importance of the cycle permeating all of life. Everything in their world of experience is conceived in terms of such cycles or of the circle; everything comes back upon itself. Black Elk so often said that all the forces of the world work in cycles or circles; the birds build their nests in circular form, the foxes have their dens in circles, the wind in its greatest power moves in a circle, and life is as a circle. I recall once how this reality was beautifully expressed in a living manner, when I noticed how this dignified old man would relate to little children. He would get down on his hands and knees and pretend he was a horse, and the children would squeal with joy on the old man's back. Here there obviously was no generation gap; he was one with the child. I once asked him how it was that he could so relate to the child, and he replied: "I who am an old man am about to return to the Great Mysterious [*Wakan Tanka*, Lakota] and a young child is a being who has just come from the Great Mysterious; so it is that we are very close together." Because of such cyclical understanding, both are very nearly at the same point.

Such attitudes could be spelled out in terms of any number of cultural expressions, but the point I want to draw from this is that we have here an example which contrasts with our own dominant concept of process which is in terms of linearity—the straight line which moves from here to there and onward indefinitely. Indeed, this theme of linearity permeates all aspects of our life. The way we read, for instance, is in lines; we have sayings in our vocabulary that tell us to "Line up!" "Let's get this straight!" Or if we refer to somebody who is a little bit crazy, we make a circular motion alongside our head, by which we indicate the reason is going in circles. There is something here from which we can learn, something about ourselves and our concept of progress, with all the loaded meanings which this term bears.

One must mention also the special nature of Native American languages, which contrasts with our understanding of language and our use of words. In Native American languages the understanding is that the meaning is in the sound, it is in the word; the word is not a symbol for a meaning which has been abstracted out, for word and meaning are together in one experience. Thus, to name a being, for example an animal, is actually to conjure up the powers latent in that animal. Added to this is the fact that when we create words we use our breath, and for these people and these traditions breath is associated with the principle of life; breath is life itself. And so if a word is born from this sacred principle of breath, this lends an added sacred dimension to the spoken word. It is because of this special feeling about words that people avoid using sacred personal names, because they contain the power of the beings named, and if you use them too much the power becomes dissipated. So usually one has to refer to a person in a very circuitous manner, or use a term which expresses relationship.

In this context one must also emphasize the positive values that could be attached to non-literacy. I use that term rather than illiteracy, which connotes the inability to read and write, which is negative and derogatory. Too often we have branded people as being backward and uncivilized if they are illiterate, whereas one can make a strong case for the advantages of growing up and living in a society which is non-literate. For in such a society all the lore which is central and sacred to the culture is borne within the individual in a living manner; you do not have to go outside of yourself, for all that is essential to life is carried with you, is ever-present. It seems that where you have people who are non-literate in this positive sense, you tend to have a special quality of person, a quality of being that cannot be described—a very different quality from that of the literate person. It has been my experience when among primal peoples in many parts of the world that there is something here that is very special.

Paralleling this primal concept of language, and of the word not as "symbol" but as an immediate event, is the quality of experiencing the visual arts and crafts. I should stress first of all that for primal peoples generally there is no dichotomy between the arts and crafts, in the manner that our art historians insist on, where art is one kind of thing that can be placed on a mantelpiece or hung on the wall, and the craft item is inferior because it is made for utilitarian ends. This seems to me a most artificial distinction and I think it is time that we outgrew it; indeed there is today evidence that we are re-evaluating such prejudiced dichotomies. For why cannot a utilitarian object also be beautiful? All necessary implements, utensils, and tools in Native American life ways are of technical excellence and are also beautiful. They must be made in special sacred ways, and the materials of the tools and objects made have to be gathered with prayer and offerings. Beauty and truth are here one! When a Pomo basket maker, for example, goes out to collect the grasses for her basket, she prays to the grasses, she enters into a relationship with them as she gathers, and makes offerings in return for having taken their life. When a woman weaves a basket she will pass the grass between her lips to moisten it, but also to breathe upon it, to give her life breath into the grass and thus give to the basket a special sacred quality that is always present in its use and tangible presence.

Through these few selected examples which have been given, I am suggesting that, where such traditions are still alive and spiritually viable, there tend to be present, within all of life's necessary activities, dimensions and expressions of the sacred. Actions of such quality could therefore be considered to manifest a ritual element in the sense that they tend to order life around and toward a Center. In this context, however, one must also speak of those special great rites and ceremonies, many often related to the seasonal cycles, which serve not just to support continuing orientations toward the sacred in everyday activities, but work for the intensification of such Presence and experience; such rites may also be the source and origin of new rites, ceremonies, and other sacred expressions through the visual arts, songs, or special dance forms.

One example of a ritual complex which is central to the lives of Plains people is the well known "vision" or "guardian spirit quest." This ritualized retreat is for the benefit of the individual man and woman, and yet means are present for the eventual sharing of received vision powers or messages with the larger community. After rigorous preparations, which always include the rites of the purifying sweat lodge and instructions by a qualified elder, the candidate goes to a high and remote place with the resolve to fast and pray continually and to suffer through acts of sacrifice and exposure to the elements for a specified number of days. The ordeal is highly ritualized and may involve the establishing of an altar, or the setting out of poles at the center and to the four directions of space. The person may also be instructed to remain within this established space and not to move about casually but to walk only out from the center to each of the poles in turn, always returning to the center. Prayers may be addressed to the powers of the four directions, and one may also use repetitive prayers such as the one the Lakota Black Elk has given us: "Grandfather, Great Mysterious, have pity on me." One may also remain silent, for it has been said that "silence is the voice of *Wakan Tanka*, the Great Mysterious." If tired, one may sleep, for dreams of power may come to the candidate in this manner; yet it is understood that the true vision is of greater power than the dream. Often the sacred experience comes in the mysterious appearance of an animal or a winged being, or perhaps in one of the powers of nature. A special message is often communicated to the seeker, and this will serve as a guide and reminder throughout the person's life. After three or four days one returns to camp where a sweat lodge has again been prepared; within this lodge the candidate will explain the vision or dream which will be interpreted by the guiding elder, who will then give instructions as to what should now be accomplished in order to insure the continuity of the participation of the spiritual throughout the person's life. From such experiences have come the "medicine bundles" with rich and complex rites specific to each bundle and their ceremonial opening on special occasions. They have also been the origin of sacred types of art forms, such as the painted shields, or special songs of power, or even the great ritual dances, such as the horse dance, involving four groups of eight horses not representing, but being the powers of the four directions of space. It is in this manner that something of the sacred experience which had come to a particular individual is shared by all members of the larger community.

What is remarkable about the rites of the vision quest among the Plains peoples is that it is accomplished not just by special people as is the case in the Arctic, but that every man or woman after the age of puberty is expected to participate either once or even repeatedly throughout his or her life.

What concerns us in this example is not just the detailed pattern of the ritual elements of the quest as such, which can encompass a multitude of very diverse possibilities, but that here we have one sample as a model of traditional ritual structures and acts which must involve initial purification, choice of appropriate site, the defining and delimiting of a special sacred place, and the fixing of a center. Further, ritualized actions are prescribed for the participant, which means that participation is not just with the mind, or a part of one's being, but with the totality of who one is. Also provided are means for continuity and development of the sacred experiences received, and the eventual responsibility for sharing something of them with the larger community.

As complement to the individually oriented "vision quest," one could mention the great communal "Sun Dance," referred to in different terms across the Plains groups. For this great complex of solemn rites, ceremonies, fasting, sacred song and dance fulfills not just the particular spiritual needs of the actively participating individuals, but also those of the entire tribal group gathered in circular camp for the occasion. The event is indeed for the welfare of the entire world. These are ceremonies, interspersed with special sacred rites, which celebrate world and life renewal at the time of spring. The ritualized dance forms again involve orientation around and towards a center which is either the sun itself or the cottonwood tree as axis of the world, standing at the center of a circular frame lodge carefully constructed in imitation of the cosmos. The ritual and ceremonial language of the total celebration speaks to and encompasses a plurality of spiritual possibilities at the levels of microcosm, macrocosm, and metacosm. It is believed by many that should the sacrificial rites of this "thirst lodge" be neglected or forgotten, the energy of the world will run out and the cycle in which we are living will close. It is an example to the world that these rites and ceremonies are far from being neglected, for today in ever increasing numbers the people are participating and are finding renewed strength and spiritual resolve.

All spiritually effective rites must accomplish three cumulative possiblities which may be termed purification, expansion in wholeness or virtue, and identity. A ritual means which embodies these possibilities may be found in the sacred nature and use of the Plains Indian tobacco pipe, the smoking of which constitutes a communion. The shape of the pipe with its stem, bowl or "heart," and foot, is identified with the human person. In purifying the pipe before a ritual smoking there is an analogy to man's own purification; for in concentrating on the hollow of the straight stem leading to the bowl comes the understanding that one's mind should be this straight and pure. In filling the bowl of the pipe a prayer is said for each grain of tobacco in such a manner that everything in the world is mentioned. The filled bowl or the heart of man, in thus containing all possibilities, is then the universe. Finally, the fire which is put to the tobacco is the Presence of the ultimate all-inclusive Principle, *Wakan Tanka,* the "Great Mysterious." In smoking the pipe, through the aid of breath the totality of all creation is absorbed within this ultimate Principle. And since in the pipe there is a grain of tobacco identified with the one who smokes, there is here enacted a sacrificial communion of identity. With this understanding, the phrase "we are all related," recited by the individual or group after the smoking, takes on the deepest possible meaning.

I will sum up by simply saying that in all that I have tried to speak of in such brief fashion, we have expressions through different means of a special quality among traditional peoples that could be called oneness of experience: a lack of dichotomizing or fragmenting, a unity in the word and in visual image. In the painted image, for example, the understanding is that in the being that is represented, or even in a depicted part of that being—the paw of a bear, let us say—all the power of the animal is present. One can draw from all Native American cultures examples to reinforce such interpretation. One final example I will use is that of the Navajo dry painting or "sand painting" as it is sometimes called. These are made in a rich ceremonial context for the curing of individuals who have gotten out of balance with their world. They are long ceremonies which can go on for four or five or up to ten days, during which time sacred chants are used with all the meaning of the word as I have tried to explain it. At a certain moment during the ceremony the ill person is placed at the center of one of the dry paintings; the understanding is that the person thus becomes identified with the power that is in the image painted on the earth with colored sand and pollen. And the singer takes some of the painted image and presses it to the body of the ill person, again to emphasize this element of identity: the painting is not a symbol of some meaning or power; the power is there present in it, and as the person identifies with it the appropriate cure is accomplished.

I conclude with this portion of a Navajo chant:

> The mountains, I become part of it . . .
> The herbs, the fir tree, I become part of it.
> The morning mists, the clouds, the gathering waters, I become
> part of it.
> The wilderness, the dewdrops, the pollen . . . I become part of it.

And in the context of other chants, there is always the conclusion that indeed, I am the universe. We are not separate, but are one.

## Nahuatl: Aztec Song

We only came to sleep
We only came to dream
It is not true
No it is not true
That we came to live on the earth

We are changed into the grass of springtime
Our hearts will grow green again
And they will open their petals
But our body is like a rose tree
It puts forth flowers and then withers

## Chapter 19

# Flowers

## *Lord Northbourne*

Flowers that are attractive by reason of their forms, colors or scents have been admired and loved and cultivated for thousands of years; perhaps never more so, at least in Europe, than at the present day. Everyone knows, or thinks he knows, what a flower is: but not until a hundred or so years ago had the modern scientific point of view been applied to flowers, as to everything else. It is therefore necessary to take that point of view into account, because so many people think that it is the only point of view from which we can learn what a flower or anything else really is, or assign to it its proper place in the scheme of things.

From a scientific point of view, then, a flower of some sort is characteristic of all the class of Angiosperms, and, whether it be conspicuous and attractive or not, it is primarily a mechanism for securing the transfer of pollen from the anther of one flower to the stigma of another of the same species, usually in the case of conspicuous flowers, on the body of an insect. The form, color and fragrance of flowers is thought to have been evolved for the purpose of attracting insects, the intervention of which compensates for the immobility of plants and makes the impregnation of the ovule by the pollen of a distant individual possible. Alternatively, as everyone knows, pollen may be transported by wind; in such cases the flower is usually small and inconspicuous, though the inflorescence that carries a number of such flowers, and sometimes the flowers themselves, may be beautiful in our eyes. In either case, still from the scientific point of view, flowers have become what they are as a result of the interaction of a number of factors mainly connected with the relationship of plants to insects or to wind, and all such factors are in principle ascertainable, even though in practice they are not likely ever all to be ascertained. In so far as flowers are the indispensable precursors of useful seeds and fruits, with honey as a by-product in some cases, there is an obvious economic relationship between flowers and mankind, but scientifically speaking, all other kinds of relationship, aesthetic or otherwise, can only be regarded as accidental. Man happens to have taken advantage of such accidents and has tried to accentuate the pleasurable aspects of his relationship to flowers in his development of floriculture, but that fact does not alter the essentially accidental or non-essential nature of the relationship itself, regarded purely from the point of view of modern science.

This point of view in fact takes account of nothing but the immediate and tangible advantage, "economic" in the broad sense of the word, of the individual or of the race; it could therefore be described as purely utilitarian. It is assumed that the qualities and way of life of every living being, including man, can in principle be regarded primarily as expedients for securing the continuity of the existence of the being or its race in the face of environmental pressures and competition from other beings or races; if any other influences are admitted they are regarded as secondary. There are scientists and philosophers of science who would say that even the above statement is tendentious, in that it makes use of such words as "advantage," "expedients" and "competition," and thereby suggests some kind of underlying purpose in the process of evolution and in existence generally; whereas according to them, there is no such purpose, terrestrial life having arisen purely through a fortuitous combination of circumstances, probably unique, and certainly destined eventually to be swallowed up in some equally fortuitous cataclysm. According to this view there exist only blind forces acting upon elementary particles, the resulting associations and dissociations of which constitute the universe and all that it contains. Thus all our experience, all our aspirations, every conception of beauty or goodness or greatness or of any kind of purpose, and of course any kind of theistic conception, while not necessarily negligible to us as human beings, can have no ultimate significance whatever. This is the philosophy of despair, of which Bertrand Russell is one of the chief exponents. It claims to expound the only intellectually acceptable basis for the development of a philosophy of life, and to represent the only possible logical and intelligent deduction from the discoveries of modern science. However that may be, the main characteristics and conclusions of the evolutionary hypothesis remain much the same, whether the process of evolution be regarded as being with or without some ultimate significance.

There are probably very few people who can accept in their hearts the view that existence is ultimately meaningless, independently of whether they are prepared to accept any particular religious or quasi-religious eschatology. But the conception of terrestrial life as a struggle for existence, in which every creature or race is fighting for its own advantage, inconsistent though it be with the general philosophy outlined above, has been thoroughly instilled into their minds by the protagonists of evolutionary ideas. It is of interest in passing to compare this point of view with another that was very prevalent in the 19th century, according to which everything on earth was created, not for its own advantage, nor for the advantage of its race, but for the benefit of mankind. It differed from the evolutionist point of view in being "creationist," and ostensibly founded on a religious rather than a scientific outlook. It perished partly because creationism was superseded by evolutionism, and partly because it met with insuperable difficulties in application, since it was necessary to argue that not only many things apparently useless to man, but also his worst enemies, were in fact created for his special and exclusive benefit. It was however very close to the more recent point of view in being essentially utilitarian; both are equally examples of the tendency to try to account for everything in terms of immediate and tangible advantage and disadvantage, which is none other than the materialist tendency. Not that considerations of immediate advantage and disadvantage are negligible or inoperative in terrestrial life, very far from it, but any theory founded on them alone is totally insufficient to account for the forms and the behavior of living beings, vegetable, animal and especially human, and no less insufficient to account for their existence, their variety and their qualities, and not least for their beauty; and that is the quality that appeals particularly to us in flowers.

The conception of a universal struggle for existence is in any case highly anthropomorphic, and it may be questioned whether it has any real meaning where a consciousness of individual existence, and *a fortiori* of being engaged in a struggle, can scarcely be said to exist. It seems probable that our view of the world of nature as a conflict rather than a harmony is no more than evidence of our own state of mind, and that it is colored far more strongly than we suppose by that state of mind, according to whether it be internally harmonious or internally distraught. The floral picture at any rate manifests a joyous superfluity that accords ill with any conception so grim as that of a universal struggle for existence as the influence above all others that made that picture what it is, and has conferred on us the inexplicable and gratuitous benediction of flowers.

Struggle there is, obviously; but it is a result of the temporal limitations that obscure the underlying harmony, the harmony that shines forth from within in the inexplicable beauty of flowers. The struggle is as it were superficial; it does not constitute the basic force that moulds the world of nature, still less did it produce the beauty of flowers, as is postulated in evolutionist theories. The theory of course is that the more brilliant the flower the better its chances of attracting insects and thereby ensuring pollination and the perpetuation of its race. It sounds plausible, but it does not even fit the facts. The attractiveness of flowers to insects bears little relation to their brilliance or size. Lubbock pulled the petals off geraniums and found that insects visited them as before. The flowers of vines, of ivy, of box, of gooseberries, of sycamores, are small and green, yet they are objects of hot competition in the insect world, more so perhaps than most conspicuous flowers. *Cotoneaster horizontalis* has the least conspicuous flowers of any of its race, and is much the most attractive to insects. Neither lilies nor magnolias seem to be particularly attractive, whereas roses and poppies and peonies are so. There are also contrasts like that between the fig and the yucca, each dependent for pollination on one species of insect, small and specialized: the flowers of the fig are entirely hidden; the large white flowers of the yucca are flaunted in great plumes on stems many feet high. An abundant source of sugar, like the waste from a sugar factory, unadvertised though it be, is far more attractive to bees than the brightest of flowers. And so on. In short, the colors and forms of uncultivated flowers cannot be accounted for by any theory that confines its attention to their purely functional or utilitarian aspect.

Let us then assume without more ado that the beauty and fragrance of flowers is not an accident nor yet is it manifested for the exclusive and tangible benefit either of the plants themselves or of man. It can of course be maintained, with no possibility of proof either way, that man alone sees beauty as such; it is anyhow a commonplace that all men do not see it in the same way and that some appear to be totally indifferent to it. Hence the saying that beauty is in the eye of the beholder, and so in one sense it is; but this saying can be interpreted in two different ways; either, on the one hand, that beauty is purely subjective and therefore has no intrinsic reality independently of its observer, or, on the other hand, that it has an intrinsic reality but is accessible to an individual only to the extent that he is attuned to it and no further. According to the first interpretation beauty is less than man and is a product of his nature; according to the second it is greater, or at least more universal, than the human individuality as such. The first interpretation alone is concordant with the scientific and evolutionary outlook; the second is not, because it takes account of something that is outside the purview of science, in that it implies that beauty is objective and universal, that its reality is independent of its manifestation in nature, and that therefore it is inherently mysterious, intangible and non-measurable. If that is so, beauty is by no means a fortuitous attribute of matter; it is something of the universal manifested in the relative, or a manifestation of the infinite in the finite, and in that case, the real importance of beauty to us does not reside in its pleasurable or aesthetic aspect, but in its symbolism, or in its didactic potentiality. The traditional association of beauty with truth is then neither sentimental nor fanciful, for the positive qualities, among which is beauty, are immutable realities; only the material and perishable forms through which the ever-present potentialities of the qualities may be more or less imperfectly manifested are ephemeral. Materialism consists precisely in restricting attention to the perishable form; whether in its scientific or in its popular guise it is therefore opposed to all that a religion not tainted with materialism teaches, namely, that the material world can only be accounted for in terms of the non-material, the visible in terms of the invisible, the measurable in terms of the non-measurable; and further that the ultimate truth is enshrined in the latter and not in the former. This is no way implies that material and measurable things should be ignored or despised in principle, but simply that they should be seen for what they are, namely, signs or symbols of a reality immeasurably greater, more comprehensive and more enduring than they are, even in their totality. Here, as always, it is a case of preserving a right balance, and this can only be done by keeping the essential principles always in view, and interpreting the facts of observation accordingly. The main principle here in view is the metaphysical superiority or transcendence of the intangible and non-measurable over the tangible and measurable, that is to say, of quality over quantity. Without quantity the universe as we know it could have no existence, but the qualities would remain as unmanifested potentialities; such a situation is conceivable. Without quality, if anything could then be said to exist, it would have no intelligibility; it would have the completely abstract character of pure number, to which, as René Guénon has shown, the conception of quantity is in the last analysis reducible; such a situation is not, strictly speaking, conceivable, since one cannot form a conception of unrelieved indistinction, pure chaos. For similar reasons it is not realizable, nevertheless it is the situation towards which the world is moving, though it can never attain to it fully.

It is therefore not really surprising that an inversion of the priorities implied in this principle has culminated, quite logically, in a sort of nihilism, in the philosophy of "unyielding despair" which Bertrand Russell announced specifically, and others of the same persuasion by implication, as the only rational basis for the ordering of human life. If the priorities are kept in the right order, the beauty of flowers, seen as the expression of a principle and not as an accident, can teach us directly, intellectually, and without recourse to sentiment of any kind, that this philosophy of despair is rubbish. But can one thus metaphorically consign to the waste-paper basket the life's work of so many able and erudite men, highly trained in logic and in exposition, and deeply convinced that they are struggling to save mankind from self-destruction? What have they done to deserve such treatment? Well, what they have done is to consign to the waste-paper basket, metaphorically or otherwise, the whole of the "perennial philosophy" that is enshrined in the sacred Scriptures of the world, all the exposition and exemplification of that philosophy given by the saints and sages whom the world has revered from time immemorial, all religion, all tradition, in short, all that has hitherto given meaning to human life. And, one must add, all that can still give meaning to it, and not a spurious meaning, as they would have it, but the only meaning it has. If they are right, they themselves must be the avatars and the prophets of a new age of realism, destined to replace millennia of delusion; but if they are wrong, the word "rubbish" applied to their work is too gentle. It is not their erudition that is in question, nor their logical consistency, nor yet their sincerity (for "sincerity" in its current sense makes no distinction between error and truth); it is the fundamental assumptions on which the logical structure of their philosophy is built. In the case of the two philosophies here contrasted, their respective starting-points are diametrically opposed, so that, even when there is a superficial resemblance in method or in development, there is still in reality no common measure between them. The one seeks to derive principles from phenomena, the other seeks to see phenomena in the light of their metaphysical principles. The first attempts an impossible task and consequently ends up in a sort of chaos or nihilism; the second attempts a task of supreme difficulty and one that can never be fully accomplished, least of all by the unaided efforts of man, but it is the task that justifies all other tasks.

Somebody may say: "Are you not doing exactly what you criticize, and trying to arrive at a principle by studying a phenomenon, for surely beauty is a phenomenon, since it is observable." Any such question misses the point that beauty as such is not a phenomenon and is not observable; what is observable is the material or psychic entity through which beauty is manifested in some degree and in some mode. The endless variety of its modes, in each of which it can achieve a sort of perfection that reflects its universality, bears witness to that very universality, to the fact that beauty is in its essence a principle and not an accident, independently of whether it be manifested in a flower or in a star or in a human soul.

Admittedly, to say that beauty is a principle or, for instance, an archetypal possibility of the highest metaphysical importance, adds nothing to the direct and incalculable impact of our experience of it. That experience can to a greater or less extent carry us "out of ourselves" by giving us a glimpse of something greater than ourselves, though its vehicle be only a humble flower. To the extent that it does so, it is an experience of the "super-natural," whether we recognize it as such or not; and it is necessarily either something like that, or it is in the last analysis but a perishable illusion devoid of ultimate significance. If it is devoid of ultimate significance, then so is everything else, ourselves included: a rejection of the super-natural logically and inevitably leads to something like a philosophy of despair. One could wish that those whose religion implies an acceptance of the super-natural would apply the same kind of logic to the development of their certitude as its rejecters apply to theirs, instead of always trying to justify it in terms of morality or of contingent advantage, which it is in the nature of the case impossible to do conclusively. The certitudes or basic assumptions that provide the starting-points of logic are necessarily themselves supra-logical, in the sense that, like existence itself or the beauty of a flower, they cannot themselves be objects of discursive proof.

There are a few people to whom flowers in general make little appeal, and there are many others whose floral likes and dislikes are at variance; the same is of course true of the perception of beauty in its many other forms. These commonplace facts may seem to support the idea that the whole issue turns on the vagaries of individual taste. But if beauty is what it has been said to be in the preceding paragraphs, its universality and transcendence imply that there must be some real or quasi-absolute criterion whereby taste can in principle be judged; the distinction between good and bad taste cannot be wholly arbitrary, nor a matter of fashion or period alone, nor even of the application of any purely human standards of judgment. Such distinctions of taste as arise entirely from individual or collective peculiarities are indeed of a very limited and fugitive importance; other distinctions can however reveal differences of approach that are more profound, because they are connected with the didactic or symbolical aspects of their objects. Distinctions of taste in the floral domain are by no means always of the first kind alone; they may indeed be more revealing than distinctions applied to human artifacts, being uncomplicated by local or national differences of style and technique.

In certain circumstances the symbolical aspect of a particular flower predominates, but that occurs only when it is used as part of some formal and established religious or traditional symbolism. One could instance the rose in the center of the cross, where the five-petalled flower symbolizes the "quintessence," the unmanifested *quinta essentia* which is central to the four elements and is their principle; the lotus as the throne of the Buddha, horizontal but with upturned petals, and lying on the face of the waters; or the *fleur-de-lys*, which we now know as iris, and the association of its triple form with the Trinity. In such cases the symbolism associated with each flower could be called a specialized symbolism, to which the beauty of the flower is incidental. Here however, we are chiefly concerned with the general symbolism of flowers in its less specialized manifestations, and with its relation to what would usually be regarded purely as questions of individual or collective taste.

One aspect of the general symbolism of flowers which is often overlooked is the following: as everybody knows, the function of flowers is exclusively concerned with the sexual reproduction of plants. In general those parts of a flower which we most admire, such as the petals, are secondary sexual characters, closely associated with the minute primary characters. The whole assembly is paraded and flaunted with joyful unconcern above the more mundane structural and nutritive organs, and it constitutes what is usually for us the most attractive feature of the plant. In this way flowers exemplify more completely and perfectly than any other living organisms the primordial innocence, beauty and unselfconsciousness of the sexual function. As a symbol and as something like a perpetual renewal of the primordial Act of creation, that function is essentially sacred; but it can be profaned and prostituted by fallen man, who has lost his innocence and unselfconsciousness and can by no means recover them. The traditional restrictions and taboos which surround it in all human societies take account of these facts. To many people, especially in these days, those restrictions seem harsh and futile, or even psychologically unsound, but they are adapted not only to the present needs of fallen man, but also and above all to the safeguarding of the fate of his soul. The latter consideration plays almost no part in contemporary discussions of what has become a burning question, but it is by far the most important, outweighing all considerations of present ease. A conscious conformity to God's laws is required of us, in exchange for our gift of freewill. The beauty of a perfect but unconscious conformity is demonstrated in flowers here and now, as a perishable symbol of that which awaits in eternity those whose conformity in this life is fully conscious.

Each manifestation of floral beauty is in some degree unique and incomparable. A wild rose, a Madonna lily, the Pasque flower, the common primrose, most crocus species, fritillaries, lily-of-the-valley, a wild cherry or apple (the latter in its true wild form is rare), Grass of Parnassus . . . But why continue? for the list might never end; but it can at least be restricted by considering only flowers that grow wild or can be cultivated out of doors in Britain. Each of the flowers named is like nothing else, and it is no use attempting to compare one with another. The writer is well aware that his own individual preferences have played a large part in the choice of those mentioned, but those preferences do not signify. Some readers may wish to delete, and some to add, but that also does not signify, provided that any plant named manifests a beauty all its own, beyond compare, or, as we so significantly say, "out of this world." There are also many less-conspicuous flowers that would qualify for inclusion if they were looked at carefully enough, not least the grasses and sedges, in which beauty of form is emphasized by a relative uniformity of color. And again there are many others which are indispensable as foils or backgrounds to set off the beauty of their brighter fellows, such as the Umbelliferae, the clovers, the bedstraws and so on. The picture is one of an endless variety of degrees and kinds of perfection, some really incomparable—that is to say, limited only by the fact that they exclude other perfections—and others of lower degree and limited in other ways. It is not wrong to use the word "perfection" in this way, although, according to the strict meaning of the word, it is an absolute and as such cannot be limited. But we are speaking of the world, and that is exactly what the world is, perfection manifested in imperfection, the absolute in the relative, the infinite in the finite; every part of the world mirrors the whole. The paradoxical or mysterious or miraculous character of the world is reflected in the gaiety, the subtlety and the extravagance of its floral adornment, at least as clearly as in any other feature.

A gardener or botanist may have noticed that all the flowers so far mentioned are species, that is to say that they occur as wild plants in this or in some other country, and are not among the innumerable hybrids or varieties that occur only in cultivation and are now conveniently described as "cultivars." These cultivars are the result of a conscious endeavor to enhance the pleasure given by flowers by selecting forms that are larger or brighter in color or more striking in form than the wild species from which they are derived; also by providing the gardener or the buyer of flowers with a much wider choice than he could obtain if he had to rely on species alone. These cultivars are commonly referred to as "improved" varieties; perhaps the commonest and the oldest kind of "improvement" consists in a multiplication of the petals, resulting in what we call a "double" flower. Double flowers, and flowers showing unusual size or brilliance as well as other departures from the normal occur occasionally in nature, and the development of most cultivars has started by the selection of such "sports," because their peculiarities can often be accentuated under the conditions of intensive cultivation. As is well known, it is this possibility of artificial selection, often resulting in great changes in the outward forms of plants, which provided Darwin with the basis of his theory of natural selection.

Whatever may be the explanation of the beauty of wild flowers, there can be no doubt that there is a conscious purpose behind the changes brought about by cultivation; it is of course the satisfaction of the desires of mankind. As those desires have never been so ambitious as they are today, nor the means of satisfying them so easy to come by, so it is with flowers. The contemporary desire for novelty, for sensationalism, for quantity (which includes size as well as number) is catered for by new methods of inducing variations and of speedy propagation. The question then is to what extent and in what sense the results of the work of flower breeders past and present can properly be designated "improvement"; or in other words, whether they are in general expressions of good taste. That work has produced many long-established favorites, the double roses and pinks, the enlarged lily-of-the-valley, the endless variety of pansies, primroses and auriculas, the double peonies, the chrysanthemums and dahlias, fuchsias and geraniums, tulips, irises and so on, some of which are seen in almost every garden, and no wonder, because they have endless brilliance and charm. They are however in danger of being superseded by more recent introductions, the bewildering multiplicity of which is presented to us in innumerable catalogues, wherein the resources of language are strained to the utmost to describe their striking colors, gigantic size and sensational effect. Without attempting to deny that some of these sensational novelties are beautiful, occasionally very beautiful, it may yet be permissible to suggest that in too many cases much more has been lost than has been gained. The new floribunda roses do not belie their name, but most of them are shapeless and often unbelievably crude in color; the total effect of a bed of modern roses is indeed startling, but it is little else; the latest gladioli have the same faults; the new daffodils look like artificial flowers which in a sense they are; cyclamens, among the most subtly elegant of flowers, have become enormous, distorted and even frilled, pansies have become huge and floppy, polyanthus primrose gigantic, sometimes frilled and even pink in color, losing all their characteristic decisive neatness; the regal pelargoniums had comparable qualities but are suffering exactly the same fate. One has sometimes got to look at the leaves to see whether a flower is a pelargonium or a petunia or a hibiscus or what. Delphiniums, larkspurs, clarkias, godetias have become like solid columns of colored crinkly paper, losing all their pristine elegance of form and marking. In short the general tendency is all towards the substitution of ostentation for elegance, crudity for subtlety, blatancy for beauty, quantity for quality. People do not seem to want to look at a flower, they want to be hit in the eye by it. The frequent sacrifice of scent to gaudiness is often lamented, but it seems equally often to be accepted as inevitable.

The views just expressed about what is happening to garden flowers are fairly widespread although those who hold them are in a minority. The "improved" varieties are on the whole much the most popular, and that is what makes it worthwhile for the nurseryman to produce them. The word "vulgar" simply means "popular," and vulgar in a derogatory sense is precisely what the taste of the majority inevitably is and always will be. We saw earlier that, beauty being what it is, the criteria of taste can never be wholly arbitrary, despite the fact that individual and collective peculiarities and fashions play a very large part in establishing them in any particular case. Those criteria cannot be defined in terms of human reactions and nothing else, the ultimate criteria can only be sought in the field of symbolism, for it is through their symbolism alone that the phenomena of this world bring us into contact with the absolute. Now it can be asserted that the symbolism of the natural is always more direct than that of the artificial, although this does not necessarily imply that the artificial—that is to say, whatever is man-made in whole or in part—must always in all circumstances be rejected in favor of the natural, for man was not given his faculties and powers for nothing. The natural is nevertheless always nearer to its origin, and its origin is the Origin of all things; the work of man, or man's interference with the natural, especially when it is directed mainly to the satisfaction of his own desires and fancies, always tends towards forgetfulness of the Origin. This forgetfulness grows as man takes more and more pride in his own supposed originality or "creativity," although in fact no man ever created anything; the most any man can do is to play about with potentialities already present in his material, and rearrange them for his advantage or amusement. However, for so long as man does not lose sight of the origin of his material, nor of the fact that its origin is also his own—and this implies among other things that he does not lose his humility—his work may be legitimate and he may not overstep the bounds of good taste. Up to a point, then, the deliberate rearrangement, encouragement or suppression of potentialities present in living things—flowering plants for example—can lead to a certain enrichment at not too heavy a cost, although the enrichment always tends to be quantitative and the loss to be qualitative. Inevitably there comes a point at which the balance tips, and thereafter erroneous tendencies reinforce one another, so that not only do losses outweigh gains, but even those gains themselves prove unsatisfying, and must constantly be replaced by others even more costly in terms of qualitative excellence. All this is aggravated by the intrusion of commercialism, with its large-scale mechanized operations, standardization and advertising. In the end it becomes virtually the dictator of taste.

That being so, one can at least see why the improved varieties produced in the earlier years of plant breeding should generally be qualitatively superior to later productions. The old-fashioned roses, the cottage pinks and carnations, the double stocks, and many other old favorites, although very artificial in that they are very "double," are nevertheless still a little "out of this world," and so are the auriculas, pansies and violas; their beauty is subtle and mysterious even when they are very "showy." The same could be said of many of the Japanese ornamental cherries, maples and peonies. Nevertheless, the enrichment represented by these more or less ancient cultivars, as well as by many of the less vulgar of their successors, is nearly always in the realm of the quantitative and sensual; the corresponding impoverishment is always in the realm of the qualitative and symbolical. And so one can see how once again the prevailing tendencies of the day are reflected in the floral domain, this time in the department of floriculture. If they are reflected less intensely there than they are in some other sectors of the field of visual aesthetics—notably in painting and sculpture—it is because the material used is the living plant, which must at least remain alive, and while it does so it can never lose all its natural characteristics.

Added to the ever-growing array of new cultivars available to gardeners, is a vast number of alien species, introduced into this country from all over the world in the past hundred years or so. A few of them have established themselves firmly in our gardens, as firmly as older introductions such as tulips, lilacs, peonies and roses, and no less worthily. We should be poorer without *Viburnum fragrans*, the regal lily, the blue-poppy, and some of the new Rhododendrons, to mention only a few of those most widely cultivated. In all, hundreds, even thousands, of exotic species are cultivated by enthusiasts and admired by many more. The hybridizers are of course hard at work "improving" them, especially the lilies. It has been said that a greater variety of plants can be grown in the British Isles than in any comparable area in the world, and this is probably not far wrong. Here indeed is a tremendous enrichment, horticulturally speaking; it may indeed represent something like an *embarras de richesses*: but if so, it is surely of a fairly harmless kind. But it is confined to the relatively restricted and artificial domain of horticulture, and as such it is a poor compensation for another result of the artificiality of modern life, the depletion of our wild flowers.

The demand for land for residential, industrial and recreational uses, chemical methods of weed-control on farms and elsewhere, and the invasion of the countryside by a motorized proletariat, pathetically longing for virgin nature but incompatible with its continued existence, these and other factors are resulting in an appallingly rapid depletion of wild flowers both in quantity and in variety. The creation of "nature reserves," desirable though it be, like many other attempts to preserve a precious heritage, cannot restore that heritage, but can only preserve it as a museum specimen, no longer alive, though better than nothing.

Not only the longing for virgin nature, but also the cult of flowers so prevalent today, are above all signs of an unconscious reaction against the ugliness associated with almost all the products of an industrialized society; and that ugliness is itself a sign, a sign of the hatefulness of all that brings it about. If a modern town were in conformity with the real needs and destiny of its inhabitants, they would love it and seek it, instead of getting out of it into the country or to the seaside at every available opportunity, often at the cost of great and prolonged discomfort and inconvenience. But they cannot help bringing the town out with them; the car, the radio, the newspapers, the cartons; and in doing so they gradually destroy the very thing they are seeking. That thing is in the last analysis, did they but know it, not so much natural beauty as communion with God. It is that, too, that the lover of flowers is really seeking, and if he knew it, he would not be so keen as he is on their supposed "improvement"; he would be more ready to accept and to marvel, and perhaps to understand.

It is mainly field botanists and Nature Conservation societies who are aware of and lament the elimination, except in a few carefully guarded sites, of many of our rarer plants, such as the Pasque flower, the fritillary and numerous orchids. Obvious to all is the reduction in buttercups, ox-eye daisies, harebell, primrose, cowslip, meadow saxifrage, wild daffodil, in short, of almost everything that formerly made our meadows flowery. There is also the more equivocal case of the weeds of arable land. Charlock may be dismissed as both vicious and ugly, but the poppy, the corn-cockle, the corn marigold, the bindweed and the cornflower have been deservedly admired, though harmful to the crops with which they compete. Under the older farming methods they could usually be kept more or less in check but they could not be eliminated; modern methods are more comprehensive. These weeds, together with their no less numerous and troublesome but less visually attractive companions in the field, are not defeated yet; but if modern chemical methods are pursued and developed for a few more decades they may well be virtually eliminated. Crops could then be grown more cheaply, but in terms of financial cost alone.

The most recent development in the same direction consists in the invention of plastic flowers. By the use of modern techniques the most conspicuous features of the forms and colors of natural or cultivated flowers can be imitated very closely; this applies particularly to lilies. If the broad decorative effect of floral arrangements were the sole criterion of the value of flowers, it would be difficult to find any plausible objection to the use of plastic flowers in appropriate circumstances. They last for ever, they need no messy water to keep them going, they are washable and can be packed away when not in use, and they eliminate all the recurrent trouble and expense associated with real flowers. The artificial flowers of the past were usually recognizable as such and did not pretend to be anything else; they were indeed often products of a real art; one could instance the charming "flowers" made out of shells in the Far East, which are the products of a gentle and unassuming form of decorative art that charms without deceiving. It is precisely their deceptiveness that condemns plastic flowers. They represent an attempt at a complete and conclusive replacement of the works of God by the works of man, a more and more complete obscuring of the reality by the appearance, a further substitution of the spurious but plausible for the genuine and guileless, death masquerading more and more successfully as life. They are like a frozen smile on the face of a corpse. Their use in churches in substitution for real flowers is nothing less than a desecration; their use elsewhere is a manifestation of bad taste pure and simple, and is correspondingly significant.

In conspicuous contrast to their durability is the evanescence of real flowers. Among the innumerable types of beauty in this world, that of flowers is both the most widespread and the most untarnished, and at the same time one of the least durable. As we have seen, their ephemerality is that of the material forms through which their beauty is manifested, and does not appertain to beauty as such; those forms are however continually and rhythmically renewed. This year's dog-rose is not the same as last year's, but its beauty is the same; the quality is eternal, only its manifestation in a material form is ephemeral. The theme of the perishability of all forms and of their rhythmical renewal is frequent in the sacred scriptures of the world. Existence is joined to eternity not only through the qualities manifested in it, but also through its rhythms, which as it were compensate the irreversible and devouring character of time. We can sense this directly when the repeated and identical vibrations of a string produce a single musical note; by extension we can perhaps learn to hear something of the "music of the spheres," wherein the rhythms of the whole creation are unified in one great song of praise.

Reginald Farrer, a great gardener who introduced many plants from the Far East, wrote in *The Rainbow Bridge* (p. 225) as follows:

> And if, amid the cataclysms of anguish that clamor round us everywhere nowadays (1918), you declare that all this babble about beauty and flowers is a vain impertinence, then I must tell you that you err, and that your perspectives are false. Mortal dooms and dynasties are brief things, but beauty is indestructible and eternal, if its tabernacle be only a petal that is shed tomorrow. Wars and agonies are shadows only cast across the path of man: each successive one seems the end of all things, but man perpetually emerges and goes forward, lured always and cheered and inspired by the immortal beauty-thought that finds form in all the hopes and enjoyments of his life. *Inter arma silent flores*[1] is no truth; on the contrary, amid the crash of doom our sanity and survival more than ever depend on the strength with which we can listen to the still

---

1. Editor's Note: This can be translated as, " In time of war, flowers are silent."

small voice that towers above the cannons, and cling to the little quiet things of life, the things that come and go and yet are always there, the inextinguishable lamps of God amid the disaster that man has made of his life.

The evanescence of flowers is not a matter for regret: it is an ever-present reminder of what we are, their recurrence is at the same time a guarantee of the immutability of the qualities that so delight us in them. Plastic flowers are therefore doubly condemned, and that by the very characteristics most commonly cited in their favor, namely, the fact that their resemblance to real flowers is so close, and the fact that they do not fade.

Ought we then not to enjoy flowers for the sake of the simple, direct and unselfconscious pleasure they afford, but rather on the contrary always be trying to philosophize about them or learn something from them by reflecting on their symbolism? By no means, because the reality that can be discerned through the symbolism of flowers is itself something that can only be apprehended directly, just as their beauty is apprehended; it cannot be attained by the analytical or imaginative powers of the mind alone, and it cannot be contained by any formula. An understanding of symbolism and reflection thereon is very far from being useless, but it cannot by itself either take the place of or bring about the direct apprehension of reality that is prefigured in our natural and unaffected delight in flowers.

One day the disciples of the Buddha were assembled to hear him preach a sermon. But he said not a word; instead, he stooped down and plucked a flower and held it up for them to see. Of all that assembly, only one showed by his smile that he understood.

## A Flower Does Not Talk

Silently a flower blooms,
In silence it falls away;
Yet here now, at this moment, at this place,
    the whole of the flower, the whole of
    the world is blooming.
This is the talk of the flower, the truth
    of the blossom:
The glory of eternal life is fully shining here.

— Zenkei Shibayama

# Acknowledgments

We would like to thank the following authors, editors and publishers for their consent to publish the articles in this anthology.

1. Frithjof Schuon, "Seeing God Everywhere"
   *Gnosis: Divine Wisdom*, Perennial Books, 1959, p. 89-102.

2. Tenzin Gyatso, His Holiness the 14th Dalai Lama, "A Tibetan Buddhist Perspective on Spirit in Nature"
   *Spirit and Nature: Why the Environment is a Religious Issue*, edited by Steven C. Rockefeller and John C. Elder, Beacon Press, 1992, p. 109-123.

3. Harry Oldmeadow, "The Firmament Sheweth His Handiwork: Re-awakening a Religious Sense of the Natural Order" (revised)
   *Sacred Web*, 2 (Winter 1998), 1998, p. 11-31.

4. Wendell Berry, "Christianity and the Survival of Creation"
   *Sex, Economy, Freedom & Community*, Pantheon Books, 1992, p. 93-116.

5. Seyyed Hossein Nasr, "The Spiritual and Religious Dimensions of the Environmental Crisis"
   *A Sacred Trust: Ecology and Spiritual Vision*, edited by David Cadman and John Carey, Temenos Academy & The Prince's Foundation, 2002, p. 118-148.

6. Oren Lyons, "Our Mother Earth"
   *I Become Part of It: Sacred Dimensions in Native American Life*, edited by D.M. Dooling and Paul Jordan-Smith, Parabola Books, 1989, p. 270-274.

7. Philip Sherrard, "The Desanctification of Nature"
   *The Rape of Man and Nature*, Golgonooza Press, 1987, p. 90-112.

8. Hari Prasad Shastri, "O Hanami: Flower Viewing"
   *Echoes of Japan*, Shanti Sadan, 1961, p. 9-12.

9. Toshihiko Izutsu, "Creation According to Ibn 'Arabî"
   *Sufism and Taoism: A Comparative Study of Key Philosophical Concepts*, University of California Press, 1983, p. 197-217.

10. James Barr, "Of Metaphysics and Polynesian Navigation"
*Avaloka: A Journal of Traditional Religion and Culture*, 3 (1-2), 1988-1989, p. 3-8.

11. Kathleen Raine, "The Underlying Order: Nature and the Imagination"
*Fragments of Infinity: Essays in Religion and Philosophy*, edited by Arvind Sharma, Prism Press, 1991, p. 198-216.

12. Arthur Versluis, "Hierophanic Nature" (revised)
*TheoSophia: Hidden Dimensions of Christianity*, Lindisfarne Press, 1994, p. 93-105.

13. Titus Burckhardt, "The Symbolism of Water"
*Mirror of the Intellect*, edited by William Stoddart, Quinta Essentia, 1987, p. 124-131.

14. Reza Shah-Kazemi, "Divine Beatitude: Supreme Archetype of Aesthetic Experience"
*Iqbal Review: Journal of the Iqbal Academy*, October, Lahore, 1999, p. 51-58.

15. J.C. Cooper, "The Yin and the Yang in Nature"
*Yin and Yang*, Aquarian Press, 1981, p. 42-55.

16. Leo Schaya, "Creation, the Image of God"
*The Universal Meaning of the Kabbalah*, Penguin, 1971, p. 61-73.

17. John Chryssavgis, "The World of the Icon and Creation: An Orthodox Perspective on Ecology and Pneumatology"
*Christianity and Ecology: Seeking the Well Being of Earth and Humans*, edited by D. Hessel and R. Radford Ruether, Harvard University Press, 2000, p. 83-96.

18. Joseph Epes Brown, "Becoming Part of It"
*I Become Part of It: Sacred Dimensions in Native American Life*, edited by D.M. Dooling and Paul Jordan-Smith, Parabola Books, 1989, p. 9-20.

19. Lord Northbourne, "Flowers"
*Looking Back on Progress*, Sophia Perennis et Universalis, 1970, p. 90-106.

The poem on the Dedication page was written by Barry McDonald and it appeared in *Cross Currents: The Journal of the Association of Religion and Intellectual Life*, Summer 1994.

# Contributors

JAMES BARR is an author, seaman, navigator and practicing Buddhist whose article "Of Metaphysics and Polynesian Navigation" first appeared in *Avaloka: A Journal of Traditional Religion and Culture.*

WENDELL BERRY is a conservationist, farmer, essayist, novelist, poet, and a former professor of English at the University of Kentucky. Described by the *New York Times* as a "prophet of rural America," Berry is a past fellow of both the Guggenheim Foundation and the Rockefeller Foundation, and an author of more than two dozen books, of which his most recent publications include *Sex, Economy, Freedom and Community* (1993), *Life is a Miracle: An Essay in Modern Superstition* (2000), *Jayber Crow* (2000) and a volume of *Selected Poetry* (1999). He is currently a Fellow of the Temenos Academy and lives and farms in his native Kentucky with his wife Tanya.

JOSEPH EPES BROWN was Professor of Religious Studies at the University of Montana and a renowned author in the field of American Indian traditions. A vital interest in the traditional life ways of the American Indians led him to the Lakota holy man Black Elk, who recounted to him the sacred rites of the Oglala Sioux, which served as the basis for his most well known book, *The Sacred Pipe* (1953). His other publications include, *The Spiritual Legacy of the American Indian* (1982), *Animals of the Soul* (1992) and *Teaching Spirits* (2001).

TITUS BURCKHARDT was an eminent member of the Traditionalist school who published many distinguished works in the fields of metaphysics, cosmology, art, architecture, alchemy, symbolism, and traditional civilization. A prolific author, he devoted all his life to the study and exposition of the different aspects of Wisdom and Tradition. His chief metaphysical work is *An Introduction to Sufi Doctrine* (1976), whilst his *Sacred Art of East and West* (2001) is an enunciation of the traditional doctrine of art as it is found in civilizations such as the Christian, Islamic, Hindu, Buddhist, and Taoist. An anthology of his writings, *Mirror of the Intellect* (1987), is particularly notable for its exposition of a wide range of subjects on traditional science and art, as well as an acute critique of their modernist counterfeits. Titus Burckhardt died in Lausanne in 1984.

J.C. COOPER was born in China where she spent much of her childhood. Informed by the perspective of the Perennial Philosophy, she wrote and lectured extensively on the subjects of comparative religion and symbolism and is the author of lucid introductory works on Chinese religion such as *Taoism, the Way of the Mystic* (1972), *Yin and Yang* (1981), and *Chinese Alchemy* (1984). In addition she wrote several works in the field of symbolism, including *Symbolism, the Universal Language* (1986), *Symbolic and Mythological Animals* (1992), and the broad ranging *An Illustrated Encyclopedia of Traditional Symbols* (1978).

REVEREND JOHN CHRYSSAVGIS is Professor of Theology and former Dean at Holy Cross Greek Orthodox School of Theology in Brookline, Massachusetts. He received his degree in Theology from the University of Athens (1980) and completed his doctoral studies in Patristic Theology at Oxford University (1983), where his studies focused on ascetic theology and the spirituality of the early Church, especially from the desert tradition of Egypt, Palestine and Sinai. During his service of the Orthodox Church in Australia, he co-founded St. Andrew's Theological College in Sydney, where he was Sub-Dean and taught Patristics and Church History. Rev. Dr. Chryssavgis also acts as theological advisor to the Patriarchal Commission on Religion and Science (Ecumenical Patriarchate), which focuses on the environment. He is the prolific author of numerous books and articles on the early Church fathers and Orthodox spirituality, including *Ascent to Heaven* (1989), *The Desert is Alive* (1994), *The Way of the Fathers* (1998), and *Soul Mending: The Art of Spiritual Direction* (2000). World Wisdom Books recently published his introductory work on early Christian monasticism entitled, *In the Heart of the Desert: The Spirituality of the Desert Fathers and Mothers* (2003).

TENZIN GYATSO, HIS HOLINESS THE 14TH DALAI LAMA is both the spiritual and temporal leader of the Tibetan people. Following the invasion of Tibet by the communist-inspired Chinese Army in 1959 and the impending threat on his life, he escaped into exile and has since resided in Dharmsala, the seat of the Tibetan Government-in-exile. He is a recipient of the Nobel Peace Prize and an author of numerous books and essays, including *Kindness, Clarity and Insight* (1984), *A Human Approach to World Peace* (1984), and *Ocean of Wisdom* (1989).

TOSHIHIKO IZUTSU was Professor Emeritus at Keio University in Japan and an outstanding authority in the metaphysical and philosophical wisdom schools of Islamic Sufism, Hindu Advaita Vedanta, Mahayana Buddhism (particularly Zen), and Philosophical Taoism. Fluent in over 30 languages, including Arabic, Persian, Sanskrit, Pali, Chinese, Japanese, Russian and Greek, his peripatetic research in such places as the Middle East, India, Europe, North America, and Asia were undertaken with a view to developing a meta-philosophical approach to comparative religion based upon a rigorous linguistic study of traditional metaphysical texts. His most important works include *Sufism and Taoism: A Comparative Study of Key Philosophical Concepts* (1983) and a posthumously published collection of essays entitled *Creation and the Timeless Order of Things* (1994).

SATISH KUMAR was born in Rajasthan in India in 1936. When he was only nine years old, he renounced the world and joined the wandering brotherhood of Jain monks. Dissuaded from his path by an inner voice at the age of eighteen, he became a campaigner for land reform, working to turn Gandhi's vision of renewed India and a peaceful world into reality. In 1973 he settled in England, taking on the editorship of *Resurgence* magazine, and has been the Editor ever since. He is the guiding spirit behind a number of ecological, spiritual and educational ventures in Britain. In 1991, Schumacher College, a residential international center for the study of ecological and spiritual values, was founded, of which he is the Director of Programmes. He is the author of *Path Without Destination* (William Morrow, 2000) and *You Are Therefore I Am* (Green Books, 2002).

OREN LYONS is a member of the Wolf Clan of the Onondaga Nation, the Firekeepers of the Haudenosaunee. He is an Associate Professor in the Department of American Studies at the State University of New York in Buffalo, and publisher of *Daybreak*, an American Indian news magazine dedicated to the seventh generation.

BARRY MCDONALD serves as Managing Director of World Wisdom Press. A strong attraction to authentic spirituality led him to many parts of the world and brought him in contact with spiritual authorities from several traditions. Thomas Yellowtail, the venerable Medicine Man and Sun Dance Chief, adopted him into his Crow tribe. He is the editor of *Every Branch in Me: Essays on the Meaning of Man* (World Wisdom, 2002) and his poetry has appeared in *CrossCurrents, Sacred Web, Sophia,* and *Sufi.* His graduate degree is from Indiana University.

SEYYED HOSSEIN NASR is University Professor of Islamic Studies at George Washington University and president of the Foundation for Traditional Studies, the publisher of *Sophia: The Journal of Traditional Studies.* He is the author of over thirty books and three hundred articles on topics ranging from comparative religion to traditional Islamic philosophy, cosmology, art, ecology, and mysticism. Among his most notable works are *Ideals and Realities of Islam* (1966), *Knowledge and the Sacred* (the 1981 Gifford Lectures), *Sufi Essays* (1991), and *Religion and the Order of Nature* (1996). The Seyyed Hossein Nasr Foundation propagates traditional teachings in general, and the various facets of traditional Islam and other religions in particular.

LORD NORTHBOURNE was a frequent contributor to the British journal *Studies in Comparative Religion* and a translator of Traditionalist works by Frithjof Schuon, René Guénon and Titus Burckhardt. His books *Religion in the Modern World* (1963) and *Looking Back on Progress* (1970) are considered by many to be especially good introductions to the Perennialist outlook.

KENNETH OLDMEADOW is co-ordinator of Philosophy and Religious Studies at La Trobe University in Australia and author of the acclaimed *Traditionalism: Religion in the Light of the Perennial Philosophy* (2000), an authoritative introduction to the perspective of Perennialism as it is found in the works of such authors as Frithjof Schuon, René Guénon, and Ananda Coomaraswamy. He is a frequent contributor to the traditional journals *Sophia* and *Sacred Web* and has published on a wide range of topics, including works on the Australian Aborigines, Hindu Advaita Vedanta, and Tibetan Buddhism.

KATHLEEN RAINE, C.B.E. is an internationally recognized English poet and Blake scholar. She is the founder of Temenos Academy, an organization that advocates the primacy of the Imagination and which promulgates a traditional view of the arts and crafts in Britain. In addition to her many seminal works on the Romantic poet William Blake such as *Blake and Antiquity* (1979), *Golgonooza, City of the Imagination: Last Studies in William Blake* (1991), and *Blake and Tradition* (2002), all of which stress a neo-Platonic interpretative outlook, other of her more representative publications include *Defending Ancient Springs* (1985) and *Yeats the Initiate* (1986).

LEO SCHAYA was born in Switzerland where he received a traditional Jewish upbringing. From his early youth he devoted himself to the study of the great metaphysical doctrines of the Orient and Occident, particularly the works of neo-Platonism, Sufism and Advaita Vedanta. He published several articles on the metaphysical and esoteric wisdom of the Jewish Kabbalah, as well as a perspicacious book on the subject entitled *The Universal Meaning of the Kabbalah* (1958).

FRITHJOF SCHUON was the foremost expositor of the Perennialist perspective in the 20th century and is best known as a philosopher in the metaphysical current of Shankara and Plato. He wrote more than 25 books on metaphysical and religious themes and was a regular contributor to journals on comparative religion in both Europe and America. Schuon's writings have been translated into over a dozen languages, and have been consistently featured and reviewed in a wide range of scholarly and philosophical publications around the world, respected by both scholars and spiritual authorities alike. Of his first work, *The Transcendent Unity of Religions* (1953), T.S. Eliot wrote: "I have met with no more impressive work in the comparative study of Oriental and Occidental religion." Frithjof Schuon died in 1998.

REZA SHAH-KAZEMI is a Research Associate at the Institute of Ismaili Studies in London. His major work is *Paths to Transcendence: Spiritual Realization according to Shankara, Ibn Arabi, and Meister Eckhart* (forthcoming). His several contributions to the traditional journals *Sophia* and *Sacred Web* deal with themes relating to the Perennial Philosophy, Tradition, and prayer. He is currently preparing a new English translation of the Imam Ali's *Nahj Al-Balagha*.

HARI PRASAD SHASTRI was born at Bareilly in Northern India and educated at Benares and Allahabad University. A gifted Sanskrit scholar well versed in the metaphysical wisdom of Advaita Vedanta, he lectured at Waseda University in Tokyo from 1916-1918 during which time he wrote a precious evocation of Buddhism in *Echoes of*

*Japan*. He afterwards moved to China for a period of eleven years and was Dean of the Foreign Department at Hardoon University and Professor of Philosophy at Nankwang College, where he founded the *Asiatic Review* and supervised the publication of the standard Chinese edition of the Buddhist Scriptures (over 5000 texts). At the instigation of his spiritual teacher Shri Dadaji of Aligarh (heir to a famous teaching line of traditional Yoga which can be traced back, through Shankara, to the Seers mentioned in the Upanishads), he traveled to Britain in 1929 where he founded Shanti Sadan, the Center of Adhyatma Yoga in the West, and made several distinguished translations of Advaita classics such as the *Avadhut Gita* of Mahatma Dattatreya (1934), *Ashtavakra Gita* (1949), the *Panchadashi* of Vidyaranya (1954), and the *Aparokshanubhuti* of Shankara (1955). Dr Shastri died in London in 1956.

PHILIP SHERRARD taught at both Oxford and London Universities where he lectured in the History of the Orthodox Church, of which he was a member since 1956. He was co-translator, with G.E.H. Palmer and Bishop Kallistos Ware, of the *Philokalia*, an influential compendium of mystical writings by the spiritual fathers of the Orthodox Church. Of his many writings, two notable works are dedicated to a critique of modern scientism and its dehumanization of man: *The Rape of Man and Nature* (1987), and *Human Image, World Image: The Death and Resurrection of Sacred Cosmology* (1992). A wide-ranging collection of articles called *Christianity: Lineaments of a Sacred Tradition* (1998) deal with topics such as Tradition, a critique of the psychology of C.G. Jung, death and dying, the problem of evil, and the revival of contemplative Hesychast spirituality in the modern world. He was co-founder, with Keith Critchlow, Brian Keeble and Kathleen Raine, of *Temenos*, a review dedicated to the traditional exposition of the arts and imagination. Philip Sherrard died in London in 1995.

ARTHUR VERSLUIS teaches literature, mythology, and writing and is the author of numerous books and articles on traditional religion, cosmology and culture, including *The Egyptian Mysteries* (1988), *Song of the Cosmos: An Introduction to Traditional Cosmology* (1991), *Sacred Earth: The Spiritual Landscape of Native America* (1992), and *TheoSophia: Hidden Dimensions of Christianity* (1994). He is currently editor of *Esoterica*, an on-line journal of traditional studies, and a former editor of *Avaloka: A Journal of Traditional Religion and Culture*.

## Contributors

**PHILIP ZALESKI**, author of *Gifts of the Spirit: Living the Wisdom of the Great Religious Traditions*, is a senior editor at *Parabola* magazine, as well as the editor of *The Best Spiritual Writing* series. He teaches religion at Smith College and has been a visiting lecturer in literature at Wesleyan University. His writing on religion and culture regularly appears in national publications including *The New York Times*, *Parabola*, *First Things* and *Reader's Digest*.

# Poets

MATSUO BASHO: considered one of the greatest of the Haiku poets in the Japanese tradition. Zen Buddhism was a formative influence in the school of poetry he founded. This poem appears in *Echoes of Japan* by H.P. Shastri (London, 1961).

YUNUS EMRE: unlettered Turkish shepherd. Sang mystical songs still popular today. The translation is by Annemarie Schimmel, as it appears in Seyyed Hossein Nasr's *Religion and the Order of Nature* (Oxford, 1996).

ESKIMO: "The Great Sea" is taken from *In the Trail of the Wind: American Indian Poems and Ritual Orations*, edited by John Bierhorst (n.p., 1971).

ORTHA NAN GAIDHEAL: translated as Song of the Gaels. This is an ancient and little known text supplied by D.M. Matheson to Whitall N. Perry, who included it in his monumental *A Treasury of Traditional Wisdom* (Cambridge, 1971).

ROBERT HERRICK: vicar of Dean Prior and one of the greatest English lyric and mystical poets. This selection is taken from *The Poetical Works of Robert Herrick*, edited by F.W. Moorman (Oxford, 1951).

HILDEGARD OF BINGEN: German abbess, visionary mystic, healer, painter, composer, preacher and social critic. The short poem following chapter 7 appears in *Religion and the Order of Nature* by Seyyed Hossein Nasr (Oxford, 1996). Responsory for Virgins , which follows chapter 17 is taken from *Hildegard of Bingen: Mystica Writings*, edited by Fiona Bowie and Oliver Davies with new translations by Robert Carver (New York, 1990).

NUR AD-DIN 'ABD AR-RAHMAN JAMI: famous Afghan Sufi poet and philosopher. This poem is selected from his *Lawa'ih* (*Flashes of Light*), translated by E.H. Whinfield and Mirza Muhammed Kazvini (London, 1914).

KEIZAN: this piece is taken from his *Denko-roku,* and is translated by W.S. Merwin in his introduction to *Sun at Midnight: Poems and Sermons of Muso Soseki* (San Francisco, 1989).

MECHTHILD OF MAGDEBURG: German visionary and poet. An early Latin translation of her book *The Flowing Light of the Godhead* is said to have inspired Dante. This translation is by Jane Hirshfield and appears in *The Enlightened Heart: An Anthology of Sacred Poetry,* edited by Stephen Mitchell (San Francisco, 1989).

"NAHUATL: AZTEC SONG": this translation, by Antonio Penafiel, is taken from *The Aztecs: People of the Sun* by Alfonso Caso (Oklahoma, 1958).

SA'D-UD-DIN MAHMUD SHABISTARI: author of *Gulshan-i-Raz (The Secret Rose Garden)* and one of the greatest of the Persian Sufi poets. The translation is by Florence Lederer (Lahore, n.d.).

HAN SHAN: one of the greatest of the T'ang Dynasty poets. His Chinese Buddhist writings are expressive of the poet's search for enlightenment and peace. This poem is translated by Burton Watson from his *Cold Mountain: 100 Poems of the T'ang Poet* Han Shan (Columbia, 1970).

REVEREND ZENKEI SHIBAYAMA: Abbot of Nanzenji Monastery in Kyoto. The translation is by Sumiko Kudo and is taken from *A Flower Does Not Talk: Zen Essays* (Boston, Massachusetts, 1977).

ANGELUS SILESIUS: born Johann Scheffler. His epigrams are perfectly suited to the intrinsic problem of any mystical writer: expressing the ineffable in words. This piece is taken from his *The Cherubinic Wanderer* (New York, 1986), and is translated by Maria Shrady.

ALFRED LORD TENNYSON: one of the great representative figures of the Victorian age whose writings encompass many poetic styles and include some of the finest idyllic poetry in the English language. This selection is taken from *The Pocket Book of Verse: Great English and American Poems* (New York, 1965).

TEWA: "The Song of the Sky Loom" derives from the Tewa people of the American Southwest. It appears in *The Magic World: American Indian Songs and Poems,* selected and edited by William Brandon (New York, 1971). The translation is by Herbert J. Spinden.

WANG WEI: along with Li Po, Tu Fu and Po Chu'i, considered one of the greatest poets of the T'ang Dynasty. This translation is from *Laughing Lost in the Mountains,* by Tony Barnstone, Willis Barnstone and Xu Haixin (New England, 1991).

LEVI YITZCHAK OF BERDITCHOV: this translation of the Hasidic mystic is by Harry Rabinowicz and is extracted from his *The Way of the Jewish Mystics* (Boston, Massachusetts 1994).

# Index

# Index

# Index

# Index

## Index

*315*

# Index

# Index

# Index

# Index

Plants, 5, 11, 20, 42, 99, 174, 178, 184, 230, 232, 237, 271, 279, 282, 287-289, 291-294

Plato, 165, 174-175, 179-180, 190, 217, 219, 303

Platonic Region of Eternal Ideas, 134

Platonic, 45, 87, 134, 216, 219

Platonism, 32, 46

Platonist, 44, 265

Pleasure, 56, 61, 63, 174, 227, 232, 288, 295

Plenitude, 3, 11, 32, 216, 220, 223

Plotinus, 174, 176, 178

Pneumatology, 253, 262, 298

Po Chu, 307

Pomo, 273

Post-modernists, 84

Praise, 2, 15, 46, 88-89, 188-189, 223, 254, 294

Prajna-Paramita, 32

Prayer, 59, 66, 104, 134, 144, 217, 220, 273, 276, 303

Prayers, 34, 59-60, 81, 86, 163, 212, 274

Preachers, 53

Prejudices, 43, 134, 269-270

Presence of Divinity, 138-139

Presence, 3, 20, 34-36, 56, 59, 74, 87-89, 111-112, 118-119, 124, 128, 138-139, 145, 153-155, 164, 186-187, 196-197, 207, 218, 247, 250, 254, 261, 270-271, 273-274, 276

Prime Matter, 149-150

Primitive Mentality, 41

Primordial Man, 33, 179, 218

Primordial Tradition, 38, 168, 179-180

Primordial, 33, 38, 43, 168, 179-180, 185, 194, 196, 198, 210, 218, 287

Principle, 1-2, 6, 9, 17, 19, 21, 34-40, 42, 44-45, 83, 86, 91-93, 97, 110, 122, 125, 127-130, 133, 139, 142-144, 146, 174, 178, 207, 215-218, 220, 242-244, 246-251, 272, 276, 279-280, 283-286

Profane, 35-36, 40-41, 47, 49, 193-194, 223, 260

Progress, 20, 22, 30, 69, 79, 269, 272, 298, 302

Promethean, 44

Prophet of Islam, 220

Prophet, 81, 92, 144-146, 172, 220, 299

Protestant, 85, 194, 197

Protestant-influenced Catholics, 193

Protestantism, 47, 193-194, 198

Proverbs, 241

Providence, 2, 56

Psalms, 29, 46, 55, 242

Purgatory, 211

Puritanical, 193

Purusha, 33

Pythagorean, 7

Pythagorean-Platonic, 114-115

Quran, 87-90, 92, 153

Quranic, 92, 141, 151-152

*Raa*, 166-167

Rainer Maria Rilke, 188

Rama, 172

Ramakrishna, 43, 221-222

Rational, 77, 79, 98, 123, 126-127, 130, 150-151, 158, 255, 284

Reality, 1-3, 8-9, 13-14, 17-19, 21-22, 32, 34-35, 39-43, 45, 65, 68, 74-76, 80-81, 84, 87, 89, 91, 95, 97, 99, 110, 112, 115-116, 118, 123, 125, 128, 135, 143, 145-146, 149-151, 155-158, 163, 172-175, 179-181, 187-188, 193, 202, 206-207, 211, 218-219, 221-222, 227, 241-247, 249, 251, 253, 257, 261, 263, 269-271, 283, 285, 293, 295

Reason, 6-7, 13, 18, 27, 55, 65-66, 74-75, 77, 95-96, 115-116, 119-120, 126-127, 134, 149, 158, 171, 182, 206, 219, 222, 265, 272, 279

Reasoning, 18, 117, 126, 229

Reflection, 4, 7, 31, 38, 50, 112, 182, 200-201, 207, 209, 218-219, 232-233, 243, 245, 247, 265, 295

Reformation, 30, 67, 113

Religion, 18, 24, 26, 31, 34-35, 38, 43, 45, 49, 54-55, 58-62, 65, 67-70, 75-87, 92, 94, 96, 98-99, 109, 113-114, 119-121, 127, 167, 180, 188, 269-270, 283-285, 298-305

Religious Education, 73

Religious Sense, 29, 91, 297

Religious, 5, 25-26, 29-32, 34, 36, 38, 49-50, 54, 58-59, 63-66, 68-69, 73, 75-77, 79-99, 119, 137-138, 194, 198, 200, 221, 264, 270, 281, 286, 297, 299, 302-303

Remembrance, 2, 12-13, 99, 215-216, 219, 223

Renaissance, 30, 44, 86, 90, 113, 173, 178

René Descartes, 113

René Guénon, 41, 73, 194, 284, 302

*Republic*, 165

*Responsory for Virgins*, 267, 305

*319*

# Index

# Index

For a glossary of all key foreign words used in books published by World Wisdom, including metaphysical terms in English, consult: www.DictionaryofSpiritualTerms.org. This on-line Dictionary of Spiritual Terms provides extensive definitions, examples and related terms in other languages.